Contents

List of Maps

AN INVITATION TO THE READER

In researching this book, we discovered many wonderful places—hotels, restaurants, shops, and more. We're sure you'll find others. Please tell us about them, so we can share the information with your fellow travelers in upcoming editions. If you were disappointed with a recommendation, we'd love to know that, too. Please write to:

Frommer's Portable Maui
Macmillan Travel
1633 Broadway
New York, NY 10019

AN ADDITIONAL NOTE

Please be advised that travel information is subject to change at any time—and this is especially true of prices. We therefore suggest that you write or call ahead for confirmation when making your travel plans. The authors, editors, and publisher cannot be held responsible for the experiences of readers while traveling. Your safety is important to us, however, so we encourage you to stay alert and be aware of your surroundings. Keep a close eye on cameras, purses, and wallets, all favorite targets of thieves and pickpockets.

WHAT THE SYMBOLS MEAN
✪ Frommer's Favorites

Our favorite places and experiences—outstanding for quality, value, or both.

The following abbreviations are used for credit cards:

AE	American Express	EURO	Eurocard
CB	Carte Blanche	JCB	Japan Credit Bank
DC	Diners Club	MC	MasterCard
DISC	Discover	V	Visa
ER	enRoute		

FIND FROMMER'S ONLINE

Arthur Frommer's Budget Travel Online (**www.frommers.com**) offers more than 6,000 pages of up-to-the-minute travel information—including the latest bargains and candid, personal articles updated daily by Arthur Frommer himself. No other Web site offers such comprehensive and timely coverage of the world of travel.

Frommer's®

PORTABLE

Maui

1st Edition

by Jeanette Foster & Jocelyn Fujii

Macmillan • USA

ABOUT THE AUTHORS

A resident of the Big Island, **Jeanette Foster** is a prolific writer widely published in travel, sports, and adventure magazines; she's also a contributing editor to *Hawaii* magazine.

Kauai-born **Jocelyn Fujii,** a resident of Honolulu, has authored *Under the Hula Moon: Living in Hawaii* and *The Best of Hawaii,* as well as articles for *The New York Times, National Geographic Traveler, Islands, Condé Nast Traveller, Travel Holiday,* and other national and international publications.

In addition to this guide, Jeanette and Jocelyn also co-author *Frommer's Hawaii* and *Frommer's Hawaii from $70 a Day.*

MACMILLAN TRAVEL

Macmillan General Reference USA, Inc.
1633 Broadway
New York, NY 10019

Find us online at **www.frommers.com**.

Copyright © 2000 by Macmillan General Reference USA, Inc.
Maps copyright © by Macmillan General Reference USA, Inc.

ISBN 0-02-863090-4
ISSN 1524-4318

Production Editor: Tammy Ahrens
Photo Editor: Richard Fox
Design by Michele Laseau
Staff Cartographers: John Decamillis and Roberta Stockwell
Page Creation by Marie Kristine Parial-Leonardo, Sean Monkhouse, and Carl Pierce

SPECIAL SALES

Bulk purchases (10+ copies) of Frommer's and selected Macmillan travel guides are available to corporations, organizations, mail-order catalogs, institutions, and charities at special discounts, and can be customized to suit individual needs. For more information write to Special Sales, Macmillan General Reference, 1633 Broadway, New York, NY 10019.

Manufactured in the United States of America

5 4 3 2 1

Planning a Trip to Maui

by Jeanette Foster

*M*aui, also called the Valley Isle, is but a small dot in the vast Pacific Ocean, but it has the potential to offer visitors dreamlike, even surreal, experiences: floating weightless in a rainbowed sea of tropical fish, standing atop a 10,000-foot volcano watching the sunrise color the sky, listening to the raindrops in a bamboo forest.

From around the globe, travelers are drawn to Maui, each in search of a unique encounter. Next to Waikiki, Maui is Hawaii's best-known destination, welcoming some 2¹/₂ million people each year to its sunny shores. As soon as you arrive at Kahului Airport, a huge banner greets you with the news that the readers of *Condé Nast Traveller* voted Maui the best island *in the world*—and they've done so 4 years running. As a result, sometimes Maui feels a little *too* well known—especially when you're stuck in bumper-to-bumper traffic around the airport. However, the congestion here pales in comparison to big-city Honolulu; Maui is really just a casual collection of small towns. Once you move beyond the resort areas, you'll find a slower, more peaceful way of life, where car horns are used only to greet friends, posted store hours mean nothing if the surf's up, and taking time to watch the sunset is part of the daily routine.

Maui has so many places to explore, things to do, sights to see—where to start? That's where we come in. In the pages that follow, we've compiled everything you need to know to plan your ideal trip to Maui: information on airlines, seasons, a calendar of events, how to make camping reservations, and much more.

1 The Island in Brief

CENTRAL MAUI

This flat, often windy corridor between Maui's two volcanoes is where you'll most likely arrive—it's where the main airport is. It's also home to the majority of the island's population, the heart of the business community, and the local government. You'll find good shopping and dining bargains here, but very few accommodations.

Maui

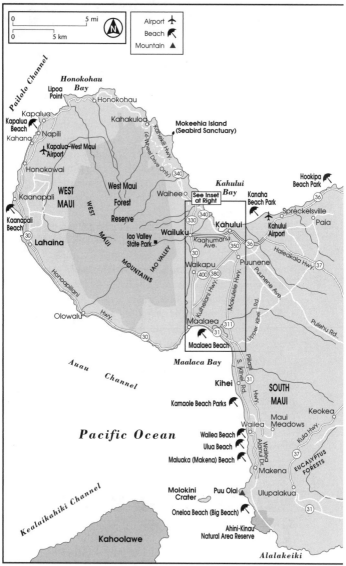

- Pailolo Channel
- Honokohau Bay
- Lipoa Point
- Honokohau
- Kapalua
- Kapalua Beach
- Kahana
- Napili
- Kahakuloa
- Kapalua-West Maui Airport
- Honokowai
- Mokeehia Island (Seabird Sanctuary)
- 4-Wheel Drive Only
- Kaanapali
- WEST MAUI
- West Maui Forest Reserve
- Waihee
- Kahului Bay
- See Inset at Right
- Hookipa Beach Park
- Kanaha Beach Park
- Kaanapali Beach
- WEST MAUI
- MOUNTAINS
- Iao Valley State Park
- IAO VALLEY
- Kahului
- Spreckelsville
- Paia
- Lahaina
- Wailuku
- Kaahumanu Ave.
- Kahului Airport
- Haleakala Hwy.
- 340
- 330
- 36
- 350
- 37
- Honoapiilani Hwy.
- Waikapu
- Puunene
- Puunene Ave.
- Olowalu
- 400 380
- Kuihelani Hwy.
- Mokulele Hwy.
- Upper Kula Rd.
- Pulehu Rd.
- 30
- 30
- 311
- Maalaea
- Maalaea Beach
- 31
- Auau Channel
- Maalaea Bay
- Kihei
- SOUTH MAUI
- S. Kihei Rd.
- Piilani Hwy.
- 31
- Kamaole Beach Parks
- Maui Meadows
- Keokea
- Pacific Ocean
- Wailea
- Wailea Beach
- Ulua Beach
- Maluaka (Makena) Beach
- Wailea Alanui Dr.
- Kula Hwy.
- 37
- EUCALYPTUS FORESTS
- Makena
- Molokini Crater
- Puu Olai
- Ulupalakua
- Kealaikahiki Channel
- Oneloa Beach (Big Beach)
- Ahini-Kinau Natural Area Reserve
- 31
- Kahoolawe
- Alalakeiki

Scale: 0 — 5 mi / 0 — 5 km

Legend:
- Airport ✈
- Beach 🏖
- Mountain ▲

2

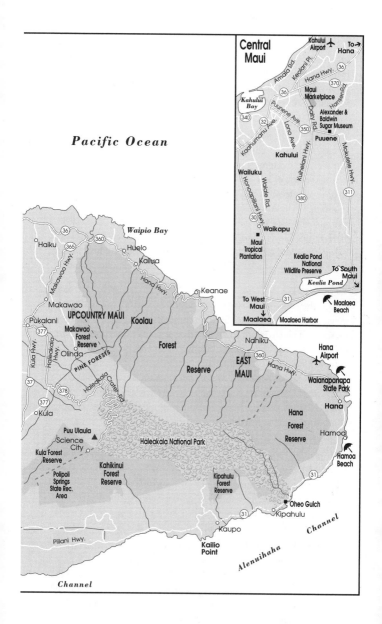

Pacific Ocean

Waipio Bay

Haiku

Huelo

Kailua

Hana Hwy.

Keanae

Makawao

UPCOUNTRY MAUI

Koolau

Pukalani

Makawao Forest Reserve

Forest

Olinda

PINE FORESTS

Nahiku

Kula

Reserve

EAST MAUI

Hana Hwy.

Hana Airport

Waianapanapa State Park

Puu Ulaula

Science City

Haleakala National Park

Hana

Hana Forest Reserve

Hamoa

Hamoa Beach

Kula Forest Reserve

Kahikinui Forest Reserve

Kipahulu Forest Reserve

Polipoli Springs State Rec. Area

Oheo Gulch

Kipahulu

Piilani Hwy.

Kaupo

Kailio Point

Alenuihaha

Channel

Channel

Central Maui

Kahului Airport

To Hana

Amala Rd.

Keolani Pl.

Hana Hwy.

Maui Marketplace

Hansen Rd.

Kahului Bay

Puunene Ave.

Dairy Rd.

Alexander & Baldwin Sugar Museum

Lono Ave.

Puunene

Kaahumanu Ave.

Kahului

Kuihelani Hwy.

Mokulele Hwy.

Wailuku

Waiale Rd.

Honoapiilani Hwy.

Waikapu

Maui Tropical Plantation

Kealia Pond National Wildlife Preserve

To South Maui

Kealia Pond

To West Maui

Maalaea

Maalaea Harbor

Maalaea Beach

KAHULUI   This is "Dream City," home to thousands of former sugarcane workers who dreamed of owning their own homes away from the plantations. A couple of small hotels located just 2 miles from the airport are convenient for 1-night stays if you have a late arrival or early departure, but this is not a place to spend your vacation.

WAILUKU   With its faded wooden storefronts, old plantation homes, and shops straight out of the 1940s, Wailuku is like a time capsule. Although most people race through on their way to see the natural beauty of **Iao Valley,** this quaint little town is worth a brief visit, if only to see a real place where real people live. Beaches surrounding Wailuku are not great for swimming, but the old town has a spectacular view of Haleakala, a couple of hostels and an excellent historic B&B, great budget restaurants, a tofu factory, some interesting bungalow architecture, a Frank Lloyd Wright building on the outskirts of town, and the always-endearing Bailey House Museum.

WEST MAUI

This is the fabled Maui you see on postcards, with jagged peaks and green valleys. The beaches here are some of Hawaii's best. And it's no secret: This stretch of coastline, from Kapalua to the historic port of Lahaina, is the island's most bustling resort area (with South Maui close behind).

If you want to book into a resort or condo on this coast, first consider which community you'd like to base yourself in. Starting at the southern end of West Maui and moving northward, the coastal communities are as listed below.

LAHAINA   This old whaling seaport teems with restaurants, T-shirt shops, and galleries, but there's still lots of real history to be found. This vintage village is a tame version of its former self, when whalers swaggered ashore in search of women and grog. The town serves as a great base for visitors: A few old hotels, quaint B&Bs, and a handful of oceanfront condos offer a variety of choices. This is the place to stay if you want to be in the center of things.

KAANAPALI   Farther north along the West Maui coast is Hawaii's first master-planned family resort. Pricey midrise hotels, which line nearly 3 miles of gold-sand beach, are linked by a landscaped parkway and separated by a jungle of plants. Golf greens wrap around the slope between beachfront and hillside properties. **Whalers Village**—an upscale seaside mall, plus the best little whale museum in Hawaii—and other restaurants are easy to reach on foot along the waterfront walkway or via resort shuttle, which also serves the small West Maui airport just to the north. Shuttles also go to Lahaina, 3 miles to the south, for shopping, dining, entertainment, and boat tours. Kaanapali is popular with meeting groups and families—especially those with teenagers, who will like all the action.

FROM HONOKOWAI TO NAPILI In the building binge of the 1970s, condominiums sprouted along this gorgeous coastline. Today, these older ocean-side units offer excellent bargains and a great location—along sandy beaches, within minutes of both the Kapalua and the Kaanapali resort areas, and close enough to the goings-on in Lahaina town.

In **Honokowai** and **Mahinahina,** you'll find mostly older units that tend to be cheaper; there's not much shopping here aside from convenience stores, but you'll have easy access to the shops and restaurants of Kaanapali.

Kahana is a little more upscale than Honokowai and Mahinahina. Most of the condos here are big high-rise types, built more recently than those immediately to the south. You'll find a nice selection of shops and restaurants in the area, and Kapalua West Maui Airport is nearby.

Napili is a much-sought-after area for condo seekers: It's quiet; has great beaches, restaurants, and shops; and is close to Kapalua. Units are generally more expensive here (although we've found a few hidden gems at affordable prices).

KAPALUA North beyond Kaanapali and the shopping centers of Napili and Kahana, the road starts to climb and the vista opens up to fields of silver-green pineapple and manicured golf fairways. Turn down the country lane of Pacific pines toward the sea, and you could only be in Kapalua. It's the very exclusive domain of two gracious and expensive hotels, set on one of Hawaii's best gold-sand beaches, next to two bays that are marine-life preserves (with fabulous surfing in winter).

Even if you don't stay here, you're welcome to come and enjoy Kapalua. Both of the fancy hotels provide public parking and beach access. The resort champions innovative environmental programs; it also has an art school, three golf courses, historic features, a collection of swanky condos and homes (many available for vacation rental at astronomical prices), and wide-open spaces that include a rain-forest preserve—all open to the general public. Kapalua is a great place to stay put. However, if you plan to "tour" Maui, you will spend a lot of your vacation driving from this location and might want to consider a more central place to stay, because even Lahaina is a 15-minute drive away.

SOUTH MAUI

This is the hottest, sunniest, driest, most popular coastline on Maui for sun worshippers—Arizona by the sea. Rain rarely falls, and temperatures stick around 85°F year-round. On former scrub land from Maalaea to Makena, where cacti once grew wild and cows grazed, are now four distinct areas—Maalaea, Kihei, Wailea, and Makena— each appealing to a different crowd.

MAALAEA   This oceanfront village centers around the small boat harbor (with a general store and a couple of restaurants) and the newly opened **Maui Ocean Center,** an aquarium/ocean complex. This quaint region offers several condominium units to choose from, but visitors staying here should be aware that it is often very windy (all the wind from the Pacific is funneled between the West Maui Mountains and Haleakala, coming out in Maalaea).

KIHEI   Kihei is less a proper town than a nearly continuous series of condos and mini-malls lining South Kihei Road. This is Maui's best vacation bargain: Budget travelers swarm over the eight sandy beaches along this scalloped, condo-packed, 7-mile stretch of coast. Kihei is neither charming nor quaint; what it lacks in aesthetics, though, it more than makes up for in sunshine, affordability, and convenience. If you want latte in the morning, beach in the afternoon, and Hawaii Regional Cuisine in the evening—all at budget prices—head to Kihei.

WAILEA   Only 25 years ago, this was wall-to-wall scrub kiawe trees, but now Wailea is a manicured oasis of multimillion-dollar resort hotels situated along 2 miles of palm-fringed gold coast. It's like Beverly Hills by the sea: warm, clear water full of tropical fish; year-round sunshine and clear blue skies; and hedonistic pleasure palaces on 1,500 acres of black-lava shore. Amazing what a billion dollars can do.

This is the playground of the stretch-limo set. The planned resort development—practically a well-heeled town—has a shopping village, three prized golf courses of its own and three more in close range, and a tennis complex. A growing number of large homes sprawl over the upper hillside, some offering excellent bed-and-breakfast units at reasonable prices. The resorts along this fantasy coast are spectacular, to say the least.

Appealing natural features include the coastal trail, a 3-mile round-trip path along the oceanfront with pleasing views everywhere you look—out to sea and to the neighboring islands, or inland to the broad lawns and gardens of the hotels. The trail's south end borders an extensive garden of native coastal plants, as well as ancient lava-rock house ruins juxtaposed with elegant oceanfront condos. But the chief attractions, of course, are those five outstanding beaches (the best is Wailea).

MAKENA   Suddenly, the road enters raw wilderness. After Wailea's overdone density, the thorny landscape is a welcome relief. Although beautiful, this is an end-of-the-road kind of place: It's a long drive from Makena to anywhere on Maui. If you're looking for an activity-filled vacation, you might want to book somewhere else, or spend a lot of time in your car. But if you crave a quiet, relaxing respite, where the biggest trip of the day is from your bed to the beach, Makena is your place.

Beyond Makena you'll discover Haleakala's last lava flow, which ran to the sea in 1790; the bay named for French explorer La Pérouse; and a chunky lava trail known as the King's Highway, which leads around Maui's empty south shore past ruins and fish camps. Puu Olai stands like Maui's Diamond Head on the shore, where a sunken crater shelters tropical fish, and empty golden-sand beaches stand at the end of dirt roads.

UPCOUNTRY MAUI

After a few days at the beach, you'll probably take notice of the 10,000-foot mountain in the middle of Maui. The slopes of Haleakala ("House of the Sun") are home to cowboys, growers, and other country people who wave back as you drive by; they're all up here enjoying the crisp air, emerald pastures, eucalyptus, and flower farms of this tropical Olympus—there's even a misty California redwood grove. You can see 1,000 tropical sunsets reflected in the windows of houses old and new, strung along a road that runs like a loose hound from Makawao, an old-paniolo-turned–New Age village, to Kula, where the road leads up to the crater and **Haleakala National Park.** The rumpled, two-lane blacktop of Highway 37 narrows on the other side of Tedeschi Winery, where wine grapes and wild elk flourish on the Ulupalakua Ranch, the biggest on Maui. A stay upcountry is usually affordable and a nice contrast to the sizzling beaches and busy resorts below.

MAKAWAO   Until recently, this small, two-street upcountry town consisted of little more than a post office, gas station, feed store, bakery, and restaurant/bar serving the cowboys and farmers living in the surrounding community; the hitching posts outside storefronts were really used to tie up horses. As the population of Maui started expanding in the 1970s, a health-food store sprang up, followed by boutiques and a host of health-conscious restaurants. The result is an eclectic amalgam of old paniolo Hawaii and the baby-boomer trends of transplanted mainlanders. **Hui No'eau Visual Arts Center,** Hawaii's premier arts collective, is definitely worth a peek. The only accommodations here are reasonably priced bed-and-breakfasts, perfect for those who enjoy great views and don't mind slightly chilly nights.

KULA   A feeling of pastoral remoteness prevails in this upcountry community of old flower farms, humble cottages, and new suburban ranch houses with million-dollar views that take in the ocean, isthmus, West Maui Mountains, Lanai and Kahoolawe off in the distance, and, at night, the string of pearls that lights the gold coast from Maalaea to Puu Olai. Everything flourishes at a cool 3,000 feet (bring a jacket), just below the cloud line, along a winding road on the way up to Haleakala National Park, and everyone here grows something—Maui onions, carnations, orchids, and proteas, that strange-looking blossom that looks like a *Star Trek* prop. The local B&Bs cater to guests seeking cool tropic nights, panoramic views, and a rural upland escape. Here you'll find the true peace and quiet that only rural farming country can offer—yet you're still just 30 to 40 minutes away from the beach and an hour's drive from Lahaina.

EAST MAUI

ON THE ROAD TO HANA   When old sugar towns die, they usually fade away in rust and red dirt. Not **Paia.** The tangle of electrical, phone, and cable wires hanging overhead symbolizes the town's ability to adapt to the times—it may look messy, but it works. Here, trendy restaurants, eclectic boutiques, and high-tech windsurf shops stand next door to the ma-and-pa grocery, fish market, and storefronts that have been serving customers since the plantation days. Hippies took over in the 1970s; although their macrobiotic restaurants and old-style artists' co-op have made way for Hawaii Regional Cuisine and galleries featuring the works of renowned international artists, Paia still manages to maintain a pleasant vibe of hippiedom. The town's main attraction, though, is **Hookipa Beach Park,** which attracts windsurfers from around the world. A few B&Bs are located just outside Paia in the tiny community of **Kuau.**

Ten minutes down the road from Paia and up the hill from the Hana Highway—the connector road to the entire east side of Maui—sits **Haiku.** Once a pineapple-plantation village, complete with cannery (today a shopping complex), Haiku offers vacation rentals and B&Bs a quiet, pastoral setting: the perfect base for those who want to get off the beaten path and experience a quieter side of Maui, but don't want to feel too removed (the beach is only 10 minutes away).

About 15 to 20 minutes past Haiku is the largely unknown community of **Huelo.** Every day, thousands of cars whiz by on the road to Hana, but most passengers barely glance at the double row of mailboxes overseen by a fading HAWAII VISITORS BUREAU sign. But down the road lies a hidden Hawaii: a Hawaii of an earlier time, where Mother Nature is still sensual and wild, where ocean waves pummel soaring lava cliffs, and where an indescribable sense of serenity prevails. Huelo is not for everyone—but those who hunger for the magic of a place still largely untouched by "progress" should check into a B&B or vacation rental here.

HANA Set between an emerald rain forest and the blue Pacific is a village probably best defined by what it lacks: golf courses, shopping malls, McDonald's. Except for two gas stations and a bank with an ATM, you'll find little of what passes for progress here. Instead, you'll discover the simple joys of fragrant tropical flowers, the sweet taste of backyard bananas and papayas, and the easy calm and unabashed small-town aloha spirit of old Hawaii. What saved "Heavenly" Hana from the inevitable march of progress? The 52-mile **Hana Highway,** which winds around 600 curves and crosses more than 50 one-lane bridges on its way from Kahului. You can go to Hana for the day—it's a 3-hour drive (and a half century away)—but 3 days are better. The tiny town has a first-class resort, a handful of great B&Bs, and some spectacular vacation rentals (where else can you stay in a tropical cabin in a rain forest?).

2 Visitor Information

For advance information, contact the **Maui Visitors Bureau,** 1727 Wili Pa Loop, Wailuku, Maui, HI 96793 (☎ **800/ 525-MAUI** or 808/244-3530; fax 808/244-1337; www. visitmaui.com). Once you're on the island, to get here from the airport, go right on Highway 36 (the Hana Highway) to Kaahumanu

Avenue (Highway 32); follow it past Maui Community College and Wailuku War Memorial Park onto East Main Street in Wailuku; at North Market Street, turn right, and then right again on Mill Street; go left on Imi Kala Street and left again onto Wili Pa Loop.

The state agency responsible for tourism is the **Hawaii Visitors and Convention Bureau** (HVCB), Suite 801, Waikiki Business Plaza, 2270 Kalakaua Ave., Honolulu, HI 96815 (☎ **800/ GO-HAWAII** or 808/923-1811; www.gohawaii.com). The HVCB also has a U.S. mainland office at 180 Montgomery St., Suite 2360, San Francisco, CA 94104 (☎ **800/353-5846**). All other HVCB offices on the mainland have been closed due to budget constraints.

MAUI ON THE WEB

Here are some useful links to Hawaii:

- **Hawaii Visitors and Convention Bureau:** www.gohawaii.com
- **Hawaii State Vacation Planner:** www.hshawaii.com
- **Hawaii State Tourism Office:** www.hawaii.gov/tourism
- **Travel and Visitor Information:** www.planet-hawaii.com/travel
- **Maui Information:** www.maui.net
- **Maui Visitors Bureau:** www.visitmaui.com
- **Kaanapali Beach Resort Association:** www.maui.net/~kbra

3 When to Go

Most visitors don't come to Maui when the weather's best in the islands; rather, they come when it's at its worst everywhere else. Thus, the **high season**—when prices are up and resorts are booked to capacity—generally runs from mid-December through March or mid-April. The last 2 weeks of December in particular are the prime time for travel to Maui; if you're planning a holiday trip, make your reservations as early as possible, count on holiday crowds, and expect to pay top dollar for accommodations, car rentals, and airfare.

The **off-seasons,** when the best bargain rates are available, are spring (from mid-April to mid-June) and fall (from September to mid-December)—a paradox, since these are the best seasons in terms of reliably great weather. If you're looking to save money, or if you just want to avoid the crowds, this is the time to visit. Hotel rates tend to be significantly lower during these off-seasons. Airfares also tend to be lower—again, sometimes substantially—and good packages and special deals are often available.

Note: If you plan to come to Maui between the last week in April and mid-May, be sure to book your accommodations, inter-island air reservations, and car rental in advance. In Japan, the last week of April is called Golden Week, because three Japanese holidays take place one after the other; the islands are especially busy with Japanese tourists during this time.

Due to the large number of families traveling in **summer** (June through August), you won't get the fantastic bargains of spring and fall. However, you'll still do much better on packages, airfare, and accommodations than you will in the winter months.

CLIMATE   Since Maui lies at the edge of the tropical zone, it technically has only two seasons, both of them warm. The dry season corresponds to summer, and the rainy season generally runs during the winter from November to March. It rains every day somewhere in the islands at any time of the year, but the rainy season can cause "gray" weather and spoil your tanning opportunities. Fortunately, it seldom rains for more than 3 days straight.

The **year-round temperature** usually varies no more than 15°F, but it depends on where you are. Maui is like a ship in that it has leeward and windward sides. The **leeward** sides (the west and south) are usually hot and dry, whereas the **windward** sides (east and north) are generally cooler and moist. If you want arid, sunbaked, desertlike weather, go leeward. If you want lush, often wet, junglelike weather, go windward. Your best bet for total year-round sun are the Kihei-Wailea and Lahaina-Kapalua coasts.

Maui is also full of **microclimates,** thanks to its interior valleys, coastal plains, and mountain peaks. If you travel into the mountains, it can change from summer to winter in a matter of hours, since it's cooler the higher up you go. In other words, if the weather doesn't suit you, go to the other side of the island—or head into the hills.

MAUI CALENDAR OF EVENTS

Please note that, as with any schedule of upcoming events, the following information is subject to change; always confirm the details before you plan your schedule around an event. For a complete and up-to-date list of events throughout the islands, point your Internet browser to **www.hawaiian.net/~mahalo/calendar/current.html**.

January
- **PGA Kapalua Mercedes Championship,** Kapalua Resort. Top PGA golfers compete for $1 million. Call ☎ **808/669-0244.** First weekend after New Year's Day.

- **Hula Bowl Football All-Star Classic,** War Memorial Stadium. An annual all-star football classic featuring America's top college players. Call ☎ **888/716-HULA** or 808/947-4141. Sunday before the Super Bowl.
- **Maui Pro Surf Meet,** Hookipa Beach and Honolua Bay. The top professional surfers from around the globe compete for some $40,000 in prize money. Call ☎ **808/575-9264.** Mid-January.
- **Celebration of Whales,** Four Seasons Resort, Wailea. Cetacean experts host discussions, whale-watching excursions, social functions, art exhibits, and entertainment. Call ☎ **808/847-8000.** Last weekend in January.

February

✪ **Chinese New Year,** Wo Hing Temple, Front Street, Lahaina. The Chinese New Year is ushered in with a lion dance, food booths, Chinese calligraphy, firecrackers, and other activities. Call ☎ **808/667-9175** or e-mail: action@maui.net.

March

- **Whalefest Week,** West Maui. A weeklong celebration with seminars, art exhibits, sailing, snorkeling and diving tours, and numerous events for children to celebrate Maui's best-known winter visitors, the humpback whales. Call ☎ **808/667-9175** or e-mail: action@maui.net. Usually early March.
- **St. Patrick's Day Parade,** Kaanapali Parkway, Kaanapali Resort. Everyone becomes Irish for a day when this hometown parade makes its way through the Kaanapali Resort area. Call ☎ **808/ 661-3271.** March 17.
- **East Maui Taro Festival,** Hana. Here's your chance to taste taro in its many different preparations, from poi to chips. Also on hand are Hawaiian exhibits, demonstrations, and food booths. Call ☎ **808/248-8972.** Usually the last weekend in March.
- **Queen Kaahumanu Festival,** Kaahuman Center, Kahului. A day of celebration for Kamehameha's first wife, with Hawaiian exhibits, entertainment, games, and storytelling. Call ☎ **808/ 877-3369.**
- **Prince Kuhio Celebration.** Various festivals throughout the state commemorate the birth of Jonah Kuhio Kalanianaole, born March 26, 1871. He might have been one of Hawaii's kings, if not for the U.S. overthrow of the monarchy and Hawaii's annexation to the United States. Prince Kuhio was elected to Congress in 1902. End of March.

✪ **Annual Ritz-Carlton Kapalua Celebration of the Arts,** Ritz-Carlton Kapalua. Contemporary and traditional artists give hands-on lessons. Call ☎ **808/669-6200.** End of March or early April.

April

- **Buddha Day,** Lahaina Jodo Mission, Lahaina. This historic mission holds a flower-festival pageant honoring the birth of Buddha. Call ☎ **808/661-4303.** April 6.

- **Da Kine Hawaiian Pro Am Windsurfing,** Hookipa Beach Park. The top competitors from around the globe flock to the world-famous windsurfing beach for this annual competition. Call ☎ **808/575-9264.**

✪ **Maui County Agricultural Trade Show and Sampling,** Ulupalakua Ranch and Tedeschi Winery, Ulupalakua. The name might be long and cumbersome, but this event is hot, hot, hot. Local product exhibits and sampling, food booths, and live entertainment. Call ☎ **808/875-0457** for this year's schedule.

May

✪ **Annual Lei Day Celebration.** May Day is Lei Day in Hawaii, celebrated with lei-making contests, pageantry, arts and crafts, and concerts throughout the islands. Call ☎ **808/879-1922** for Maui events. May 1.

- **Outrigger Canoe Season**. From May to September, nearly every weekend, canoe paddlers across the state participate in outrigger canoe races. Call ☎ **808/961-5797.**

- **In Celebration of Canoes,** A Street Festival, Front Street, Lahaina. Daylong events with food booths, music, parades, cultural demonstrations, and more, all in celebration of the Hawaiian canoe. Call ☎ **808/667-9175.**

- **Maui Music Festival,** Kapalua Resort. Weekend of events featuring the top musicians in the state. Call ☎ **808/661-3271.**

June

✪ **King Kamehameha Celebration,** statewide. It's a state holiday with a massive floral parade, *hoolaulea* (party), and much more. Call ☎ **808/667-9175** for Maui events. First weekend in June.

July

- **Makawao Parade and Rodeo,** Makawao. The annual parade and rodeo event has been taking place in this upcountry cowboy town for generations. Call ☎ **808/572-9565** or 808/572-2076 for this year's date.

✪ **Kapalua Wine Symposium,** Kapalua. Famous wine and food experts and oenophiles gather at the Ritz-Carlton and Kapalua Bay hotels for formal tastings, panel discussions, and samplings of new releases. Call ☎ **800/669-0244** for this year's dates and schedule.

August

- **Maui Onion Festival,** Whalers Village, Kaanapali, Maui. Everything you ever wanted to know about the sweetest onions in the world. Food, entertainment, tasting, and Maui Onion Cook-Off. Call ☎ **808/661-4567.** First week in August.

September

✪ **Aloha Festivals,** various locations statewide. Parades and other events celebrate Hawaiian culture. Call ☎ **800/852-7690,** or 808/545-1771 for a schedule of events.

✪ **Earth Maui,** Kapalua Resort, Kapalua. A weeklong series of events to encourage appreciation of Maui's natural environment, plus hiking and snorkeling trips. Call ☎ **800/527-2582** or 808/ 669-0244 for this year's schedule of events.

- **A Taste of Lahaina,** Lahaina Civic Center. Some 20,000 people show up to sample 35 signature entrees of Maui's premier chefs during the weekend-long festival, which includes cooking demonstrations, wine tastings, and live entertainment. Call ☎ **808/667-9175** or e-mail: action@maui.net. Usually mid-September.

- **Hana Relays,** Hana Highway. Hundreds of runners, in relay teams, will crowd the Hana Highway from Kahalui to Hana (you might want to avoid the road this day). Call ☎ **808/871-6441.** Usually the third Saturday in September.

October

- **Run to the Sun,** Paia to Haleakala. The world's top ultramarathoners make the journey from sea level to the top of 10,000-foot Haleakala, some 37 miles. Call ☎ **808/871-6441.**

- **Maui County Fair,** War Memorial Complex, Wailuku. The oldest county fair in Hawaii features a parade, amusement rides, live entertainment, and exhibits. Call ☎ **808/242-2721.** Early October.

✪ **Aloha Classic World Wavesailing Championship,** Hookipa Beach. The top windsurfers in the world gather for this final event in the Pro Boardsailing World Tour. If you're on Maui, don't miss it—it's spectacular to watch. Call ☎ **808/575-9151.**

✪ **Halloween in Lahaina.** There's Carnival in Rio, Mardi Gras in New Orleans, and Halloween in Lahaina. Come to this giant costume party (some 20,000 people show up) on the streets of Lahaina; Front Street is closed off for the party. It'll be the greatest memory of your trip. Call ☎ **808/667-9175.**

November

- **Hawaii International Film Festival,** various locations on Maui. A cinema festival with a cross-cultural spin, featuring filmmakers from Asia, the Pacific Islands, and the United States. Call ☎ **808/528-FILM** or www.hiff.org. Mid-November.
- **Festival of Art & Flowers,** Lahaina. The weekend before Thanksgiving is celebrated in Lahaina with flowers: cut flower displays, floral arrangements, demonstrations, lei-making contests, art exhibits, and entertainment. Call ☎ **808/667-9175** or e-mail: action@maui.net.

December

- **Old-Fashioned Holiday Celebration,** Lahaina. The second Saturday in December, in the Banyan Tree Park on Front Street, is a day of Christmas carolers, Santa Claus, live music and entertainment, a crafts fair, baked goods, and activities for children. Call ☎ **808/667-9175** or e-mail: action@maui.net.
- **Festival of Lights,** island-wide. Festivities include parades and tree-lighting ceremonies. Call ☎ **808/667-9175** on Maui, or 808/567-6361 on Molokai. Early December.

✪ **First Night,** Maui Arts and Cultural Center. Hawaii's largest festival of arts and entertainment takes place on three different islands. For 12 hours, musicians, dancers, actors, jugglers, magicians, and mimes perform, food is available, and fireworks bring in the New Year. Alcohol-free. Call ☎ **808/242-7469.** December 31.

4 Tips for Travelers with Special Needs

FOR TRAVELERS WITH DISABILITIES

Travelers with disabilities are made to feel very welcome on Maui. Hotels are usually equipped with wheelchair-accessible rooms, and tour companies provide many special services. The **Commission on Persons with Disabilities,** 919 Ala Moana Blvd., Suite 101, Honolulu, HI 96814 (☎ **808/586-8121**), and the **Hawaii Center for Independent Living,** 414 Kauwili St., Suite 102, Honolulu, HI 96817 (☎ **808/522-5400;** fax 808/586-8129; www.hawaii.gov/

health/cpd_indx.htm; e-mail: cpdppp@aloha.net), can provide information and send you a copy of the *Aloha Guide to Accessibility* ($15).

A World of Options, a 658-page book of resources for travelers with disabilities, covers everything from biking trips to scuba outfitters. It costs $45 and is available from **Mobility International USA**, P.O. Box 10767, Eugene, OR 97440 (☎ **541/343-1284,** voice and TDD; www.miusa.org). For information on travel destinations, services, accommodations, and transportation, contact **Access/Abilities**, P.O. Box 458, Mill Valley, CA 94942 (☎ **415/ 388-3250;** www.accessabil.com).

On the Internet, check out **Access-Able Travel Source** (www.access-able.com), which provides information for disabled travelers. **Accessible Vans of Hawaii,** 186 Mehani Circle, Kihei, HI 96753 (☎ **800/303-3750** or 808/879-5521; fax 808/879-0640; www.accessiblevans.com), has details on renting a van in Hawaii.

For travelers with disabilities who want to do their own driving, hand-controlled cars can be rented from **Avis** (☎ **800/331-1212**) and **Hertz** (☎ **800/654-3131**). The number of hand-controlled cars in Maui is limited, so be sure to book well in advance. Hawaii recognizes other states' windshield placards indicating that the driver of the car has a disability; these can give you access to specially marked handicapped parking spaces, so be sure to bring yours with you.

Vision-impaired travelers who use a Seeing-Eye dog can now travel to Maui without the hassle of quarantine. A recent court decision ruled that visitors with Seeing-Eye dogs need only present documentation that the dog has had rabies shots and that it is a trained Seeing-Eye dog in order to bypass quarantine. Previously, all dogs and cats in Hawaii had to spend 4 months in quarantine, since Hawaii is rabies-free (quarantine has been reduced to 1 month, Seeing-Eye dogs exempted). For more information, contact the **Animal Quarantine Facility** (☎ **808/483-7171;** www.hawaii.gov).

FOR GAY & LESBIAN TRAVELERS

Known for its acceptance of all groups, Hawaii welcomes gays and lesbians just as it does any other group.

The best guide for gay and lesbian visitors is Matthew Link's *Rainbow Handbook Hawaii,* available for $14.95 by writing P.O. Box 100, Honaunau, HI 96726 (☎ **800/260-5528;** www. rainbowhandbook.com).

To get a sense of the local gay and lesbian community, contact **Both Sides Now,** P.O. Box 5042, Kahului, HI 96733-5042

(☎ **808/244-4566;** fax 808/874-6221; www.maui-tech.com/glom; e-mail: gaymaui@maui.net), which publishes a monthly newspaper on news, issues, and events for Maui's gay, lesbian, bisexual, and transgendered community.

For the latest information on the gay marriage issue, contact the **Hawaii Marriage Project** (☎ **808/532-9000**).

Pacific Ocean Holidays, P.O. Box 88245, Honolulu, HI 96830 (☎ **800/735-6600** or 808/923-2400; www.gayhawaii.com), offers vacation packages that feature gay-owned and gay-friendly lodgings. It also publishes the *Pocket Guide to Hawaii: A Guide for Gay Visitors & Kamaaina,* a list of gay-owned and gay-friendly businesses throughout the islands. Send $5 for a copy (mail order only; no phone orders, please), or access the online version on the Web site.

5 Money-Saving Package Deals

Booking an all-inclusive travel package that includes some combination of airfare, accommodations, rental car, meals, airport and baggage transfers, and sightseeing can be the most cost-effective way to travel to Maui. You can sometimes save so much money by buying all the pieces of your trip through a packager that your transpacific airfare ends up, in effect, being free.

The best place to start looking for a package deal is in the travel section of your local Sunday newspaper. Also check the ads in the back of such national travel magazines as *Travel & Leisure, National Geographic Traveler,* and *Condé Nast Traveler.* **Liberty Travel** (☎ **888/271-1584** to be connected with the agent closest to you; www.libertytravel.com), for instance, one of the biggest packagers in the Northeast, usually boasts a full-page ad in Sunday papers. You won't find much in the way of service, but you will get a good deal. **American Express Travel** (☎ **800/AXP-6898**; www. americanexpress.com/travel) can also book you a well-priced Hawaiian vacation; it also advertises in many Sunday travel sections.

Hawaii is such an ideal destination for vacation packages that some packagers book Hawaiian vacations as the majority of their business. **Pleasant Hawaiian Holidays** (☎ **800/2-HAWAII** or 800/242-9244; www.pleasantholidays.com or www.2hawaii.com) is by far the biggest and most comprehensive packager to Hawaii; it offers an extensive, high-quality collection of 50 condos and hotels in every price range.

Other reliable packagers include the airlines themselves, which often package their flights together with accommodations. Among the

---

Package-Buying Tip

For one-stop shopping on the Web, go to **www.vacationpackager. com**, a search engine that can link you up to many different package-tour operators, who can then help you plan a custom-tailored trip to Maui. Be sure to look under "Maui," "Hawaii," and the "Hawaiian Islands."

---

airlines offering good-value package deals to Hawaii are **American Airlines FlyAway Vacations** (☎ **800/321-2121;** www. 2travel.com/americanair/hawaii.html), **Continental Airlines Vacations** (☎ **800/634-5555** or 800/301-3800; www. coolvacations.com), **Delta Dream Vacations** (☎ **800/872-7786;** www.deltavacations.com), **TWA Getaway Vacations** (☎ **800/ GETAWAY** or 800/438-2929; www.twa.com), and **United Vacations** (☎ **800/328-6877;** www.unitedvacations.com). If you're traveling to the islands from Canada, ask your travel agent about package deals through **Air Canada Vacations** (☎ **800/776-3000;** www.aircanada.ca).

GREAT DEALS AT HAWAII'S TOP HOTEL CHAINS

Hawaii's three major hotel chains—which together represent nearly 100 hotels, condominiums, resorts, a historic B&B, and even restored plantation homes—have a host of packages that will save you money.

With some 28 properties in Hawaii, including 4 on Maui, **Outrigger** (☎ **800/OUTRIGGER;** fax 800/622-4852; www. outrigger.com) offers excellent affordable accommodations, all with consistently dependable, clean, and well-appointed rooms. The chain's price structure is based entirely on location, room size, and amenities. You'll be comfortable at any of the chain's outposts: The small rooms at the budget Outriggers are just as tastefully appointed as the larger, more expensive Outrigger rooms right on the beach. Package deals include discounted rates for spring and fall stays, a car package, deals on multinight stays, family plans, cut rates for seniors, and even packages for scuba divers (2 days of two-tank boat dives and a 3-night stay start at $311 per person, double occupancy).

The **Aston** chain (☎ **800/92-ASTON;** fax 808/922-8785; www.aston-hotels.com), which celebrated 50 years in Hawaii in 1998, has some 29 hotels, condominiums, and resort properties scattered throughout the islands, with eight on Maui. They range dramatically in price and style, from the oceanfront Maui Lu Resort to the economical Aston Maui Islander. Aston offers package deals galore, including family plans; discounted senior rates; car, golf, and shopping packages; and deals on multinight stays, including a wonderful "Island Hopper" deal that allows you to hop from island to island and get 25% off on 7 nights or more at Aston properties.

Marc Resorts Hawaii (☎ **800/535-0085;** fax 800/633-5085; www.marcresorts.com) has 22 properties on every island but Lanai, ranging from the luxury Embassy Suite Resort in Kaanapali to the affordable Molokai Shores condominium on Molokai. The chain offers package deals for seniors, multinight stays, honeymooners, and golfers, as well as corporate discounts and car-rental deals.

6   Getting There

If possible, fly directly to Maui; doing so can save you a 2-hour layover in Honolulu and another plane ride. If you're headed for Molokai or Lanai, you'll have to connect through Honolulu.

If you think of the island of Maui as the shape of a head and shoulders of a person, you'll probably arrive on its neck, at **Kahului Airport.**

At press time, four airlines fly directly from the mainland to Kahului: **United Airlines** (☎ **800/241-6522;** www.ual.com) offers daily nonstop flights from San Francisco and Los Angeles; **Hawaiian Airlines** (☎ **800/367-5320;** www.hawaiianair.com) has direct flights from Los Angeles (daily) and Seattle (four times a week); **American Airlines** (☎ **800/433-7300;** www.americanair.com) flies direct from Los Angeles; and **Delta Airlines** (☎ **800/221-1212;** www.delta-air.com) offers direct flights from San Francisco and Los Angeles. The other carriers fly to Honolulu, where you'll have to pick up an inter-island flight to Maui. Both **Aloha Airlines** (☎ **800/367-5250;** www.alohaair.com) and **Hawaiian Airlines** (☎ **800/367-5320;** www.hawaiianair.com) offer jet service from Honolulu. See "Inter-island Flights," below.

For information on airlines serving Hawaii from places other than the U.S. mainland, see chapter 2, "For Foreign Visitors."

LANDING AT KAHULUI AIRPORT   If there's a long wait at baggage claim, step over to the state-operated **Visitor Information Center,** where you can pick up brochures and the latest issue of *This Week Maui,* which features great regional maps of the islands, and ask about island activities. After collecting your bags from the poky, automated carousels, step out, take a deep breath, proceed to the

---

Packing Tip

You may be surprised to learn that it really can get cold on Maui. If you plan to see the sunrise from the top of Haleakala, bring a warm jacket—40°F upcountry temperatures, even in summer when it's 80°F at the beach, are not uncommon. It's always a good idea to bring long pants and a windbreaker, sweater, or light jacket. And be sure to bring along rain gear if you'll be in Maui from November to March.

---

curbside car-rental pickup area, and wait for the appropriate rental-agency shuttle van to take you a half mile away to the car-rental checkout desk. (All major rental companies have branches at Kahului; see "Getting Around," below.)

If you're not renting a car, the cheapest way to get to your hotel is **SpeediShuttle** (☎ **808/875-8070**), which can take you between Kahului Airport and all the major resorts between 5am and 9pm daily. Rates vary, but figure on $20 for two passengers to Wailea (one way) and $40 for two to Kapalua (one way). Be sure to call before your flight to arrange pickup.

If you're staying in the Lahaina-Kaanapali area, transportation service is available through **Airporter Shuttle** (☎ **800/533-8765** or 808/661-6667), which runs every half hour from 9am to 4pm; the cost is $13 one way, $19 round-trip.

You'll see taxis outside the airport terminal, but note that they are quite expensive—expect to spend around $60 to $75 for a ride from Kahului to Kaanapali and $50 from the airport to Wailea.

If possible, avoid landing on Maui between 3 and 6pm, when the working stiffs on Maui are "pau work" (finished with work) and a major traffic jam occurs at the first intersection.

AVOIDING KAHULUI   You can avoid Kahului Airport altogether by taking an **Island Air** (☎ **800/323-3345;** www. alohaair.com) flight to **Kapalua–West Maui Airport,** which is convenient if you're planning to stay at any of the hotels in Kapalua or at the Kaanapali resorts. If you're staying in Kapalua, it's only a 10- to 15-minute drive to your hotel; it takes 10 to 15 minutes to Kaanapali (as opposed to 35 or 40 minutes from Kahului). Island Air also flies into tiny **Hana Airport,** but you have to make a connection at Kahului to get there.

A newcomer on the interisland commuter scene is Kahului-based **Pacific Wings** (☎ **888/873-0877** or 808/575-4546; fax 808/ 873-7920; www.pacificwings.com), which flies eight-passenger, twin-engine Cessna 402C aircraft. It currently offers flights from Kahului to Hana, Molokai, and Waimea (on the Big Island), with plans to expand to flights to Kapalua, Lanai, and Honolulu.

INTER-ISLAND FLIGHTS

Don't expect to jump a ferry between any of the Hawaiian islands. Today, everyone island-hops by plane. In fact, almost every 20 minutes of every day from just before sunrise to well after sunset (usually around 8pm), a plane takes off or lands at the Kahului Airport on the interisland shuttle service. If you miss a flight, don't worry; they're like buses—another one will be along real soon.

Aloha Airlines (☎ **800/367-5250** or 808/244-9071; www. alohaair.com) is the state's largest provider of interisland air transport service. It offers 180 regularly scheduled daily jet flights throughout Hawaii, using an all-jet fleet of Boeing 737 aircraft. Aloha's sibling company, **Island Air** (☎ **800/323-3345** or 808/484-2222; www.alohaair.com), operates deHavilland DASH-8 and DASH-6 turboprop aircraft and serves Hawaii's small inter-island airports on Maui, Molokai, and Lanai.

Hawaiian Airlines (☎ **800/367-5320** or 808/871-6132; www.hawaiianair.com), Hawaii's first interisland airline (which also flies daily to Hawaii from the West Coast; see above), has carried more than 100 million passengers to and around the state. It's one of the world's safest airlines, having never had a fatal incident since it began operations in 1929.

MULTI-ISLAND PASSES   At press time, the standard interisland fare was around $100 one way between islands. However, both airlines offer multiple-flight deals that you might want to consider.

Nonresidents of Hawaii can purchase the Aloha Airlines **Visitor Seven-Day Island Pass.** For just $321 per person, including tax, you get unlimited travel on Aloha and Island Air for 7 consecutive days; Aloha also offers a 1-month version for $999. If you're traveling for more than a week but less than a month, you can buy a **Coupon Book** for $315, which contains six blank tickets that you can use—for yourself or any other traveler—any time within 1 year of purchase. This is probably the best deal if you're island-hopping two or three times in the course of your stay.

Hawaiian Airlines offers a variety of discounts based on the number of flights you're taking and the number of passengers flying. The **Hawaiian Island Pass** gives you unlimited interisland flights for $299 per person for 5 consecutive days, $369 for 7 days, and $409 for 2 weeks. Because Hawaiian Airlines also flies to and from the

mainland United States, you may also be able to apply your transpacific flight toward discounts on your interisland travel; be sure to
inquire when booking.

TRAVEL DEALS FOR NET SURFERS

Grab your mouse and start surfing before you hit the real waves in
Maui—you could save a bundle by finding great deals on the
Internet.

Several major airlines offer a free e-mail service known as
E-Savers, via which they'll send you their best bargain airfares on
a weekly basis. Once a week, subscribers receive a list of discounted
flights to and from various destinations, both international and domestic. Here's the catch: These fares are usually available only if you
leave the next Saturday (or sometimes Friday night) and return on
the following Monday or Tuesday. Some of the participating airlines
include **American Airlines** (www.americanair.com), **Continental
Airlines** (www.flycontinental.com), **Northwest Airlines** (www.
nwa.com), **TWA** (www.twa.com), and **US Airways** (www.
usairways.com).

Internet Airfares (www.air-fare.com) is one of the best sites for
searching for low airfares. **Airlines of the Web** (www.itn.net/
airlines) has a unique feature: the Low Fare Ticker, which allows you
to monitor fares around the clock (particularly useful during fare
wars). **AirSaver.com** (www.airsaver.com) specializes in consolidated
tickets. **Cheap Fare Finder** (www.cheapfarefinder.com) will search
for the cheapest fare, then arrange to have your ticket waiting for you
at the airport.

Arthur Frommer's Budget Travel (www.frommers.com) is
home of the Encyclopedia of Travel, *Arthur Frommer's Budget
Travel* magazine and daily newsletter, and lots of information on
Maui.

Travelocity (www.travelocity.com) and **Microsoft Expedia**
(www.expedia.com) are multipurpose travel sites. **Epicurious
Travel** (travel.epicurious.com) and **Smarter Living** (www.
smarterliving. com) allow you to sign up for all the airline e-mail
lists at once.

Pleasant Hawaiian Holidays (pleasantholidays.com) now offers
its low-cost deals on the Web; check out the site's 360-degree
"Surround Video" tours of hotels and destinations. **The Hottest
Airfares on Earth** (www.etn.nl/hotfares.htm) is a clearinghouse of
information on airfares, packages, and hotel deals from low-cost
ticket suppliers, tour operators, and travel agents. **Travel Shop**

(www.aonestoptravel.com) has access to consolidated rates on every aspect of travel to Hawaii, and promises to meet or beat any quote you get from a travel agent or airline. Finally, check out the Hawaii package deals at **Travelzoo.com** (www.travelzoo.com).

7 Getting Around

The only way to really see Maui is by rental car. There's no real island-wide public transit.

DRIVING AROUND MAUI

Maui has only a handful of major roads: One follows the coastline around the two volcanoes that form the island, Haleakala and Puu Kukui; one goes up to Haleakala's summit; one goes to Hana; one goes to Wailea; and one goes to Lahaina. It sounds simple, right? Well, it isn't, because the names of the few roads change en route. Study the island map on pages 2 and 3 before you set out.

The best and most detailed road maps are published by *This Week Magazine,* a free visitor publication available on Maui. For island maps, check out those published by the University of Hawaii Press. Updated periodically, they include a detailed network of island roads, large-scale insets of towns, historical and contemporary points of interest, parks, beaches, and hiking trails. These maps cost about $3 each, or about $15 for a complete set. If you can't find them in a bookstore near you, write to **University of Hawaii Press,** 2840 Kolowalu St., Honolulu, HI 96822. If you seek topographical maps, write the **Hawaii Geographic Society,** P.O. Box 1698, Honolulu, HI 96806 (☎ **808/546-3952;** fax 808/536-5999).

TRAFFIC ADVISORY   The road from Central Maui to Kihei and Wailea, Mokulele Highway (Hwy. 311), is a dangerous strip that's often the scene of head-on crashes involving intoxicated and speeding drivers; be careful. Also, be alert on the Honoapiilani Highway (Hwy. 30) en route to Lahaina, since drivers who spot whales in the channel between Maui and Lanai often slam on the brakes and cause major tie-ups and accidents.

If you get into trouble on Maui's highways, look for the flashing blue strobe lights on 12-foot poles; at the base are emergency, solar-powered call boxes (programmed to dial 911 as soon as you pick up the handset). There are 29 emergency call boxes on the island's busiest highways and remote areas, including along the Hana and Haleakala highways and on the north end of the island in the remote community of Kahakuloa.

Another traffic note: Buckle up your seat belt—Hawaii has stiff fines for noncompliance.

CAR RENTALS

All the major car-rental agencies have offices on Maui, usually at both Kahului and West Maui airports. They include: **Alamo** (☎ 800/327-9633; www.goalamo.com), **Avis** (☎ 800/321-3712; www.avis.com), **Budget** (☎ 800/935-6878; www.budgetrentacar.com), **Dollar** (☎ 800/800-4000; www.dollarcar.com), **Hertz** (☎ 800/654-3011; www.hertz.com), and **National** (☎ 800/227-7368; www.nationalcar.com).

There are also a few frugal car-rental agencies offering used cars at discount prices. **Word of Mouth Rent-a-Used-Car,** in Kahului (☎ 800/533-5929 or 808/877-2436), offers a four-door compact without air-conditioning for $115 a week, plus tax; with air-conditioning, it's $130 a week, plus tax. **AA Rent-a-Dent,** 220 Papa Place, Kahului (☎ 808/893-0057; fax 808/893-0211; www.keysmarketing.com/rentadent), has used cars in good condition; the weekly rate is $129, plus tax.

MULTI-ISLAND DEALS   If you're going to visit multiple islands, it's usually easiest and cheapest to book with one company and carry your contract through on each island for your entire stay; just drop off your car on the island you're leaving, and there will be one waiting for you on the next island with the same company. By booking your cars this way, as one interisland rental, you can usually take advantage of weekly rates that you'd be excluded from if you treated each rental separately. Both **Avis** (☎ **800/321-3712;** www.avis.com) and **Hertz** (☎ **800/654-3011;** www.hertz.com) can do this for you; inquire about interisland rental arrangements when booking.

INSURANCE   Hawaii is a no-fault state, which means that if you don't have collision-damage insurance, you are required to pay for all damages before you leave the state, whether or not the accident was your fault. Your personal car insurance may provide rental-car coverage; read your policy or call your insurer before you leave home. Bring your insurance identification card if you decline the optional insurance, which usually costs from $12 to $20 a day. Obtain the name of your company's local claim representative before you go. Some credit-card companies also provide collision-damage insurance for their customers; check with yours before you rent.

Hassle-free Discounts on Activities

You can save 10–25% on nearly 100 different activities statewide by buying an **Activity Owners Association of Hawaii Gold Card,** 355 Hukilike St., #202, Kahului, HI 96732 (☎ **800/398-9698** or 808/871-7947; www.maui.org), for just $30. The AOA Gold Card gives your entire family (up to four people) discounts on car rentals, helicopter tours, sailing tours, dinner cruises, horseback riding, kayaking, luaus, submarine tours, and more. Note that you must buy the card before you arrive in Hawaii.

OTHER TRANSPORTATION OPTIONS

TAXIS   For island-wide 24-hour service, call **Alii Taxi** (☎ 808/661-3688 or 808/667-2605). You can also try **Kihei Taxi** (☎ 808/879-3000), **Wailea Taxi** (☎ 808/874-5000), or **Yellow Cab of Maui** (☎ 808/877-7000) if you need a ride.

SHUTTLES   SpeediShuttle (☎ **808/875-8070**) can take you between Kahului Airport and all the major resorts from 5am to 9pm daily (for details, see "Landing at Kahului Airport," under "Getting There," above).

Free shuttle vans operate within the resort areas of Kaanapali, Kapalua, and Wailea; if you're staying in those areas, your hotel can fill you in on exact routes and schedules.

FAST FACTS: Maui

American Express   For 24-hour traveler's check refunds and purchase information, call ☎ **800/221-7282.** Local offices are located in South Maui, at the **Grand Wailea Resort** (☎ 808/875-4526), and in West Maui, at the **Ritz-Carlton Kapalua** (☎ 808/669-6018) and the **Westin Maui** at Kaanapali Beach (☎ 808/661-7155).

Area Code   All of the islands are in the **808** area code. Note that if you're calling one island from another, you must dial 1-808 first, and you'll be billed at long-distance rates (which can be more expensive than calling the mainland).

Dentist   Emergency dental care is available at **Maui Dental Center,** 162 Alamaha St., Kahului (☎ **808/871-6283**).

Doctor   No appointment is necessary at **West Maui Healthcare Center,** Whalers Village, 2435 Kaanapali Pkwy., Suite H-7 (near

Leilani's Restaurant), Kaanapali (☎ **808/667-9721;** fax 808/
661-1584), which is open 365 days a year, nightly until 10pm. In
Kihei, call **Urgent Care,** 1325 S. Kihei Rd., Suite 103 (at Lipoa
Street, across from Star Market), Kihei (☎ **808/879-7781**), open
daily from 6am to midnight; doctors are on call 24 hours a day.

Emergencies   Dial ☎ **911** for the police, ambulance, and fire
department. District stations are located in Lahaina (☎ **808/
661-4441**) and in Hana (☎ **808/248-8311**). For the **Poison
Control Center,** call ☎ **800/362-3585.**

Hospitals   For medical attention, go to **Maui Memorial
Hospital,** in Central Maui at 221 Mahalani, Wailuku (☎ 808/
244-9056); East Maui's **Hana Medical Center,** on Hana
Highway (☎ 808/248-8924); or **Kula Hospital,** in upcountry
Maui at 204 Kula Hwy., Kula (☎ 808/878-1221).

Smoking   It's against the law to smoke in public buildings,
including airports, grocery stores, retail shops, movie theaters,
banks, and all government buildings and facilities. Hotels have
no-smoking rooms available, restaurants have no-smoking sections,
and car-rental agencies have smoke-free cars. Most bed-and-
breakfasts prohibit smoking indoors.

Taxes   Hawaii's sales tax is 4%. Hotel occupancy tax is 7.25%,
and hoteliers are allowed by the state to tack on an additional
.1666% excise tax. Thus, expect taxes of about 11.42% to be added
to every hotel bill.

Time   Hawaii standard time is in effect year-round. Hawaii is
2 hours behind Pacific standard time and 5 hours behind eastern
standard time. In other words, when it's noon in Hawaii, it's
2pm in California and 5pm in New York during standard time
on the mainland. There's no daylight-savings time here, so when
daylight-savings time is in effect on the mainland, Hawaii is 3 hours
behind the West Coast and 6 hours behind the East Coast; in
summer, when it's noon in Hawaii, it's 3pm in California and 6pm
in New York.

Hawaii is east of the international date line, putting it in the
same day as the U.S. mainland and Canada, and a day behind
Australia, New Zealand, and Asia.

Weather   For the current weather, call ☎ **808/871-5054;**
for Haleakala National Park weather, call ☎ **808/572-9306;**
for marine weather and surf and wave conditions, call ☎ **808/
877-3477.**

For Foreign Visitors

by Jeanette Foster

The pervasiveness of American culture around the world might make the United States feel like familiar territory to foreign visitors, but leaving your own country for the States—especially the unique island state of Hawaii—still requires an additional degree of planning. This chapter will help prepare you for the more common problems, expected and unexpected, that visitors to the islands might encounter.

1 Preparing for Your Trip

ENTRY REQUIREMENTS

Immigration laws are a hot political issue in the United States these days, and the following requirements might have changed somewhat by the time you plan your trip. Check at any U.S. embassy or consulate for current information and requirements. You can also go to the **U.S. State Department's** Web site at **www.state.gov**.

DOCUMENT REGULATIONS   Canadian citizens may enter the United States without visas; they need only proof of residence.

The U.S. State Department has a **Visa Waiver Pilot Program** allowing citizens of certain countries to enter the United States without a visa for stays of up to 90 days. At press time, these included Andorra, Argentina, Australia, Austria, Belgium, Brunei, Denmark, Finland, France, Germany, Iceland, Ireland, Italy, Japan, Liechtenstein, Luxembourg, Monaco, the Netherlands, New Zealand, Norway, San Marino, Slovenia, Spain, Sweden, Switzerland, and the United Kingdom. Citizens of these countries need only a valid passport and a round-trip air or cruise ticket in their possession upon arrival. If they first enter the United States, they may then visit Mexico, Canada, Bermuda, and/or the Caribbean islands and return to the United States without needing a visa. Further information is available from any U.S. embassy or consulate.

Citizens of all other countries must have (1) a valid **passport** with an expiration date at least 6 months later than the scheduled end of their visit to the United States, and (2) a **tourist visa,** which can be obtained without charge from the nearest U.S. consulate.

To obtain a visa, you must submit a completed application form (either in person or by mail) with a $1^{1}/_{2}$-inch-square photo, and you must demonstrate binding ties to a residence abroad. Usually you can obtain a visa at once or within 24 hours, but it may take longer during the summer rush from June to August. If you cannot go in person, contact the nearest U.S. embassy or consulate for directions on applying by mail. Your travel agent or airline office may also be able to provide you with visa applications and instructions. The U.S. consulate or embassy that issues your visa will determine whether you will be issued a multiple- or single-entry visa and any restrictions regarding the length of your stay.

British subjects can obtain up-to-date passport and visa information by calling the **U.S. Embassy Visa Information Line** (☎ 0891/ 200-290) or the **London Passport Office** (☎ 0990/210-410 for recorded information).

Foreign driver's licenses are recognized in Hawaii, although you might want to get an international driver's license if your home license is not written in English.

MEDICAL REQUIREMENTS   Inoculations are not needed to enter the United States unless you are coming from, or have stopped over in, areas known to be suffering from epidemics, particularly cholera or yellow fever.

If you have a disease requiring treatment with medications containing narcotics or drugs requiring a syringe, carry a valid signed prescription from your physician to allay any suspicions that you may be smuggling drugs.

CUSTOMS   Every adult visitor may bring in, free of duty, 1 liter of wine or hard liquor, 200 cigarettes or 100 cigars (but no cigars from Cuba) or 3 pounds of smoking tobacco, and $100 worth of gifts. These exemptions are offered to travelers who spend at least 72 hours in the United States and who have not claimed them within the preceding 6 months. It is altogether forbidden to bring into the country foodstuffs (particularly cheese, fruit, cooked meats, and canned goods) and plants (vegetables, seeds, tropical plants, and so on). Foreign tourists may bring in or take out up to $10,000 in U.S. or foreign currency with no formalities; larger sums must be declared to customs on entering or leaving by filing form CM 4790. For more information, contact **U.S. Customs** (☎ 202/927-1770; www.customs.ustreas.gov).

In addition, you cannot bring fresh fruits and vegetables into Hawaii, even if you're coming from the U.S. mainland and have no

need to clear customs. Every passenger is asked shortly before landing to sign a certificate declaring that he or she does not have fresh
fruits or vegetables in his or her possession.

INSURANCE   There is no nationwide health system in the
United States, and the cost of medical care in Hawaii is extremely
high. Accordingly, we strongly advise every traveler to secure health
insurance coverage before setting out. You may want to take out a
comprehensive travel policy that covers (for a relatively low premium) sickness or injury costs (medical, surgical, and hospital); loss
or theft of your baggage; trip-cancellation costs; guarantee of bail in
case you are arrested; and costs of accident, repatriation, or death.
Such packages (such as **Europ Assistance** in Europe) are sold by
automobile clubs at attractive rates, as well as by insurance companies and travel agencies. **Worldwide Assistance Services** (☎ **800/
821-2828**) is the Europ Assistance agent in the United States.

Insurance for British Travelers   Most big travel agents offer their
own insurance, and they will probably try to sell you their package
when you book a holiday. Think before you sign. Britain's Consum-
ers' Association recommends that you insist on seeing the policy and
reading the fine print before buying travel insurance. The **Association of British Insurers** (☎ **0171/600-3333**) gives advice by
phone and publishes the free *Holiday Insurance,* a guide to policy
provisions and prices. You might also shop around for better deals:
try **Columbus Travel Insurance Ltd.** (☎ **0171/375-0011**) or, for
students, **Campus Travel** (☎ **0171/730-2101**).

MONEY

CURRENCY   The American monetary system has a decimal base:
one U.S. **dollar** ($1) = 100 **cents** (100¢). Dollar bills commonly
come in $1 ("a buck"), $5, $10, $20, $50, and $100 denominations
(the last two are usually not welcome when paying for small
purchases and are not accepted in taxis or movie theaters).

There are six denominations of coins: 1¢ (1 cent or a "penny"),
5¢ (5 cents or a "nickel"), 10¢ (10 cents or a "dime"), 25¢ (25 cents
or a "quarter"), 50¢ (50 cents or a "half-dollar"), and the rare
$1 piece.

EXCHANGING CURRENCY   Exchanging foreign currency for
U.S. dollars can be painless on Maui. Most major banks will exchange your foreign currency for U.S. dollars, and banks generally
offer the best rates. Most major hotels also offer exchange services,
but the rate of exchange is usually not as good. Aside from desks at

banks and hotels, there are no currency-exchange services on Maui, but there are currency services at the Honolulu International Airport.

TRAVELER'S CHECKS   It's actually cheaper and faster to get cash at an automated-teller machine (ATM) than to fuss with traveler's checks. Maui has ATMs almost everywhere. If you do bring traveler's checks, those denominated in U.S. dollars are readily accepted at most hotels, restaurants, and large stores. Do not bring traveler's checks denominated in any currency other than U.S. dollars.

CREDIT CARDS   The method of payment most widely used is the credit card: Visa (BarclayCard in Britain), MasterCard (Eurocard in Europe, Access in Britain, Chargex in Canada), American Express, Diners Club, Discover, and Carte Blanche. You can save yourself trouble by using "plastic money" rather than cash or traveler's checks in most hotels, restaurants, and retail stores (a growing number of food and liquor stores now accept credit cards). You must have a credit card to rent a car on Maui.

SAFETY

GENERAL SAFETY   Although tourist areas are generally safe, crime is on the increase everywhere in the United States, and Maui is no exception. Visitors should always stay alert. It's wise to ask the island tourist office if you're in doubt about which neighborhoods are safe. Avoid deserted areas, especially at night. Generally speaking, you can feel safe in areas where there are many people and open establishments.

Avoid carrying valuables with you on the street, and don't display expensive cameras or electronic equipment. Hold onto your pocketbook, and place your billfold in an inside pocket. In theaters, restaurants, and other public places, keep your possessions in sight. When you go to the beach, do not leave valuables such as your wallet or passport on your beach towel when you go into the water.

Remember also that hotels are open to the public, and in a large hotel, security may not be able to screen everyone entering. Always lock your room door—don't assume that once inside your hotel you are automatically safe and no longer need to be aware of your surroundings.

DRIVING SAFETY   Safety while driving is particularly important. Question your rental agency about personal safety, or ask for a brochure of traveler safety tips when you pick up your car. Ask the agency to provide written directions or a map with the route marked in red showing how to get to your destination.

Recently, more crime has involved burglary of tourist rental cars in hotel parking structures and at beach parking lots. Park in well-lighted and well-traveled areas if possible. Leaving your rental car unlocked and empty of your valuables is probably safer than locking your car with valuables in plain view. Never leave any packages or valuables in sight. If someone attempts to rob you or steal your car, do not try to resist the thief or carjacker—report the incident to the police department immediately.

For more information on driving rules and getting around by car in Maui, see "Getting Around," in chapter 1.

2 Getting to & Around the United States

Airlines serving Hawaii from other than the U.S. mainland include **Air Canada** (☎ 800/776-3000; www.aircanada.ca); **Canada 3000** (☎ 888/CAN-3000; www.canada3000.com); **Canadian Airlines** (☎ 800/426-7000; www.cdnair.ca); **Air New Zealand** (☎ 0800/ 737-000 in Auckland, 64-3/379-5200 in Christchurch, or 800/ 926-7255 in the U.S.; www.airnz.com), which runs 40 flights per week between Auckland and Hawaii; **Qantas** (☎ 008/177-767 in Australia or 800/227-4500 in the U.S.; www.qantas.com), which flies between Sydney and Honolulu daily (plus additional flights 4 days a week); **Japan Air Lines** (☎ 03/5489-1111 in Tokyo or 800/525-3663 in the U.S.; www.jal.co.jp); **All Nippon Airways** (ANA) (☎ 03/5489-1212 in Tokyo or 800/235-9262 in the U.S.; www.ana.co.jp); **China Airlines** (☎ 02/715-1212 in Taipei or 800/227-5118 in the U.S.; www.china-airlines.com); **Garuda Indonesian** (☎ 251/2235 in Jakarta or 800/342-7832 in the U.S.); **Korean Airlines** (☎ 02/656-2000 in Seoul, 800/223-1155 on the East Coast, 800/421-8200 on the West Coast, or 800/438-5000 from Hawaii; www.koreanair.co.kr); and **Philippine Airlines** (☎ 631/816-6691 in Manila or 800/435-9725 in the U.S.).

Travelers coming from Europe can take advantage of the **APEX** (Advance Purchase Excursion) fares offered by all major U.S. and European carriers. Aside from these, attractive values are offered by **Icelandair** (☎ 354/5050-100 in Reykjavik, 0171/388-5599 in London, or 800/223-5500 in the U.S.; www.icelandair.is) on flights from Luxembourg to New York, and by **Virgin Atlantic Airways** (☎ 0293/747-747 in Britain or 800/862-8621 in the U.S.; www.fly.virgin.com) from London to New York/Newark. You can then catch a connecting domestic flight to Honolulu.

Some large American airlines—such as **American Airlines, Delta, Northwest, TWA,** and **United**—offer travelers on transatlantic or transpacific flights special discount tickets under the name **Visit USA,** allowing travel between any U.S. destinations at reduced rates. These tickets are not on sale in the United States and must, therefore, be purchased before you leave your foreign point of departure. This system is the best, easiest, and fastest way to see the United States at low cost. You should obtain information well in advance from your travel agent or the office of the airline concerned, since the conditions attached to these discount tickets can be changed without advance notice.

The **ETN** (European Travel Network) operates a Web site offering discounts on international airfares to the United States, accommodations, car rentals, and tours: **www.discount-tickets.com**.

Visitors arriving by air should cultivate patience and resignation before setting foot on U.S. soil. Getting through immigration control can take as long as 2 hours on some days, especially during summer weekends. Add the time it takes to clear customs, and you'll see that you should make very generous allowance for delay in planning connections between international and domestic flights—an average of 2 to 3 hours at least.

For further information about travel to Maui, see "Getting There" and "Getting Around," in chapter 1.

FAST FACTS: For the Foreign Traveler

Climate   See "When to Go," in chapter 1.

Currency & Currency Exchange   See "Preparing for Your Trip," above.

Electricity   Maui, like the U.S. mainland and Canada, uses 110 to 120 volts AC (60 cycles), compared to 220 to 240 volts AC (50 cycles) in most of Europe, Australia, and New Zealand. In addition to a 100-volt transformer, small appliances of non-American manufacture, such as hair dryers or shavers, will require a plug adapter, with two flat, parallel pins.

Embassies & Consulates   All embassies are located in Washington, D.C. Some consulates are located in major cities, and most nations have a mission to the United Nations in New York City. If your country isn't listed below, call directory information in Washington, D.C. (☎ **202/555-1212**) for the number of your national embassy.

The embassy of **Australia** is at 1601 Massachusetts Ave. NW, Washington, DC 20036 (☎ 202/797-3000; www.austemb.org). There are consulates in New York, Honolulu, Houston, Los Angeles, and San Francisco.

The embassy of **Canada** is at 501 Pennsylvania Ave. NW, Washington, DC 20001 (☎ 202/682-1740; www.cdnemb-washdc.org). Canadian consulates are in Buffalo (New York), Detroit, Los Angeles, New York, and Seattle.

The embassy of **Ireland** is at 2234 Massachusetts Ave. NW, Washington, DC 20008 (☎ 202/462-3939). Irish consulates are in Boston, Chicago, New York, and San Francisco.

The embassy of **Japan** is at 2520 Massachusetts Ave. NW, Washington, DC 20008 (☎ 202/238-6700; www.embjapan.org). Japanese consulates are located in Atlanta, Kansas City, San Francisco, and Washington, D.C.

The embassy of **New Zealand** is at 37 Observatory Circle NW, Washington, DC 20008 (☎ 202/328-4800; www.emb.com/nzemb). New Zealand consulates are in Los Angeles, Salt Lake City, San Francisco, and Seattle.

The embassy of the **United Kingdom** is at 3100 Massachusetts Ave. NW, Washington, DC 20008 (☎ 202/462-1340). Other British consulates are in Atlanta, Boston, Chicago, Cleveland, Houston, Los Angeles, New York, San Francisco, and Seattle.

Emergencies   Call ☎ **911** to report a fire, call the police, or get an ambulance.

Gasoline (Petrol)   One U.S. gallon equals 3.8 liters, and 1.2 U.S. gallons equals 1 Imperial gallon. You'll notice that several grades (and price levels) of gasoline are available at most gas stations. You'll also notice that their names change from company to company. The ones with the highest octane are the most expensive, but most rental cars take the least expensive "regular" gas with an octane rating of 87.

Mail   If you aren't sure what your address will be in the United States, mail can be sent to you, in your name, c/o **General Delivery** at the main post office of the city or region where you expect to be (call ☎ **800/275-8777** for information on the nearest post office). The addressee must pick up the mail in person and produce proof of identity (driver's license, passport, or the like). Your mail will be held for pickup for up to 1 month.

Mailboxes, generally found at intersections, are blue with a blue-and-white eagle logo and carry the inscription U.S. POSTAL SERVICE.

If your mail is addressed to a U.S. destination, don't forget to add the five-figure postal code, or **ZIP code,** after the two-letter abbreviation of the state to which the mail is addressed. The abbreviation for Hawaii is **HI.**

International airmail rates are 60¢ for half-ounce letters (40¢ for letters to Mexico and 46¢ for letters to Canada) and 50¢ for postcards (35¢ to Mexico and 40¢ to Canada). All domestic first-class mail goes from Hawaii to the U.S. mainland by air, so don't bother paying the extra amount to send a letter back to your grandmother in Michigan.

Taxes   The United States has no VAT (value-added tax) or other indirect taxes at a national level. Every state and city has the right to levy its own local tax on all purchases, including hotel and restaurant checks, airline tickets, and so on. In Hawaii, sales tax is 4%; there's also a 7.25% hotel room tax, so the total tax on your hotel bill will be 11.42%.

Telephone & Fax   The telephone system in the United States is run by private corporations, so rates, particularly for long-distance service and operator-assisted calls, can vary widely—especially on calls made from public phones. Local calls—that is, calls to other locations on Maui—made from public phones cost 35¢.

Generally, hotel surcharges on long-distance and local calls are astronomical. You are usually better off using a **public pay telephone,** which you will find clearly marked in most public buildings and private establishments, as well as on the street.

Most **long-distance and international calls** can be dialed directly from any phone. For calls to Canada and to other parts of the United States, dial 1 followed by the area code and the seven-digit number. For international calls, dial 011 followed by the country code, the city code, and the telephone number of the person you want to call.

In Hawaii, interisland phone calls are considered long-distance and often are as costly as calling the U.S. mainland.

For **reversed-charge or collect calls,** and for **person-to-person calls,** dial 0 (zero, not the letter "O"), followed by the area code and number you want; an operator will then come on the line, and you should specify that you are calling collect, or person-to-person, or both. If your operator-assisted call is international, ask for the overseas operator.

Note that calls to area codes **800, 888,** and **877** are toll-free. However, calls to numbers in area codes **700** and **900** (chat lines, bulletin boards, "dating" services, and so on) can be very expensive—usually a charge of 95¢ to $3 or more per minute.

For **local directory assistance** ("information"), dial ☎ 411; for **long-distance information,** dial 1, then the appropriate area code and 555-1212.

Fax facilities are widely available and can be found in most hotels and many other establishments. Try **Mailboxes Etc., Kinko's,** or any photocopying shop.

There are two kinds of **telephone directories** in the United States. The so-called **White Pages** lists private households and business subscribers in alphabetical order. The inside front cover lists emergency numbers for police, fire, ambulance, the coast guard, poison-control center, crime-victims hot line, and so on. The first few pages are devoted to community-service numbers, including a guide to long-distance and international calling, complete with country codes and area codes. Also in the front are detailed maps of Maui, postal ZIP codes, and a calendar of events. Printed on yellow paper, the **Yellow Pages** lists all local services, businesses, and industries according to activity, with an index in the front. Drugstores (pharmacies) are also listed by geographical location, restaurants by type of cuisine and geographical location, bookstores by special subject and/or language, and places of worship by religious denomination.

Time   See "Fast Facts: Maui," in chapter 1.

Tipping   Tipping is so ingrained in the American way of life that the annual income tax of tip-earning service personnel is based on how much they should have received in light of their employers' gross revenues. Accordingly, they may have to pay tax on a tip you didn't actually give them!

Here are some rules of thumb:

In **hotels,** tip bellhops at least $1 per piece of luggage ($2 to $3 if you have a lot of luggage), and tip the housekeeping staff $1 per person, per day. Tip the doorman or concierge only if he or she has provided you with some specific service (for example, calling a cab for you or obtaining difficult-to-get theater tickets). Tip the valet parking attendant $1 every time you get your car.

In **restaurants, bars,** and **nightclubs,** tip service staff 15% to 20% of the check, tip bartenders 10% to 15%, and tip valet-parking attendants $1 per vehicle. Tip the doorman only if he has provided you with some specific service (such as calling a cab for you). Tipping is not expected in cafeterias and fast-food restaurants.

Tip **cab drivers** 15% of the fare.

As for **other service personnel,** tip skycaps at airports at least $1 per piece ($2 to $3 if you have a lot of luggage), and tip hairdressers and barbers 15% to 20%.

Tipping gas-station attendants and ushers at movies and theaters is not expected.

Toilets   You won't find public toilets or "rest rooms" on the streets in most U.S. cities, but they can be found in bars, fast-food outlets, restaurants, hotels, museums, department stores, or service stations (although the cleanliness of toilets at service stations, parks, and beaches is more open to question). Note, however, that restaurants and bars may reserve their rest rooms for the use of their customers; some establishments display a notice that toilets are for the use of patrons only. You can ignore this sign or, better yet, avoid arguments by paying for a cup of coffee or a soft drink, which will qualify you as a patron.

3

Accommodations

by Jeanette Foster

Maui has accommodations to fit every kind of dream vacation, from luxury oceanfront suites and historic bed-and-breakfasts to reasonably priced condos that will sleep a family of four. Before you book, be sure to read "The Island in Brief," which will help you decide on your ideal location.

Remember to consider *when* you will be traveling to the islands. Maui has two seasons: high and low. The highest season, during which rooms are always booked and rates are at the top end, runs from mid-December to March. The second high season, when rates are high but bookings are somewhat easier, is summer, June to September. The low season, with fewer tourists and cheaper rates, is April to June and September to mid-December.

Finally, remember to add Maui's 11.42% accommodations tax to your final bill. Parking is free unless otherwise noted.

1 Central Maui

WAILUKU
MODERATE

✪ **Old Wailuku Inn at Ulupono.** 2199 Kahookele St. (at High St., across from the Wailuku School), Wailuku, HI 96732. ☎ **800/305-4899** or 808/244-5897. Fax 808/242-9600. www.aitv.com/ulupono. 7 units. TV TEL. Year-round $120–$180 double. Rates include gourmet breakfast. Extra person $20. AE, CB, DC, DISC, MC, V.

This 1924 former plantation manager's home offers a genuine old Hawaii experience. The theme is Hawaii of the 1920s and 1930s. Guest rooms are wide and spacious, with exotic ohia-wood floors, high ceilings, and traditional Hawaiian quilts. The mammoth bathrooms (some with claw-foot tubs, some with Jacuzzis) have plush towels and "earth-friendly" toiletries on hand. A full gourmet breakfast is served on the enclosed back lanai or delivered to your room. You'll feel right at home watching the world go by from an old wicker chair on the lanai.

Located in the old historic area of Wailuku, the inn is just a few minutes' walk from the Maui County seat, the state building, the courthouse, and a wonderful stretch of antiques shops. It's fully equipped to handle business travelers, with automated message service, modem jacks, and multiple phones in each room; fax and copy services and computers are available for guest use.

2　West Maui

LAHAINA

VERY EXPENSIVE

Puunoa Beach Estates. 45 Kai Pali Pl., Lahaina, HI 96761. ☎ **800/642-6284** or 808/667-1666. Fax 808/661-1025. www.puunoa-beach-estates.com. 10 units. A/C TV TEL. High season $580 2-bedroom (sleeps up to 4), $695 2-bedroom with loft (sleeps up to 6), $730 3-bedroom (sleeps up to 6), $800 3-bedroom with loft (sleeps up to 8); low season $550 2-bedroom, $580 2-bedroom with loft, $605 3-bedroom, $665 3-bedroom with loft. 3-night minimum. Rates include full-size car and grocery package upon arrival. AE, DISC, JCB, MC, V.

Only 10 oceanfront residences dot this tropical 3-acre complex, offering a little corner of heaven in Lahaina. The town house–style units are huge (from the 1,700-square-foot two-bedroom to the 2,100-square-foot three-bedroom with loft), and all have private oceanfront lanais. These elegant homes have everything you can imagine (and at these prices, they should): top-of-the-line kitchen equipment, a separate dining area, two TVs, private bathroom with every bedroom, and a whirlpool tub in the master bedroom. Other extras include daily maid service, resident manager on-site, swimming pool with pavilion, whirlpool spa and sauna, barbecue area, and paddle tennis courts.

MODERATE

If you dream of an oceanfront condo but your budget is on the slim side, also consider **Lahaina Roads,** 1403 Front St. (reservations c/o Klahani Travel, 505 Front St., Lahaina, HI 96761; ☎ **800/ 669-MAUI** or 808/667-2712; fax 808/661-5875; e-mail: robyn@maui.net), which offers small, reasonably priced units in an older building in the quiet part of town ($100 one-bedroom, $180 two-bedroom; 3-night minimum). Another option is **Lahaina Shores Beach Resort,** 475 Front St. (☎ **800/628-6699;** www. lahaina-shores.com), a large, oceanfront condo complex with studio and one-bedroom units from $120 to $175.

Lahaina & Kaanapali

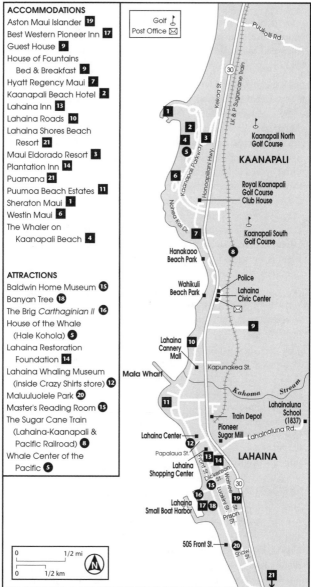

ACCOMMODATIONS
Aston Maui Islander 19
Best Western Pioneer Inn 17
Guest House 9
House of Fountains
  Bed & Breakfast 9
Hyatt Regency Maui 7
Kaanapali Beach Hotel 2
Lahaina Inn 13
Lahaina Roads 10
Lahaina Shores Beach
  Resort 21
Maui Eldorado Resort 3
Plantation Inn 14
Puamana 21
Puumoa Beach Estates 11
Sheraton Maui 1
Westin Maui 6
The Whaler on
  Kaanapali Beach 4

ATTRACTIONS
Baldwin Home Museum 15
Banyan Tree 18
The Brig Carthaginian II 16
House of the Whale
  (Hale Kohola) 5
Lahaina Restoration
  Foundation 14
Lahaina Whaling Museum
  (inside Crazy Shirts store) 12
Maluuluolele Park 20
Master's Reading Room 15
The Sugar Cane Train
  (Lahaina-Kaanapali &
  Pacific Railroad) 8
Whale Center of the
  Pacific 5

Golf
Post Office ✉

Puukolii Rd.
Kekaa St.
LK & P Sugarcane Train
Kaanapali North
Golf Course
KAANAPALI
Honoapiilani Hwy.
Kaanapali Parkway
Royal Kaanapali
Golf Course
Club House
Nohea Kai Dr.
Kaanapali South
Golf Course
Hanakaoo
Beach Park
Police
Wahikuli
Beach Park
Lahaina
Civic Center
✉
Lahaina
Cannery
Mall
Mala Wharf
Kapunakea St.
Kahoma Stream
Lahainaluna
School
(1837)
Train Depot
Pioneer
Sugar Mill
Lahainaluna Rd.
Lahaina Center
LAHAINA
Papalaua St.
Front St.
Dickenson St.
Wainee St.
Luakini St.
Lahaina
Shopping Center
Prison St.
Lahaina
Small Boat Harbor
505 Front St.
Shaw St.

0   1/2 mi
0   1/2 km
N

✪ **Aston Maui Islander.** 660 Wainee St. (between Dickenson and Prison sts.), Lahaina, HI 96761. ☎ **800/92-ASTON,** 800/367-5226, or 808/667-9766. Fax 808/661-3733. www.aston-hotels.com. 372 units. A/C TV TEL. High season $99 double, $125–$135 studio with kitchenette, $155 1-bedroom with kitchen (sleeps up to 4), $220 2-bedroom with kitchen (sleeps up to 6), $299 3-bedroom with kitchen (sleeps up to 8); low season $95 double, $115–$125 studio with kitchenette, $135 1-bedroom with kitchen, $195 2-bedroom with kitchen, $297 3-bedroom with kitchen. Extra rollaway bed $18, cribs free. AE, CB, DC, DISC, JCB, MC, V. Parking $1.

These units are one of Lahaina's great buys, especially those with kitchenettes; the larger ones are perfect for families on a budget. This wooden complex isn't on the beach, but it is on a quiet side street (a rarity in Lahaina) and within walking distance of restaurants, shops, attractions, and, yes, the beach (just 3 blocks away). All of the good-sized rooms, decorated in tropical-island style, are comfortable and quiet. The entire complex is spread across 10 landscaped acres and includes tennis courts (with lights for night play until 10pm), a pool, a sundeck, a barbecue, and a picnic area. The aloha-friendly staff will be happy to take the time to answer all of your questions.

Best Western Pioneer Inn. 658 Wharf St. (in front of Lahaina Pier), Lahaina, HI 96761. ☎ **800/457-5457** or 808/661-3636. Fax 808/667-5708. www.bestwestern.com. 50 units. A/C TV TEL. Year-round $99–$159 double. Extra person $15. AE, CB, DC, DISC, MC, V. Parking $4 in lot 2 blocks away.

This historic hotel has come a long way from its origins as a turn-of-the-century whalers' saloon and inn. Until the 1970s, a room at the Pioneer Inn overlooking Lahaina Harbor went for $20 and included a can of Raid insect repellent; the honky-tonk bar downstairs went until the wee hours of the morning, so no one slept. But those days are long gone—and this old waterfront hotel has never looked better.

This once-rowdy home-away-from-home for sailors and whalers now seems almost respectable, like visiting your great-grandma's house—old but nice, even charming (a word never before associated with this relic). The hotel is a two-story plantation-style structure with big verandas that overlook the streets of Lahaina and the harbor. All rooms have been totally remodeled, with vintage bathrooms and new curtains and carpets; they even have VCRs now. There's a new outdoor pool, three restaurants, the historic whalers' saloon (without the honky-tonk music), 20 shops, and the Lahaina Harbor just 50 feet away. The quietest rooms face either the garden court-yard—devoted to refined outdoor dining accompanied by live (but quiet) music—or the square-block-sized banyan tree next door. We recommend room no. 47, over the banyan court, with a view of the ocean and the harbor. If you want a front-row seat for all the Front Street action, book no. 48.

House of Fountains Bed & Breakfast. 1579 Lokia St. (off Fleming Rd., north of Lahaina town), Lahaina, HI 96761. ☎ **800/789-6865** or 808/667-2121. Fax 808/667-2120. www.alohahouse.com. 6 units (private bathrooms have shower only). A/C TV. $85–$125 double. Rates include full breakfast. Extra person $15. AE, DISC, MC, V. From Hwy. 30, take the Fleming Rd. exit; turn left on Ainakea; after 2 blocks, turn right on Malanai St.; go 3 blocks, and turn left onto Lokia St.

Talk about escape: A young German couple ran away to Maui for their honeymoon, fell in love with the island, bought a big house above Lahaina, and turned it into one of the area's best B&Bs. Their 7,000-square-foot contemporary home, in a quiet residential subdivision at the north end of town, is popular with visitors from around the world. This place is immaculate (hostess Daniela Clement provides daily maid service). The oversized rooms are fresh and quiet, with white ceramic-tile floors, bright tropical fabrics, and wicker furnishings; the four downstairs rooms all open onto flower-filled private patios. Guests share a pool, Jacuzzi, well-equipped guest kitchen, and barbecue area, and you're welcome to curl up on the living-room sofa facing the fireplace (not really needed in Lahaina) with a book from the library. Breakfast is served in the sunny dining room. Self-service laundry facilities are available for $2. The nearest beach is about 10 minutes away.

✪ **Lahaina Inn.** 127 Lahainaluna Rd. (near Front St.), Lahaina, HI 96761. ☎ **800/669-3444** or 808/661-0577. Fax 808/667-9480. www.lahainainn.com. 12 units (most bathrooms have shower only). A/C TEL. $99–$159 double. Rates include continental breakfast. AE, DISC, JCB, MC, V. Next-door parking $5. Children under 14 not accepted.

If the romance of historic Lahaina catches your fancy, a stay here will really underscore the experience. Built in 1938 as a general store, swept by fire in the mid-1960s, and reopened as a hotel in the 1970s, this place deteriorated into a fleabag with an eyesore of a bar at street level. Then, in 1986, rescue came in a classy way: It was saved from extinction by Rick Ralston, the Waikiki airbrush artist who became the Crazy Shirts mogul—and a one-man historic restoration society. About a million dollars of T-shirt money has brought this place back to life as a charming, antique-filled inn right in the heart of Lahaina.

If you like old hotels that have genuine historic touches, you'll love this place. As in many old hotels, some of these Victorian antique–stuffed rooms are small; if that's a problem for you, ask for a larger unit. All come with private bathrooms and lanais. The best room in the house is no. 7 ($99), which overlooks the beach, the town, and the island of Lanai; you can watch the action below or close the door and ignore it. Downstairs is one of Hawaii's finest bistros, David Paul's Lahaina Grill (see chapter 4).

✪ **Plantation Inn.** 174 Lahainaluna Rd. (between Wainee and Luakini sts., 1 block off Hwy. 30), Lahaina, HI 96761. ☎ **800/433-6815** or 808/667-9225. Fax 808/667-9293. www.theplantationinn.com. 18 units (some bathrooms have shower only). A/C TV TEL. Year-round $135–$215 double. Rates include full breakfast. AE, CB, DC, DISC, JCB, MC, V.

Attention, romance-seeking couples: Look no further. This charming inn looks like it's been here 100 years or more, but looks can be deceiving: The Victorian-style hotel is actually of 1990s vintage—an artful deception. The rooms are romantic to the max, tastefully done with period furniture, hardwood floors, stained glass, and ceiling fans; there are four-poster canopy beds and armoires in some rooms, brass beds and wicker in others. All come equipped with soundproofing (a plus in Lahaina), VCR, fridge, private bathroom, and lanai; the suites have kitchenettes. The rooms wrap around the large pool and deck. Also on the property are a spa and an elegantly decorated pavilion lounge, as well as Gerard's, an excellent French restaurant. It can be pricey, but hotel guests get a discount on dinner (you'll kick yourself if you don't eat here). Breakfast is served around the pool and in the pavilion lounge; ours featured fresh fruit, followed by a choice of Gerard's French toast or his homemade yogurt and granola.

Puamana. Front St., at the extreme southern end of Lahaina, a half mile from downtown (P.O. Box 11108), Lahaina, HI 96760. ☎ **800/669-6284** or 808/ 667-2712. Fax 808/661-5875. E-mail: robyn@maui.com. 40 units. TV TEL. $100–$175 1-bedroom double, $140–$250 2-bedroom, $300–$350 3-bedroom. 3-night minimum. AE, MC, V.

These 28 acres of town houses situated right on the water are the ideal choice for those who want the option of retreating from downtown Lahaina into the serene quiet of an elegant neighborhood. Private and peaceful are apt descriptions for this complex: Each unit is a privately owned individual home, with no neighbors above or below. Most are exquisitely decorated, and all come with a full kitchen, TV, lanai, barbecue, and at least two bathrooms. There are three pools (one for adults only), a tennis court, table tennis, and on-site laundry facilities (some units have washers and dryers as well). Puamana was once a private estate in the 1920s, part of the sugar plantation that dominated Lahaina; the plantation manager's house has been converted into a clubhouse with oceanfront lanai, library, card room, sauna, and office.

INEXPENSIVE

✪ **Guest House.** 1620 Ainakea Rd. (off Fleming Rd., north of Lahaina town), Lahaina, HI 96761. ☎ **800/621-8942** or 808/661-8085. Fax 808/661-1896. www.ourworld.compuserve.com/homepages/guesthouse. 5 units (1 unit shares a bathroom with hosts). A/C TV TEL. $69–$99 double. Rates include full breakfast. Extra person $15. AE, DISC, MC, V. Take Fleming Rd. off Hwy. 30; turn left on Ainakea; the house is 2 blocks down.

This is one of Lahaina's great bed-and-breakfast deals: a charming house with more amenities than the expensive Kaanapali hotels just down the road. The roomy home features parquet floors, floor-to-ceiling windows, and a pool—surrounded by a deck and comfortable lounge chairs—that's larger than some at high-priced condos. Every guest room is air-conditioned and has a ceiling fan, small fridge, TV, and private phone; four of the rooms each have a quiet lanai and a romantic hot tub. The large kitchen (with every gadget imaginable) is available for guests' use. The Guest House also operates Trinity Tours and offers discounts on car rentals and just about every island activity.

KAANAPALI
VERY EXPENSIVE

✪ **Sheraton Maui.** 2605 Kaanapali Pkwy., Lahaina, HI 96761. ☎ **800/STAY-ITT** or 808/661-0031. Fax 808/661-9991. www.sheraton-maui.com. 510 units. A/C TV TEL. $310–$465 double, from $600 suite. Extra person $40; children 17 and under stay free using existing bedding. AE, CB, DC, DISC, MC, V. Valet parking $8, self-parking $5.

Terrific facilities for families and fitness buffs and a premier beach location make this beautiful resort an all-around great place to stay. The first to set up camp in Kaanapali (in 1963), the hoteliers took the best location on the beach: the curving white-sand cove next to Black Rock (a lava formation that rises 80 feet above the beach), where they built into the side of the cliff. The grand dame of Kaanapali Beach reopened in 1997 after a $160 million, 2-year renovation; the resort is virtually new, with six buildings set in well-established tropical gardens. The lobby has been elevated to take advantage of panoramic views, and a new lagoonlike pool features lava-rock waterways, wooden bridges, and an open-air spa.

The new emphasis is on family appeal, with a class of rooms dedicated to those traveling with children (665-square-foot units with two double beds and a pull-down wall bed) and other kid-friendly amenities. Every room is outfitted with minifridges, free Kona coffee for the coffeemakers, irons, hair dryers, and even toothbrushes and toothpaste. Other pluses include a "no hassle" check-in policy: The valet takes you and your luggage straight to your room, thus no time wasted standing in line at registration. But not everything has changed, thankfully. Cliff divers still swan-dive off the torch-lit lava-rock headland in a traditional sunset ceremony—a sight to see. And the views of Kaanapali Beach, with Lanai and Molokai in the distance, are some of the best in Kaanapali.

Dining/Diversions: Three restaurants, with cuisine ranging from teppanyaki to steaks and seafood, plus a snack bar and three bars and cocktail lounges.

Amenities: Free summer children's program, in-room dining from 6:30am to 10:30pm, valet laundry, baby-sitting, express checkout, in-house doctors' office, two pools, three tennis courts, conference facilities, activities desk, fitness center, game center, full beach services, 24-hour coin-op laundry, and hospitality suite for early arrivals or late departures.

Westin Maui. 2365 Kaanapali Pkwy., Lahaina, HI 96761. ☎ **800/228-3000** or 808/667-2525. Fax 808/661-5831. www.westin.com. 793 units. A/C MINIBAR TV TEL. $265–$495 double, from $800 suite. Extra person $30 ($50 in Royal Beach Club rooms). Special wedding/honeymoon and other packages available. "Resort fee" of $6 for such amenities as free local phone calls, use of fitness center, complimentary coffee and tea, free parking, and free local paper. AE, DC, DISC, ER, JCB, MC, V.

The "Aquatic Playground"—an 87,000-square-foot pool area with five free-form heated pools joined by swim-through grottoes, waterfalls, and a 128-foot-long water slide—sets this resort apart from its peers along Kaanapali Beach. This is the Disney World of water-park resorts—and your kids will be in water-hog heaven. The fantasy theme extends from the estatelike grounds into the interior's public spaces, which are filled with the shrieks of tropical birds and the splash of waterfalls; the oversized architecture, requisite colonnade, and $2 million art collection make a pleasing backdrop for all of the action. Guests seem to love it: The resort has taken top honors in various readers' surveys, from *Condé Nast Traveller* to *Travel & Leisure*. With lots of indoor and outdoor meeting spaces, it's also a big hit with wedding parties and groups.

The majority of the rooms (refurbished in 1995) in the two 11-story towers overlook the aquatic playground, the ocean, and the island of Lanai in the distance. In addition to the standard features, each comes with a safe, an ironing board and iron, a coffeemaker, and its own lanai. The top-floor Royal Beach Club rooms feature a hospitality lounge and special amenities.

Dining/Diversions: Several outdoor restaurants and lounges, ranging from a sushi bar to a seafood buffet; see chapter 4 for a review of the Villa, a romantic restaurant near waterfalls.

Amenities: Twice-daily maid service, nightly turndown, multilingual staff, American Express and Hertz desks, and secretarial services. Guest Services will help you plan sightseeing and activities. Extensive health club and spa facilities. Extensive supervised kids' program weekdays. Five pools, Jacuzzi, water aerobics classes, scuba lessons for beginners and refresher courses, and guided outdoor adventure hikes. Coin-op laundry, ATM, and hospitality suite for early check-ins and late departures. Beauty salon, retail shops, business center, and conference facilities. Golf, tennis, and shopping are all at hand. A wedding coordinator, known as the director of romance, can help you throw an unforgettable wedding.

EXPENSIVE

Hyatt Regency Maui. 200 Nohea Kai Dr., Lahaina, HI 96761. ☎ **800/ 233-1234** or 808/661-1234. Fax 808/667-4714. www.hyatt.com. 815 units. A/C MINIBAR TV TEL. $260–$495 double, from $600 suite. Extra person $25 ($45 in Regency Club rooms); children 18 and under stay free using existing bedding. Packages available. AE, DC, DISC, JCB, MC, V. Valet parking $8, free self-parking.

People either absolutely love or hate this fantasy resort, the southernmost of the Kaanapali properties. It has lots of imaginative touches: a collection of exotic species (flaming pink flamingos, unhappy-looking penguins, and an assortment of loud parrots and macaws in the lobby), nine waterfalls, and an eclectic Asian and Pacific art collection. This huge place covers some 40 acres; even if you don't stay here, you might want to walk through the expansive tree-filled atrium and the parklike grounds, with their dense riot of plants and fantasy pools with grottoes, slides, and a suspended walking bridge. There's even an artificial beach in case the adjacent public beach is just too crowded.

All the rooms are pleasantly decorated in rich colors, floral prints, and Asian lamps—a welcome change from the typical beiges—and feature separate sitting areas and private lanais. In-room extras include safes, hair dryers, coffeemakers, and irons and ironing boards.

Dining/Diversions: Swan Court is a romantic setting for dinner; the Cascades Grille and Sushi Bar serves steak, seafood, and sushi; and Spats offers Italian fare. There's also the casual poolside Pavilion, numerous lounges, a swim-up cocktail bar, and the "Drums of the Pacific" dinner show.

Amenities: Twice-daily maid service, concierge, room service, activities desk, and baby-sitting on request. Two Regency Club floors have private concierge, complimentary breakfast, sunset cocktails, and snacks. Camp Hyatt kids' program offers daytime and evening supervised activities for 3- to 12-year-olds. The Great Pool; health club with weight and exercise rooms, Jacuzzi, sauna, and massage studio; six hard-surface tennis courts; three nearby golf courses; game room; and a small lending library. Snorkeling gear, bicycles, kayaks, boogie boards, and video and underwater cameras are available for rent. *Kiele V*, the Hyatt's 55-foot catamaran, sponsors snorkel trips, whale-watching excursions, and evening cruises.

✪ **Maui Eldorado Resort.** 2661 Kekaa Dr., Lahaina, HI 96761. ☎ **800/ 688-7444** or 808/661-0021. Fax 808/667-7039. www.outrigger.com. 98 units. AC TV TEL. $175–$200 studio double, $235–$260 1-bedroom (sleeps up to 4), $310–$350 2-bedroom (sleeps up to 6). Numerous packages available, including 7th night free, car packages, senior rates, and more. AE, CB, DC, DISC, JCB, MC, V.

These spacious condominium units—all with full kitchen, washer/ dryer, and daily maid service—were built at a time when land in Kaanapali was cheap, contractors took pride in their work, and visitors expected large, spacious rooms with views from every window. You'll find it hard to believe that this was one of Kaanapali's first properties in the late 1960s—this first-class choice still looks like new. The Outrigger chain has managed to keep prices down to reasonable levels, especially if you come in spring or fall. It's a great place for families, with its big units, grassy areas that are perfect for running off excess energy, and beachfront that's usually safe for swimming.

Amenities: Daily maid service, travel desk, fax services, personal safe, three pools, beach cabana, barbecue areas, shops, and laundry facilities.

✪ **The Whaler on Kaanapali Beach.** 2481 Kaanapali Pkwy. (next to Whalers Village), Lahaina, HI 96761. ☎ **800/367-7052** or 808/661-4861. Fax 435-655-4844. www.ten-io.com/vri. 360 units; 150 in rental pool. A/C TV TEL. High season $195–$210 studio double, $260–$390 1-bedroom (sleeps up to 4), $430–$510 2-bedroom (sleeps up to 6); low season $195–$205 studio, $235– $355 1-bedroom, $370–$480 2-bedroom. 2-night minimum. Extra person $15; crib $10. Packages available. AE, MC, V.

Location, location, location—in the heart of Kaanapali, right on the world-famous beach, lies this oasis of elegance, privacy, and luxury. The relaxing atmosphere strikes you as soon as you enter the open-air lobby, where light reflects off the dazzling koi in the meditative lily pond. No expense has been spared on these gorgeous accommodations; all have full kitchens, washer/dryers, marble bathrooms, 10-foot beamed ceilings, and blue-tiled lanais. Add to that a rarity in Kaanapali these days: free parking. Every unit boasts spectacular views, which include vistas of both Kaanapali's gentle waves and the humpback peaks of the West Maui Mountains.

Dining/Diversions: Next door is Whalers Village, where you'll find Peter Merriman's terrific Hula Grill and a handful of other restaurant and bar choices.

Amenities: Daily maid service, pool and spa, exercise room, five tennis courts. The Kaanapali Golf Club's 36 holes are across the street, and all the ocean activities Maui has to offer are just out back.

MODERATE

Kaanapali Beach Hotel. 2525 Kaanapali Pkwy., Lahaina, HI 96761. ☎ **800/ 262-8450** or 808/661-0011. Fax 808/667-5978. www.kaanapalibeachhotel.com. 433 units. A/C TV TEL. $150–$250 double, from $210 suite. Extra person $25. Car, bed-and-breakfast, golf, and romance packages available, as well as discount rates for seniors. AE, CB, DC, DISC, JCB, MC, V.

This old beach hotel, set in a garden by the sea, is Maui's most genuinely Hawaiian place to stay. It isn't a luxury property, but it's not bad, either. Three low-rise wings are set around a wide, grassy lawn with coco palms and a whale-shaped pool, bordering a fabulous stretch of beach. The spacious, spotless motel-like rooms are done in wicker and rattan, with Hawaiian-style bedspreads and a lanai that looks toward the courtyard and the beach. The beachfront rooms are separated from the water only by Kaanapali's landscaped walking trail.

The Kaanapali Beach Hotel is older and less high-tech than its upscale neighbors, but it has an irresistible local style and a real Hawaiian warmth that are absent in many other Maui hotels. Tiki torches, hula, and Hawaiian music create a festive atmosphere in the expansive open courtyard every night. As part of the hotel's extensive Hawaiiana program, you can learn to cut pineapple, weave lauhala (the leaf of the hala tree), and even dance the *real* hula; there's also an arts-and-crafts fair 3 days a week, a morning welcome reception weekdays, and a Hawaiian library.

The hotel's three restaurants feature native Hawaiian dishes as well as modern Hawaiian cuisine; there's also a poolside bar that fixes a mean piña colada. Amenities include a concierge, babysitting, a United Airlines desk, coin-op laundry, in-room movies, convenience shops and salon, conference rooms, beach-equipment rentals, free scuba and snorkeling lessons, and access to tennis and Kaanapali golf.

HONOKOWAI, KAHANA & NAPILI
VERY EXPENSIVE

Embassy Vacation Resort. 104 Kaanapali Shores Place (in Honokowai), Lahaina, HI 96761. ☎ **800/669-3155** or 808/661-2000. Fax 808/661-1353. www.maui.net/~embassy. 413 units. A/C TV TEL. $260–$400 1-bedroom suite (sleeps up to 4), $550 2-bedroom suite (sleeps up to 4). Rates include full breakfast and 2-hour cocktail party daily. Extra person $20; children 18 and under stay free using existing bedding. AE, CB, DC, DISC, MC, V. Parking $5. Take the first turn off Hwy. 30 after Kaanapali onto Lower Honoapiilani Rd.; turn left at Kaanapali Shores Place.

Kids will love this place. The all-suite property features a mammoth 1-acre pool with a 24-foot water slide, a great beach for swimming and snorkeling, and complete entertainment centers in every unit that will satisfy even the surliest teenager: 35-inch TV (with HBO), VCR (a vast video library is on-site), and stereo. With roomy condolike suites (ranging from 820 to 1,100 square feet) that feature hotel-style amenities, all-you-can-eat breakfasts, and free daily cocktail parties included in the price, Mom and Dad will be happy, too.

You can't miss this place; the shockingly pink pyramid-shaped building is visible from the highway. It's composed of three towers, each set around a central atrium amid tropical gardens with interlocking waterfalls and waterways; a huge wooden deck overlooks the koi-filled ponds and streams. Every unit has a full-sized sofa bed, a good-sized lanai, a minikitchen (microwave, small fridge, wet bar, and coffeemaker with free Kona coffee), two phones, a soaking tub big enough for two, and a second TV in the bedroom.

Dining/Diversions: There are three on-site dining choices: the oceanfront North Beach Grille, the poolside Ohana Bar and Grill, and a sandwich/snack bar, The Deli Planet.

Amenities: Concierge, laundry facilities, dry cleaning, tour desk, children's program (during holidays and in summer). Pool, health club, Jacuzzi, sauna, sundeck, 18-hole minigolf. Kaanapali's shops, golf, tennis, and restaurants are just minutes away.

EXPENSIVE

✪ **Napili Kai Beach Club.** 5900 Honoapiilani Rd. (at the extreme north end of Napili, next door to Kapalua), Lahaina, HI 96761. ☎ **800/367-5030** or 808/ 669-6271. Fax 808/669-0085. www.napilikai.com. 162 units. TV TEL. $170–$265 studio double, $270–$550 1-bedroom suite (sleeps up to 4), $270–$550 2-bedroom (sleeps up to 6). Extra person $10. Packages available. AE, MC, V.

Just south of the Bay Club restaurant in Kapalua, nestled in a small, white-sand cove, lies this comfortable oceanfront complex. Clusters of one- and two-story units with double-hipped Hawaii-style roofs

Accommodations from Honokowai to Kapalua

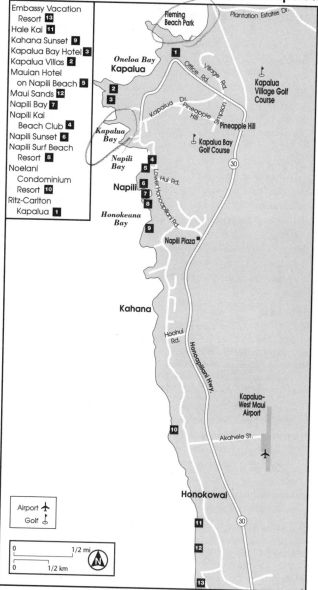

Embassy Vacation
  Resort **13**
Hale Kai **11**
Kahana Sunset **9**
Kapalua Bay Hotel **3**
Kapalua Villas **2**
Mauian Hotel
  on Napili Beach **5**
Maui Sands **12**
Napili Bay **7**
Napili Kai
  Beach Club **4**
Napili Sunset **6**
Napili Surf Beach
  Resort **8**
Noelani
  Condominium
  Resort **10**
Ritz-Carlton
  Kapalua **1**

Plantation Estates Dr.

Fleming
Beach Park

Oneloa Bay
Kapalua

Office Rd.
Village Rd.

Kapalua
Village Golf
Course

Kapalua Dr.
Pineapple
Hill

Simpson

Pineapple Hill

Kapalua
Bay

Kapalua Bay Golf Course

30

Napili
Bay

Lower Honoapiilani Rd.

Hui Rd.

Napili

Honokeana
Bay

Napili Plaza

Kahana

Hoohui
Rd.

Honoapiilani Hwy.

Kapalua-
West Maui
Airport

Akahele St.

Honokowai

30

Airport ✈
Golf ⚲

0	1/2 mi
0	1/2 km

N

face their very own gold-sand, safe-swimming beach; many have a view of the Pacific, with Molokai and Lanai in the distance. The older beachfront Lahaina Building units—with ceiling fans only—are a good buy at $215. Those who prefer air-conditioning should book into the Honolua Building, where, for the same price, you'll get a fully air-conditioned room set back from the shore around a grassy park-like lawn and pool. All units (except eight hotel rooms) have a fully stocked kitchenette with full-sized fridge, stove, microwave, toaster oven, and coffeemaker; some have dishwashers.

Dining: The Sea House Restaurant serves three meals; the Whale Watcher's Bar takes care of cocktails.

Amenities: Daily maid service, laundry facilities, dry cleaning, free children's activities (available Easter, June 15 to August 31, and Christmas), activities desk. Beach pagoda, two shuffleboard courts, barbecue areas, four pools, two 18-hole putting greens, nearby tennis courts, and golf just minutes away. Complimentary beach chairs, mats, swim masks, and snorkels; complimentary tennis rackets and golf putters. Complimentary coffee at the beach pagoda every morning, free tea in the lobby every afternoon, and a free mai tai party once a week.

MODERATE

Hale Kai. 3691 Lower Honoapiilani Rd. (in Honokowai), Lahaina, HI 96761. ☎ **800/446-7307** or 808/669-6333. Fax 808/669-7474. www.halekai. com. 40 units. TV TEL. High season $110 1-bedroom double, $140–$145 2-bedroom (sleeps up to 4), $180 3-bedroom (sleeps up to 6); low season $95 1-bedroom, $125–$130 2-bedroom, $180 3-bedroom. 3-night minimum. Extra person $10; children 3 and under stay free. MC, V.

This small, two-story condo complex is ideally located, right on the beach and next door to a county park; shops, restaurants, and ocean activities are all within a 6-mile radius. The units are older but in excellent shape, and come with a full kitchen and TV/VCR. Many guests clamor for the oceanfront pool units, but we find the park-view units cooler, and they still have ocean views (upstairs units also have cathedral ceilings). Book early, because units fill up fast; repeat guests make up most of the clientele.

❂ **Kahana Sunset.** 4909 Lower Honoapiilani Rd. (at the northern end of Kahana, almost in Napili), c/o P.O. Box 10219, Lahaina, HI 96761. ☎ **800/ 669-1488** or 808/669-8011. Fax 808/669-9170. E-mail: sun2set@maui.net. 49 units; 29 in rental pool. A/C TV TEL. High season $160–$180 1-bedroom (sleeps up to 6), $165–$265 2-bedroom (sleeps up to 6); low season $120–$160 1-bedroom, $140–$200 2-bedroom. 3-night minimum. AE, MC, V. From Hwy. 30, turn *makai* (toward the ocean) at the Napili Plaza (Napilihau St.), then left on Lower Honoapiilani Rd.

Lying in the crook of a sharp horseshoe curve on Lower Honoa-piilani Road is this series of wooden condo units, stair-stepping down the slide of a hill to a postcard-perfect white-sand beach. The unique location, nestled between the coastline and the road above, makes Kahana Sunset a very private place to stay. A small pool and Jacuzzi sit in the midst of a grassy lawn; down by the sandy beach are gazebos and picnic areas. The units feature full kitchens, washer/dryers, large lanais with terrific views, and sleeper sofas. This is a great complex for families: The beach out front is safe for swimming, the grassy area is away from traffic, and the units are roomy enough for all. The two-bedroom units have parking just outside, making carrying luggage and groceries that much easier.

Maui Sands. Maui Resort Management, 3600 Lower Honoapiilani Rd. (in Honokowai), Lahaina, HI 96761. ☎ **800/367-5037** or 808/669-1902. Fax 808/669-8790. www.mauigetaway.com. 76 units. A/C TV TEL. $85–$140 1-bedroom (sleeps up to 3), $115–$170 2-bedroom (sleeps up to 5). 7-night minimum. Extra person $9. MC, V.

The Maui Sands was built back when property wasn't as expensive and developers took the extra time and money to surround all their condo units with lush landscaping. It's hard to get a unit with a bad view: All face either the ocean (with views of Lanai and Molokai) or tropical gardens blooming with brilliant heliconia and sweet-smelling ginger. Each roomy unit has a big lanai and full kitchen. With two big bedrooms plus space in the living room for a fifth person (or even a sixth), the larger units are good deals for families. There's a narrow beach out front and a pool and laundry facilities on-site. In case you have any problems or questions, the management agency is just across the street.

Mauian Hotel on Napili Beach. 5441 Lower Honoapiilani Rd. (in Napili), Lahaina, HI 96761. ☎ **800/367-5034** or 808/669-6205. Fax 808/669-0129. www.mauian.com. 44 units. High season $145–$175 double; low season $125–$155 double. Rates include continental breakfast. Extra third or fourth person $10 each; children under 5 stay free. AE, DISC, MC, V.

This is a great place to get away from it all: The Mauian is perched above a beautiful half-mile-long, white-sand beach with great swimming and snorkeling; there's a pool with chaise longues, umbrellas, and tables on the sundeck; and the verdant grounds are bursting with tropical color. The renovated rooms feature hardwood floors, Indonesian-style furniture, and big lanais with great views. Return guests are drawn back by the small touches, such as the fresh flowers in rooms upon arrival (plus chilled champagne for guests celebrating a special occasion). There are no phones and no TVs in the rooms (this place really is about getting away from it all), but the large Ohana (family) room does have a TV with VCR and an extensive library for those who can't bear the solitude, plus complimentary coffee; phones and fax service are available in the business center. Great restaurants are just a 5-minute walk away, Kapalua Resort is up the street, and the nightly sunsets off the beach are spectacular.

✪ **Noelani Condominium Resort.** 4095 Lower Honoapiilani Rd. (in Kahana), Lahaina, HI 96761. ☎ **800/367-6030** or 808/669-8374. Fax 808/669-7904. www.noelani-condo-resort.com. 50 units. TV TEL. $97–$107 studio double, $127–$135 1-bedroom (sleeps up to 3), $167–$177 2-bedroom (sleeps up to 4), $197–$207 3-bedroom (sleeps up to 6). 3-night minimum. Rates include continental breakfast on first morning. Extra person $10; children under 17 stay free. Packages for honeymooners, seniors, and AAA members available. AE, MC, V.

This oceanfront condo is a great value, whether you stay in a studio or a three-bedroom unit (ideal for large families). Everything is first class, from the furnishings to the oceanfront location, with a sandy cove next door at the new county park. There's good snorkeling off the cove, which is frequented by spinner dolphins and turtles in the summer and humpback whales in winter. All units feature full kitchens, entertainment centers, and spectacular views. Our favorites are in the Antherium building, where the one-, two-, and three-bedrooms have oceanfront lanais just 20 feet from the water. There are two freshwater swimming pools (one heated for night swimming) and an oceanfront Jacuzzi. Guests are invited to a continental breakfast orientation on their first day and mai tai parties at night.

INEXPENSIVE

✪ **The Napili Bay.** 33 Hui Dr. (off Lower Honoapiilani Hwy., in Napili), c/o Maui Beachfront Rentals, 256 Papalaua St., Lahaina, HI 96767. ☎ **888/661-7200** or 808/661-3500. Fax 808/661-5210. www.mauibeachfront.com. 33 units. TV TEL. $65–$100 for up to 4. 5-night minimum. MC, V.

One of Maui's best secret bargains is this small, two-story complex, located right on Napili's half-mile white-sand beach. It's perfect for a romantic getaway: The atmosphere is comfortable and relaxing, the ocean lulls you to sleep at night, and birdsong wakes you in the morning. The beach here is one of the best on the coast, with great swimming and snorkeling—in fact, people staying at much more expensive resorts down the road frequently haul all their beach paraphernalia here for the day. The compact studio apartments have everything you need to feel at home, from a full kitchen to a big TV, comfortable queen bed, and roomy lanai that's great for watching the sun set over the Pacific. Louvered windows and ceiling fans keep the units cool during the day. Our favorite is no. 201, a corner unit with fabulous views and a king bed.

Within walking distance of restaurants and a convenience store, the complex is just a mile from a shopping center, 10 minutes from world-class golf and tennis, and 15 minutes from Lahaina. A resident on-site manager is a walking encyclopedia of information on where to go and what to do while you're on Maui. All this for as little as $65 a night—unbelievable! Book early, and tell 'em Frommer's sent you.

Napili Sunset. 46 Hui Rd. (in Napili), Lahaina, HI 96761. ☎ **800/447-9229** or 808/669-8083. Fax 808/669-2730. www.napilibay.com. 42 units. TV TEL. High season $95 studio double, $185 1-bedroom double, $265 2-bedroom (sleeps up to 4); low season $75 studio, $159 1-bedroom, $219 2-bedroom. 3-night minimum. Extra person $12; children under 3 stay free. MC, V.

Housed in three buildings (two on the ocean and one across the street) and located just down the street from Napili Bay (see above), these clean, older, but well-maintained units offer good value. At first glance, the plain two-story structures don't look like much, but the location, the bargain prices, and the friendly spirit of the staff are the real hidden treasures here. In addition to daily maid service, the units each have a free in-room safe, full kitchen (with dishwasher), ceiling fans, sofa bed in the living room, small dining room, and small bedrooms. Laundry facilities are on-site (you provide the quarters, they provide the free detergent). The beach—one of Maui's best—can get a little crowded, because the public beach access is through this property (and everyone on Maui seems to want to come here). The studio units are all located in the building off the beach and a few steps up a slight hill; they're good-sized, with complete kitchens and either a sofa bed or a queen Murphy bed, and they overlook the small swimming pool and garden. The one- and two-bedroom units are all on the beach (the downstairs units have lanais that lead right to the sand). The staff makes sure each unit has the basics—paper towels, dishwasher soap, coffee filters, condiments— to get your stay off to a good start.

KAPALUA
VERY EXPENSIVE

Kapalua Bay Hotel & Villas. 1 Bay Dr., Kapalua, HI 96761. ☎ **800/ 367-8000** or 808/669-5656. Fax 808/669-4694. www.kapaluabayhotel.com.

209 units. A/C MINIBAR TV TEL. $275–$525 double, $375–$525 villa suite, from $800 1- and 2-bedroom suites. Extra person $50; children 17 and under stay free using existing bedding. AE, CB, DC, JCB, MC, V.

Few Hawaiian resorts have the luxury of open space like this one. It sits seaward of 23,000 acres of green fields lined by spiky Norfolk pine windbreaks. The 1970s-style rectilinear building sits down by the often windy shore, full of angles that frame stunning views of ocean, mountains, and blue sky. The tastefully designed maze of oversized rooms fronts a palm-fringed gold-sand beach that's one of the best in Hawaii, as well as an excellent Ben Crenshaw golf course. Each guest room has a sitting area with a sofa, a king or two double beds, and an entertainment center; plantation-style shutter doors open onto private lanais with a view of Molokai across the channel. The renovated bathrooms feature two granite vanities, a large soaking tub, and a glass-enclosed shower.

The one- and two-bedroom villas are situated on the ocean at the very private Oneloa Bay. Each one has several lanais, a full kitchen, a washer/dryer, ceiling fans, an oversized tub, and access to three swimming pools with cabanas and barbecue facilities.

Dining: The most appealing dining spot is the Bay Club, in its own plantation-style building overlooking the sea, specializing in seafood for lunch and dinner. The casual Gardenia Court serves three meals.

Amenities: 24-hour room service, twice-daily maid service, ice service every afternoon and on request, resort shuttle, complimentary transfer to Kapalua–West Maui Airport, secretarial services, and baby-sitting. Two pools, an exercise facility, a famous trio of golf courses (each with its own pro shop), and 10 Plexi-pave tennis courts for day and night play (villa guests have access to two additional tennis courts). Kamp Kapalua, for kids ages 5 to 12, offers activities ranging from snorkeling and surfing to lei making and cookie baking. Adults can plan similar activities through the hotel's Beach Activity Center. The Kapalua Shops are within easy walking distance.

✪ **Ritz-Carlton Kapalua.** 1 Ritz-Carlton Dr., Kapalua, HI 96761. ☎ **800/ 262-8440** or 808/669-6200. Fax 808/665-0026. www.kapaluamaui.com. 548 units. A/C MINIBAR TV TEL. $265–$395 double, from $375 suite. Extra person $40 ($80 in Club Floor rooms). Wedding/honeymoon, golf and other packages available. AE, DC, DISC, MC, V. Valet parking $10, free self-parking.

Of all the Ritz-Carltons in the world, this is probably the best. It's in the best place (Hawaii) near the best beach (Kapalua), and it's got a friendly staff who go above and beyond the call of duty to make sure that your vacation is a dream come true. The Ritz is a complete universe, one of those resorts where you can sit by the pool with a book for two whole weeks. It rises proudly on a knoll, in a singularly spectacular setting between the rain forest and the sea, with a commanding view of Molokai.

The style is fancy plantation, elegant but not imposing. The public spaces are open, airy, and graceful, with plenty of tropical foliage and landscapes by artist Sarah Supplee that recall the not-so-long-ago agrarian past. Rooms are up to the usual Ritz standard, outfitted with marble bathrooms, private lanais, in-room fax capability, and voice mail. Hospitality is the keynote here; you'll find the exemplary service you expect from Ritz-Carlton seasoned with good old-fashioned Hawaiian aloha.

Dining/Diversions: Dining is excellent at the Anuenue Room (also great for elegant Sunday brunch), the outdoor Terrace (for breakfast and dinner), and poolside (for lunch). Whether you prefer your gourmet fare regular or macrobiotic, it'll be memorable, thanks to executive chef Patrick Callarec and crew. It's a small hike to the beach, so fortunately the Beach House serves daytime drinks and light fare. Cocktails are served in the Lobby Lounge, which doubles as an espresso bar in the morning. A new pool bar serves drinks by the three pools.

Amenities: 24-hour room service, twice-daily towels, nightly turndowns; private club floors with concierge, continental breakfast, afternoon drinks, private lounge, and other extras. Airport and golf shuttle, secretarial services, daily kids' programs, lei greetings, and multilingual staff. Three top-rated golf courses, a tennis complex, three pools, a nine-hole putting green, a croquet lawn, beach volleyball, a fitness center and salon, guests-only full-day guided backcountry hikes, and a historic plantation-style wedding chapel.

EXPENSIVE

Golfers and families will like the upscale **Kapalua Villas,** 500 Office Rd., Kapalua, HI 96761 (☎ **800/545-0018** or 808/669-8088; fax 808/669-5234; www.kapaluavillas.com), which come fully equipped and can accommodate groups ($185 to $245 one-bedroom condo, $250 to $400 two-bedroom condo, $1,195 three-bedroom home, $2,500 to $3,000 four-bedroom home, $4,000 to $5000 five-bedroom home). Guests have some access to the resort's amenities (some amenities are an additional fee) and enjoy special golf rates.

3   South Maui

KIHEI

We recommend two booking agencies that represent a host of condominiums and unique homes in the Kihei/Wailea area: **Kihei Maui Vacation,** P.O. Box 1055, Kihei, HI 96753 (☎ **800/ 541-6284** or 808/879-7581; www.kmvmaui.com), and **Condominium Rentals Hawaii,** 362 Huku Lii Place, Suite 204, Kihei, HI 96753 (☎ **800/367-5242** or 808/879-2778; www.crhmaui.com).

EXPENSIVE

Maalaea Surf Resort. 12 S. Kihei Rd. (at S. Kihei Rd. and Hwy. 350), Kihei, HI 96743. ☎ **800/423-7953** or 808/879-1267. Fax 808/874-2884. 34 units in rental pool. A/C TV TEL. $205–$230 1-bedroom double, $277–$307 2-bedroom (sleeps up to 4). Extra person $15. MC, V.

Located at the quiet end of Kihei Road, this two-story condominium complex sprawls over 5 acres of lush tropical gardens. This is the place for people who want a quiet, relaxing vacation on a well-landscaped property, with a beautiful white-sand beach right outside. The large, luxury town houses all have ocean views, big kitchens, and VCRs. Maid service (Monday through Saturday) is included in the price.

✪ **Maui Hill.** 2881 S. Kihei Rd. (across from Kamaole Park III, between Keonekai St. and Kilohana Dr.), Kihei, HI 96753. ☎ **800/92-ASTON** or 808/ 879-6321. Fax 808/879-8945. www.aston-hotels.com. 140 units. A/C TV TEL. High season $205 1-bedroom, $235 2-bedroom, $315 3-bedroom; low season $170 1-bedroom, $200 2-bedroom, $280 3-bedroom. AE, CB, DC, DISC, JCB, MC, V.

Located on a hill above the heat of Kihei town, this large, Spanish-style resort combines all the amenities and activities of a hotel—large pool, hot tub, tennis courts, Hawaiiana classes, and more—with large luxury condos that have full kitchens, lots of space, and plenty of privacy. Nearly all units have ocean views, a dishwasher, a washer/dryer, a queen sofa bed, a big lanai, and daily maid service. Beaches are within easy walking distance. The management here goes out of its way to make sure that your stay is as perfect as you planned it.

Amenities: Daily maid service, concierge service, weekly complimentary continental breakfast, and weekly manager's party. Large pool, hot tub, putting green, tennis courts, shuffleboard, 14 barbecue areas, and classes in Hawaiiana such as lei making and crafts. A variety of restaurants and shops is just a short walk away along South Kihei Road.

South Maui Coast Accommodations

Ann and Bob Babson's Bed & Breakfast and Sunset Cottage 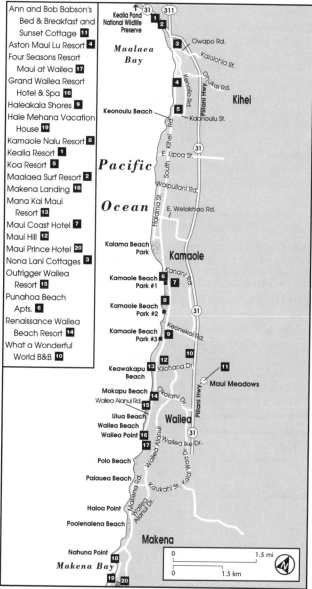 11
Aston Maui Lu Resort 4
Four Seasons Resort Maui at Wailea 17
Grand Wailea Resort Hotel & Spa 16
Haleakala Shores 9
Hale Mehana Vacation House 19
Kamaole Nalu Resort 8
Kealia Resort 1
Koa Resort 5
Maalaea Surf Resort 2
Makena Landing 18
Mana Kai Maui Resort 13
Maui Coast Hotel 7
Maui Hill 12
Maui Prince Hotel 20
Nona Lani Cottages 3
Outrigger Wailea Resort 15
Punahoa Beach Apts. 6
Renaissance Wailea Beach Resort 14
What a Wonderful World B&B 10

Kealia Pond National Wildlife Preserve

31 311

1
2

3

Owapo Rd.

Maalaea Bay

Kalolohia St.

4

Keonoulu Beach

Kaonoulu St.

Kihei

Piilani Hwy

Ohukai Rd.

Keala Rd.

5

Pacific

E. Lipoa St.

31

Ocean

Waipuilani Rd.

South Kihei Rd.

Halama St.

E. Welakaho Rd.

Kalama Beach Park

Kamaole

Kamaole Beach Park #1

Kanani Rd.

6
7

Kamaole Beach Park #2

8

31

Kamaole Beach Park #3

Keonekai Rd.

9

10

12

11

Keawakapu Beach

13

Kilohana Dr.

Maui Meadows

Mokapu Beach

14

Okolani Dr.

Wailea Alanui Rd.

15

Ulua Beach
Wailea Beach
Wailea Point

16

Wailea

Piilani Hwy

17

Wailea Ike Dr.

31

Polo Beach

Wailea Alanui

Wailea Alanui Rd.

Palauea Beach

Kaukahi St.

Wailea Alanui Dr.

Kaulana Dr.

Haloa Point

Poolenalena Beach

Makena

Nahuna Point

18

Makena Bay

19 20

0	1.5 mi
0	1.5 km

MODERATE

✪ **Aston Maui Lu Resort.** 575 S. Kihei Rd. (between Kaonoulu and Ohukai sts.), Kihei, HI 96753. ☎ **800/92-ASTON** or 808/879-5881. Fax 808/879-4627. 120 units. A/C TV TEL. High season $120–$185; low season $99–$165. Packages available. AE, DC, DISC, JCB, MC, V.

They just don't make them like this anymore. Located at the quieter northern end of Kihei, the Polynesian-style Maui Lu offers a nostalgic old-Hawaii atmosphere on its 28 green acres by the sea. Ask for a beach unit if you'd like to be right on the sand; the rest of the resort is across the road and up on a rise, around a pool shaped like the island of Maui. Each big, airy room is outfitted with rattan furniture, ceiling fans, Hawaiian art, two double beds, a coffeemaker, and a small fridge. Tennis and laundry facilities are available. The restaurant, Ukulele Grill, has an inspired local chef and a reasonably priced continental/Hawaiian gourmet menu; it serves breakfast, dinner, and Sunday brunch.

Haleakala Shores. 2619 S. Kihei Rd. (across from Kamaole Park III, at Keonekai St.), Kihei, HI 96753. ☎ **800/869-1097** or 808/879-1218. Fax 808/879-2219. 144 units; 76 in rental pool. TV TEL. High season $120 2 bedroom (sleeps up to 4), 7-night minimum; low season $90 2-bedroom, 5-night minimum. Extra person $10. MC, V.

This is a great buy for frugal travelers and for families on a budget. Each large unit (some 1,200 square feet) sleeps up to six people and comes with two bedrooms, two bathrooms, private lanai, full kitchen with dishwasher, and washer/dryer. The great location, just across the street from Kamaole Park III, makes it an easy walk to restaurants and shopping. Even the parking situation is ideal: There's a free covered garage. Okay, now for the bad news: The units were built in 1974, and most still sport 1970s-style decor. Also, they can be noisy, thanks to traffic on Kihei Road (ask for a unit inside the complex) and thin walls (you can hear your neighbors' TV and conversations quite clearly). If you manage to get a quiet unit and can overlook the nostalgic decor, these units are winners.

Kamaole Nalu Resort. 2450 S. Kihei Rd. (between Kanani and Keonekai rds., next to Kamaole Beach Park II), Kihei, HI 96753. ☎ **800/767-1497** or 808/879-1006. Fax 808/879-8693. www.mauigateway.com/~kamaole. 36 units. TV TEL. High season $145–$165 double; low season $100–$130 double. 3-night minimum. Extra person $10–$15. MC, V.

Located between two beach parks, Kamaole I and Kamaole II, this six-story condominium boasts fabulous ocean views. The property, right across the street from a shopping complex, has an ocean-side pool and barbecue facilities that are great for a sunset cookout. The units have large living rooms and private lanais; the kitchens are a bit small but come fully equipped. We recommend no. 306 for its wonderful bird's-eye ocean view. Be warned: Since the building is located on Kihei Road, the units can be noisy.

✪ **Koa Resort.** 811 S. Kihei Rd. (between Kulanihakoi St. and Namauu Place), c/o Bello Realty, P.O. Box 1776, Kihei, HI 96753. ☎ **800/541-3060** or 808/879-3328. Fax 808/875-1483. www.bellomaui.com. 54 units. TV TEL. High season $105–$180 double; low season $85–$160 double. No credit cards.

Located just across the street from the ocean, Koa Resort consists of five two-story wooden buildings on more than 5^1/$_2$ acres of landscaped grounds. The spacious, privately owned one-, two-, and three-bedroom units are decorated with care and come with a fully equipped kitchen. The larger units have both showers and tubs, whereas the smaller units have showers only. All feature large lanais, ceiling fans, and washer/dryers. The property has two tennis courts, a pool, a hot tub, and an 18-hole putting green. For maximum peace and quiet, ask for a unit far from Kihei Road.

Maui Coast Hotel. 2259 S. Kihei Rd. (1 block from Kamaole Beach Park I), Kihei, HI 96753. ☎ **800/895-6284** or 808/874-6284. Fax 808/875-4731. www.maui.net/~mch. 265 units. A/C TV TEL. $129–$139 double, $149–$159 suite, $179 1-bedroom (sleeps up to 4), $225 2-bedroom (sleeps up to 4). Extra person $10. Rental-car packages available. AE, DC, DISC, JCB, MC, V.

Built in 1993, this off-beach midrise stands out as one of the only moderately priced new hotels in Hawaii. That's big news—especially on Maui, where luxury abounds. More great news: For the price of a room (or a one- or two-bedroom apartment), the Maui Coast's Extra Value package gives you a rental car for free. The chief advantages of this hotel are price and location—about a block from Kamaole Beach Park I, with plenty of bars, restaurants, and shopping within walking distance. Rooms are clean and simple; they remind us of college dorms, only with lots of extras: sitting areas, coffeemakers and free coffee, hair dryers, whirlpool tubs, minifridges, safes, ceiling fans, and furnished, private lanais. There's a casual restaurant, a sushi bar, and a poolside bar with nightly entertainment. Additional amenities include room service, an activities desk, laundry, two pools (one for the kids), two Jacuzzis, tennis courts, and a gift shop. This ain't the Ritz, but you'll be very comfortable here—and your wallet will thank you.

INEXPENSIVE

✪ **Ann and Bob Babson's Bed & Breakfast and Sunset Cottage.** 3371 Keha Dr. (in Maui Meadows), Kihei, HI 96753. ☎ **800/824-6409** or 808/

874-1166. Fax 808/879-7906. www.mauibnb.com. 4 units. TV TEL. $80–$110 double (including breakfast Mon–Sat), $115–$125 cottage double. 4-night minimum. Extra person $15. MC, V.

In addition to the wonderful accommodations on their property, Ann and Bob Babson also operate a B&B booking service, where they go above and beyond the call of duty to find the ideal place for you. But we highly recommend staying right here on their landscaped half-acre, which boasts 180° views of the islands of Lanai, Kahoolawe, and Molokini, and sunsets not to be missed. Accommodations include two rooms in the house (one with panoramic ocean views, skylights, and a whirlpool tub), a one-bedroom suite downstairs, and a two-bedroom cottage.

Kealia Resort. 191 N. Kihei Rd. (north of Hwy. 31, at the Maalaea end of Kihei), Kihei, HI 96753. ☎ **800/265-0686** or 808/879-0952. Fax 808/ 875-1540. www.apmimaui.com. 51 units. TV TEL. $65–$90 studio double, $85–$130 1-bedroom double, $145–$175 2-bedroom (sleeps up to 4). 4-night minimum. Extra person $10. MC, V.

This oceanfront property at the northern end of Kihei is well maintained and nicely furnished—and the price is excellent. As tempting as the $65 studio units may sound, don't give in: They face noisy Kihei Road and are near a major junction, so big trucks downshifting can be especially noisy at night. Instead, go for one of the oceanview units, which all have full kitchens, washer/dryers, and private lanais. The grounds, which abut a 5-mile stretch of beach, feature a recently retiled pool with sundeck. The management goes out of its way to provide opportunities for guests to meet; social gatherings include free coffee-and-doughnut get-togethers every Friday morning and pupu parties on Wednesday.

Mana Kai Maui Resort. 2960 S. Kihei Rd. (between Kilohana and Keonekai rds., at the Wailea end of Kihei), Kihei, HI 96753. ☎ **800/367-5242** or 808/ 879-2778. Fax 808/876-5042. www.crhmaui.com. 132 units. A/C TV TEL. $80–$100 double, $150–$195 1-bedroom (sleeps up to 4), $185–$230 2-bedroom (sleeps up to 6). AE, DC, DISC, MC, V.

This eight-story complex, situated on a beautiful white-sand cove, is an unusual combination of hotel and condominium. The hotel rooms, which constitute half of the total number of units, are small but nicely furnished. The condo units feature full kitchens and open living rooms with sliding-glass doors that lead to small lanais overlooking the sandy beach and ocean. Some units are beginning to show their age, but they're all clean and comfortable. There are laundry facilities on each floor, the open-air restaurant called Five Palms, a pool on the property, and one of the best snorkeling beaches on the coast just steps away.

Nona Lani Cottages. 455 S. Kihei Rd. (just south of Hwy. 31), P.O. Box 655, Kihei, HI 96753. ☎ **800/733-2688** or 808/879-2497. Fax 808/891-0273. E-mail: kong_fam@sprynet.com. 11 units. A/C TV. $60 double, $70–$85 cottage. 4-night minimum. Extra person $7–$10 (children 5 and under pay an extra $5). No credit cards.

Picture this: right across the street from a white-sand beach, a grassy expanse dotted with eight small cottages tucked among palm and fruit trees. Built in 1975, the 400-square-foot cottages are tiny, but they contain all the necessities: a small but complete kitchen, two twin beds that double as couches in the living room, a separate bedroom with queen bed, and a lanai with table and chairs—ideal for watching the ocean waves as you eat your breakfast. The cottages are slightly worn, but the setting and the privacy make up for it. There are no phones in the cabins (a blessing if you're trying to escape civilization), but there is a public phone near the coin-op laundry.

If the cabins are booked, or if you want a bit more luxury in your accommodations, you might opt for one of the private guest rooms in host David Kong's main house. Each beautiful room features cathedral-like open-beam ceilings, plush carpet, koa bed frames, air-conditioning, and private entrance.

✪ **Punahoa Beach Apartments.** 2142 Iliili Rd. (off S. Kihei Rd., 100 yards from Kamaole Beach I), Kihei, HI 96753. ☎ **800/564-4380** or 808/879-2720. Fax 808/875-3147. E-mail: pb6110@aol.com. 12 units. TV TEL. High season $93 studio double, $127 1-bedroom double, $130 2-bedroom double; low season $66 studio double, $85 1-bedroom, $94 2-bedroom. 5-night minimum. Extra person $12. AE, MC, V.

Book this place. The location is fabulous: off noisy, traffic-ridden Kihei Road, on a quiet side street with ocean frontage. A grassy lawn rolls about 50 feet down to the beach; there's great snorkeling just offshore and a popular surfing spot next door; and shopping and restaurants are all within walking distance. All of the beautifully decorated units in this small, four-story building have lanais with great ocean views and fully equipped kitchens. Rooms go quickly during the winter months, so book early.

✪ **What a Wonderful World B&B.** 2828 Umalu Place (off Keonakai St., near Hwy. 31), Kihei, HI 96753. ☎ **808/879-9103.** Fax 808/874-9352. E-mail: amauibnb@maui.net. 4 units. A/C TV TEL. $65 double, $75 studio double, $85–$95 one-bedroom apt. Rates include full gourmet breakfast. Children 11 and under stay free. AE, DC, DISC, MC, V.

We couldn't believe what we'd discovered here: an impeccably done B&B with thought and care put into every room, a great location, and excellent rates. Then we met hostess Eva Tantillo, who has not only a full-service travel agency, but also a master's degree—along with several years of experience—in hotel management. The result? One of Maui's finest bed-and-breakfasts, centrally located in Kihei (a half mile to Kamaole II Beach Park, 5 minutes from Wailea golf courses, and convenient to shopping and restaurants). Choose from one of four units: the master suite (with small fridge, coffeemaker, and barbecue grill on the lanai), studio apartment (with fully equipped kitchen), or two one-bedroom apartments (also with fully equipped kitchens). Each comes with private bathroom, phone, and entrance. Guests are welcome to use the barbecue, laundry facilities, and hot tub. Eva serves a gourmet family-style breakfast on her lanai, which has views of white-sand beaches, the West Maui Mountains, and Haleakala.

WAILEA

For a complete selection of condominium units throughout Wailea and Makena, contact **Destination Resorts Hawaii,** 3750 Wailea Alanui Dr., Wailea, HI 96753 (☎ **800/367-5246** or 808/ 879-1595; fax 808/874-3554; www.destinationresortshi.com). The luxury units represented include one-bedroom doubles ($140 to $435), two-bedroom units that sleep up to four ($170 to $510), and three-bedroom units that sleep up to six ($450 to $600; extra person $20). Minimum stays vary by property.

VERY EXPENSIVE

✪ **Four Seasons Resort Wailea.** 3900 Wailea Alanui Dr., Wailea, HI 96753. ☎ **800/334-MAUI** or 808/874-8000. Fax 808/874-6449. www.fshr.com. 463 units. A/C MINIBAR TV TEL. $295–$690 double, from $545 suite. Extra person $80 ($140 in Club Floor rooms); children under 18 stay free using existing bedding. Packages available. AE, DC, JCB, MC, V.

All of the luxury hotels in Wailea are fabulous, boasting terrific views and luxurious accommodations. What sets the Four Seasons apart is its relaxing, casual atmosphere, combined with service so great you hardly notice it. If money's not a factor, this is the place to spend it. And bring the kids too: There's a complete activities program designed just for them.

It's hard to beat this modern version of a Hawaiian palace by the sea. Although it sits on the beach between two other hotels, you won't feel like you're on chockablock resort row: The Four Seasons inhabits its own separate world, thanks to an open courtyard of pools and gardens. The spacious (about 600 square feet) rooms feature furnished private lanais (nearly all with ocean views) that are great for watching whales in winter and sunsets year-round.

The grand bathrooms have deep marble tubs, showers for two, and lighted French makeup mirrors. Other amenities include safes, irons and ironing boards, hair dryers, and plush terry-cloth robes.

Service is attentive but not cloying. At the pool, guests lounge in casbahlike tents, pampered with special touches like iced Evian and chilled towels. And you'll never see a housekeeping cart in the hall: The cleaning staff works in teams, so they're as unobtrusive as possible and in and out of your room in minutes.

This ritzy neighborhood is home to great restaurants and shopping, the Wailea Tennis Center (known as Wimbledon West), and six golf courses—not to mention that great beach, with gentle waves and islands framing the view on either side.

Dining/Diversions: Seasons, the signature restaurant of the resort, recently lost chef George Mavrothalassitis, who was lured back to Honolulu to start his own restaurant—but his Hawaii Regional Cuisine is still served here in a memorable setting. The Seaside Restaurant offers a casual atmosphere by day; at night, it's transformed into Ferraro's at Seaside, serving authentic Italian fare. The poolside Pacific Grill offers lavish breakfast buffets and dinners featuring Hawaii Regional Cuisine.

Amenities: Twice-daily maid service, 24-hour room service, same-day dry cleaning and laundry, 1-hour and overnight pressing, free overnight shoe shine or sandal repair, complimentary valet and shuttle around resort, airport limousine service, rental cars at concierge desk, 24-hour medical service, lei greeting and oshibori towel on arrival, and early arrival/late departure facility. Voice mail, safes, hair dryers, irons and ironing boards, and terry-cloth robes. Special amenities on Club Floors, including breakfast, afternoon tea and snacks, cocktails, pupus, and open bar. Two pools (one for adults only), 41 pool and beach cabanas, two whirlpools (one for adults only), fitness center with weight room and steam room, tennis (two lighted Plexi-pave courts with rackets and tennis balls provided), putting green, and nearby golf. Beach pavilion with snorkels, boogie boards, kayaks, and other water-sports gear; 1 hour free use of snorkel equipment; complimentary use of bicycles; complimentary exercise and tennis attire on loan. Game room, video library, salon, shops, conference facilities. Year-round kids' program with loads of activities and a complete children's facility, plus a teen recreation center; children's video library and toys.

✪ **Grand Wailea Resort Hotel & Spa.** 3850 Wailea Alanui Dr., Wailea, HI 96753. ☎ **800/888-6100** or 808/875-1234. Fax 808/879-4077. www.grandwailea.com. 814 units. A/C MINIBAR TV TEL. $380–$580 double, from $1,100 suite. Extra person $30 ($50 in Napua Club rooms and suites). AE, DC, DISC, JCB, MC, V.

Here's where grand becomes grandiose. The pinnacle of Hawaii's brief fling with fantasy megaresorts, this monument to excess is extremely popular with families, incentive groups, and conventions; it's the grand prize in Hawaii vacation contests and the dream of many honeymooners.

This hotel really is too much. It has a Japanese restaurant decorated with real rocks hewn from the slopes of Mount Fuji; 10,000 tropical plants in the lobby; an intricate pool system with slides, waterfalls, rapids, and a water-powered elevator to take you up to the top; Hawaii's most elaborate spa (not even the Romans had it this good); Hawaii's most expensive hotel suite, a 5,500-square-foot pad with a 180° view of paradise; a restaurant in an artificial tide pool; a floating New England–style wedding chapel; and nothing but ocean-view rooms, outfitted with every amenity you could ask for. And it's all crowned with a $30 million collection of original art, much of it created expressly for the hotel by Hawaii artists and sculptors. There's also a fantastic beach out front.

Dining/Diversions: Six restaurants and 12 bars range from fine dining to casual poolside snacks, serving everything from Japanese and Italian specialties to local seafood and spa cuisine.

Amenities: Lei greeting, complimentary valet parking, 24-hour room service, twice-daily towel service, same-day laundry and dry cleaning, multilingual concierge, infant care center, art and hotel tours, Budget Rent-A-Car and American Express tour desks, and 100 Napua Club rooms (with attendants, complimentary continental breakfast, cocktails, and tea service). Hawaii's largest spa, the 50,000-square-foot Spa Grande, with a blend of European-, Japanese-, and American-style techniques; 2,000-foot-long Action Pool, featuring a 10-minute swim/ride through mountains and grottoes; complimentary dive and windsurf lessons; seaside wedding chapel; conference facilities. Kids enjoy a computer center, video game room, arts and crafts, 60-seat children's theater, and outdoor playground. Five golf courses, including two 18-hole championship courses, are nearby.

✪ **Renaissance Wailea Beach Resort.** 3550 Wailea Alanui Dr., Wailea, HI 96753. ☎ **800/9-WAILEA** or 808/879-4900. Fax 808/879-6128.

www.renaissancehotels.com. 345 units. A/C TV TEL. $290–$515 double, from $820 suite. Extra person $40; children 18 and under stay free using existing bedding. AE, CB, DC, DISC, MC, V. Parking $3.

This is the place for visitors in search of the luxury of a Wailea hotel, but in a smaller, more intimate setting. Located on 15 acres of rolling lawn and tropical gardens, Renaissance Wailea has the feeling of a small boutique hotel. Perhaps it's the resort's U-shaped design, the series of small coves and beaches, or the spaciousness of the rooms—whatever the reason, it just doesn't feel crowded here.

Each room has a sitting area, large lanai, TV and VCR, three phones (with data ports), fridge, and safe. The bathrooms include such extras as double vanities (one with lighted makeup mirror) and *hapi* coats (Japanese-style cotton robes). Bedspreads, drapes, and towels in all rooms have recently been upgraded. Rooms in the Mokapu Beach Club, an exclusive two-story building just steps from a crescent-shaped beach, feature such extras as private check-in, in-room continental breakfast, and access to a private pool and beach cabanas.

Dining/Diversions: The casual, open-air Palm Court offers buffets and oven-baked pizzas. Hana Gion features a sushi bar and teppanyaki grill. Maui Onion, a casual poolside restaurant surrounded by lush gardens and a cascading waterfall, serves breakfast and lunch. Every Monday, there's a traditional luau at sunset.

Amenities: Room service (from 6am to 11pm), lei greeting, concierge, complimentary in-room coffee and daily newspaper, complimentary video library, traditional Hawaiian craft classes, massage therapy, baby-sitting, Camp Wailea children's program. Complete fitness center, two freshwater swimming pools, two whirlpools, nearby golf and tennis, shopping arcade, hair salon, basketball court, Ping-Pong, and shuffleboard.

EXPENSIVE

Outrigger Wailea Resort. 3700 Wailea Alanui Dr., Wailea, HI 96753. ☎ **800/OUTRIGGER** or 808/879-1922. Fax 800/622-4852. www.outrigger.com. 516 units. A/C TV TEL. $229–$399 double, from $499 suite. Packages available. AE, CB, DC, DISC, JCB, MC, V.

This classic 1970s-style hotel is like a tropical garden by the sea. It was the first resort built in Wailea (in 1976), yet it remains the most Hawaiian of them all. Airy and comfortable, with touches of Hawaiian art throughout and a terrific aquarium that stretches forever behind the front desk, it just feels right.

What's truly special about this hotel is how it fits into its environment without overwhelming it. Eight buildings, all low-rise except for an eight-story tower, are spread along 22 gracious acres of lawns and gardens spiked by coco palms, with lots of open space and a half mile of oceanfront on a point between Wailea and Ulua beaches. The vast, parklike expanses are a luxury on this now-crowded coast.

All of the rooms have private lanais and separate dressing and bathroom areas with marble-topped basins. The Outrigger chain took over management of the hotel in 1999 and plans to make the necessary renovations to restore this once grande dame to her former glory.

Dining/Diversions: At press time, Outrigger had just taken over the hotel and promised to upgrade the dining facilities.

Amenities: Room service (from 6:30am to 11pm), same-day laundry and valet, multilingual concierge. Three pools, gift shop, newsstand, beauty salon, barber shop. Three championship golf courses nearby.

MAKENA
EXPENSIVE

✪ **Hale Mehana Vacation House.** 176 Makena Rd. (by the Keawalai Church in South Makena), Kihei, HI 96753. ☎ **808/879-2957.** Fax 808/877-2046. E-mail: dugal@maui.net. TV TEL. 1 three-bedroom/two-bathroom home. $200 double. 5-night minimum. Extra person $25; maximum 6 people. No credit cards.

Located right on the ocean at Makena (with the waves lapping just a few feet from the magnificent deck), Hale Mehana ("warm-hearted house") consists of the entire upstairs floor of a luxury home. Not a penny has been spared to make this property a dream oceanfront accommodation. A huge deck wraps around the house, offering breathtaking views of Molokini and Kahoolawe in the distance and easy access to swimming, snorkeling, and kayaking. The living area has big picture windows, polished wooden floors, a huge sofa, and a complete entertainment center. The kitchen opens onto the living/dining area, taking advantage of those incredible views; it contains every possible appliance a cook could want. The master bedroom is simply fabulous: a huge bay window looks out on the ocean, and the large master bathroom has a Jacuzzi big enough for two. Two small-ish bedrooms share a full bathroom. Makena golf and tennis courts are just 2 minutes away, and Wailea restaurants and shopping are a 5-minute drive.

Maui Prince Hotel. 5400 Makena Alanui, Makena, HI 96753. ☎ **800/ 321-MAUI** or 808/874-1111. Fax 808/879-8763. www.westin.com. 304 units. A/C MINIBAR TV TEL. $230–$395 double, $440–$840 suite. Packages available. AE, DC, JCB, MC, V.

If you're looking for a vacation in a beautiful, tranquil spot with a golden-sand beach, here's your place. But if you plan to tour Maui, this is definitely out of your way: It's at the end of the road—far, far away from anything else on the island.

When you first see the stark white hotel, it looks like a high-rise motel stuck in the woods—from the outside. Inside, you'll discover an atrium garden with a koi-filled waterfall stream, an ocean view from every room, and a simplicity to the furnishings that makes some people feel uncomfortable and others blissfully clutter-free. Rooms are small but come with private lanais with great views.

Dining/Diversions: Japanese cuisine tops the menu at the elegant Hakone, which also has a sushi bar. For dinner, the Prince Court specializes in Hawaii Regional Cuisine, while the casual Cafe Kiowai offers seasonal and international specialties. The Makena Clubhouse Restaurant serves lunch and snacks. The Molokini Lounge has local Hawaiian music nightly.

Amenities: Lei greeting, complimentary early morning coffee and tea, complimentary valet parking, multilingual concierge, same-day dry cleaning and laundry, daily kids' program, early arrival and late departure services. Tennis (six Plexi-pave courts, two lit for night play), 36 holes of Robert Trent Jones–designed golf, separate pools for adults and children, fitness center, six-station fitness trail, conference facilities, library.

INEXPENSIVE

✪ **Makena Landing.** 5100 Makena Rd. (next to the county beach park), Makena, HI 96753. ☎ **808/879-6286.** 2 units. TV TEL. $95 double. 3-night minimum. Extra person $10. No credit cards.

This has to be the most fabulous location for a bed-and-breakfast: right on the ocean at Makena Landing. The view is incredible; the sunsets are to die for; some of the best swimming, snorkeling, diving, and shoreline fishing are within walking distance; and the hosts are the nicest people you'll ever meet. The property has been in the Lu'uwai family for seven generations; hosts Boogie and Vi are both native Hawaiians, and they're brimming with generosity.

To ensure privacy, the two units are at opposite ends of the two-story cedar house. Both have private entrances, full bathrooms, kitchens, and private balconies that overlook the ocean, with

Molokini and Kahoolawe off in the distance. The kitchens have everything you can think of, and Vi makes sure that you have all the fixings for breakfast. Outside are a barbecue area and a sundeck; here you'll have the ocean splashing at your feet, and a ringside seat to watch the humpback whales from December to April.

4 Upcountry Maui

MAKAWAO, OLINDA & HALIIMAILE
MODERATE

✪ **Olinda Country Cottages & Inn.** 2660 Olinda Rd. (near the top of Olinda Rd., a 15-min. drive from Makawao), Makawao, HI 96768. ☎ **800/932-3435** or 808/572-1453. Fax 808/573-5326. www.mauibnbcottages.com. 5 units. TV TEL. $95 double (includes continental breakfast), $125 suite double (includes 1st morning's breakfast in fridge), $140–$155 cottage double (sleeps up to 5; includes 1st morning's breakfast in fridge). 2-night minimum for rooms and suite, 3- to 5-night minimum for cottages. Extra person $15. No credit cards.

Set on the slopes of Haleakala in the crisp, clean air of Olinda (just 15 minutes from the restaurants and shops of Makawao), this charming B&B is on an 8 1/2-acre protea farm, surrounded by 35,000 acres of ranch lands (with miles of great hiking trails). The 5,000-square-foot country home has large windows with incredible panoramic views of all of Maui. Upstairs are two guest rooms with antique beds, private full bathrooms, and a separate entryway. Connected to the main house but with its own private entrance, the Pineapple Sweet has a full kitchen, an antique-filled living room, a marble-tiled full bathroom, and a separate bedroom. A separate 1,000-square-foot cottage is the epitome of cozy country luxury, with a fireplace, a bedroom with a queen bed, cushioned window seats (with great sunset views), and open-beam cathedral ceilings. The 950-square-foot Hidden Cottage (in a truly secluded spot surrounded by protea flowers) features three decks, 8-foot French glass doors, a full kitchen, a washer/dryer, and a private tub for two on the deck. Beaches are about a half-hour drive away.

INEXPENSIVE

If you'd like your own private cottage, consider **Peace of Maui,** 1290 Haliimaile Rd. (just outside Haliimaile town), Haliimaile, HI 96768 (☎ **808/572-5045;** www.peaceofmaui.com), with full kitchen, bedroom, day bed, and large deck; the cottage goes for $65. Children are welcome.

Banyan Tree House. 3265 Baldwin Ave. (next to Veteran's Cemetery, just 0.8 mile below Makawao), Makawao, HI 96768. ☎ **808/572-9021.** Fax 808/285-5152. www.banyantreehouse.com. 3 units. $85 cottage double, $225 3-bedroom/3-bathroom house (sleeps up to 6). 2- to 3-night minimum for house. MC, V.

Huge monkeypod trees (complete with swing and hammock) extend their branches over this 2¹/₂-acre property like a giant green canopy. The restored 1920s plantation manager's house is decorated with Hawaiian furniture from the 1930s; the large guest rooms have big, comfortable beds and private, marble-tiled bathrooms. A fireplace stands at one end of the huge living room, a large lanai runs the entire length of the house, and the hardwood floors shine throughout. The two guest cottages have been totally renovated and also feature hardwood floors and marble bathrooms. The small cottage has a queen bed, private bathroom, microwave, coffeemaker, and access to the fridge in the laundry room. The larger cottage has two beds, private bathroom, small kitchenette, and TV. Guests have use of laundry facilities. The quiet neighborhood and nostalgic old Hawaii ambience give this place a comfortable, easygoing atmosphere. Restaurants and shops are just minutes away in Makawao, and the beach is a 15-minute drive.

KULA
MODERATE
✪ **Silver Cloud Ranch.** Old Thompson Rd. (1.2 mi. past Hwy. 37). RR 2, Box 201, Kula, HI 96790. ☎ **800/532-1111** or 808/878-6101. Fax 808/878-2132. www.maui.net/~slvrcld. 12 units. $85–$125 double in main house, $105–$145 studio double in bunkhouse, $150 cottage double. Rates include full breakfast. Extra person $15. AE, DISC, MC, V.

Old Hawaii lives on at Silver Cloud Ranch. The former working cattle spread has a commanding view of four islands, the West Maui Mountains, and the valley and beaches below. The Lanai Cottage, a favorite among honeymooners, is nestled in a flower garden and has an ocean-view lanai, claw-foot tub, full kitchen, and wood-burning stove to warm chilly nights; a futon is available if you're traveling with a third person. The best rooms in the main house are on the second floor: the King Kamehameha Suite (with king bed) and the Queen Emma Suite (with queen bed). Each has a royal view, though some prefer Emma's. The Paniolo Bunkhouse, once used by real cowboys, is now fully restored and houses five studios, each with private bathroom, kitchenette, and views of the Pacific or Haleakala (go for the ocean view). All guests are free to use the main house and kitchen.

You'll find it cool and peaceful up here at 2,800 feet (bring a sweater). One-lane Thompson Road makes an ideal morning walk (about 3 miles round-trip), and you can go horseback riding next door at Thompson Ranch. There's a TV available if you feel deprived, but after a few Maui sunsets, you won't even remember why you bothered to ask.

INEXPENSIVE

✪ **Kili's Cottage.** Kula, c/o Hawaii's Best Bed & Breakfasts, P.O. Box 563, Kamuela, HI 96743. ☎ **800/262-9912** or 808/885-4550. Fax 808/885-0559. www.bestbnb.com. 1 three-bedroom/two-bathroom house. TV TEL. $95 double. 2-night minimum. Rates include breakfast fixings. Extra person $10. DISC.

If you're looking for a quiet getaway in the cool elevation of Kula, this sweet cottage with large lanai, situated on 2 acres, is the perfect place. The amenities are numerous: full kitchen, gas barbecue, washer/dryer, views, even toys for the kids. Hostess Kili Namau'u, who is also the director of a Hawaiian-language immersion school, greets each guest with royal aloha—from the flowers (picked from the garden outside) that fill the house to the welcome basket of tropical produce grown on the property.

Kula Cottage. 206 Puakea Place (off Lower Kula Rd.), Kula, HI 96790. ☎ **808/878-2043** or 808/871-6230. Fax 808/871-9187. www. gilbertadvertising.com/kulacottage. 1 cottage. TV TEL. $85 double. 2-night minimum. Rates include continental breakfast. No credit cards.

We can't imagine having a less-than-fantastic vacation here. Tucked away on a quiet street amid a half-acre of blooming papaya and banana trees, Cecilia and Larry Gilbert's romantic honeymoon cottage is very private—it even has its own driveway and carport. The 700-square-foot cottage has a full kitchen (complete with dishwasher), washer/dryer, and three huge closets that offer enough storage space for you to move in permanently. An outside lanai has a big gas barbecue and an umbrella table and chairs. Cecilia delivers a continental breakfast daily (visitors rave about her homemade bread in the guest book). If you're an animal lover, Hana, the dog, will be more than happy to be a surrogate pet to you during your vacation; otherwise, Cecilia makes sure that Hana stays out of your way. Groceries and a small take-out lunch counter are within walking distance; it's a 30-minute drive to the beach.

✪ **Nohona Laule'a.** 763-2 Kamehameiki Rd. (off Kula Hwy.), Kula, HI 96790. ☎ **808/878-6646.** Fax 808/878-6646. 1 two-bedroom cottage. TV TEL. $85 double. 3-night minimum. Extra person $10. No credit cards.

What a deal—an impeccable two-bedroom cottage for $85 for two! Located on a windy road at about 2,500 feet, Nohona Laule'a ("peaceful dwelling") is 4 acres of tropical paradise with the cottage smack-dab in the middle. The 700-square-foot cottage, decorated in Asian style, features open-beam ceilings, skylights, a complete gourmet kitchen, a full bathroom, a living room, a huge deck, and a washer/dryer. The whole cottage has great island views: One bedroom, with Japanese shoji doors and two twin beds, looks out onto Haleakala; the other, with a double bed, has a big picture window overlooking the garden and the north shore beyond. The living room has a comfortable couch, a wooden rocker, and another huge picture window. Owners Brian and Sue Kanegai are congenial hosts; Sue greets guests with her delicious mango or banana bread. True to its name, this place is indeed peaceful. Kick back in a comfortable chair on the big deck and survey the blooming landscape at your feet.

5 East Maui: On the Road to Hana

KUAU
INEXPENSIVE

✪ **Mama's Beachfront Cottages.** 799 Poho Place (off the Hana Hwy., in Kuau), Paia, HI 96779. ☎ **800/860-HULA** or 808/579-9764. Fax 808/579-8594. www.maui.net/~mamas. 6 units. TV TEL. $90 1-bedroom apt. (sleeps up to 4), $225 2-bedroom apt. (sleeps up to 6). 3-night minimum. AE, DC, DISC, MC, V.

The fabulous location (nestled in a coconut grove on the secluded Kuau beach), beautifully decorated interior (with island-style rattan furniture and works by Hawaiian artists), and plenty of extras (Weber gas barbecue, 27-inch TVs, and all the beach toys you can think of) make this place a must-stay for people looking for a centrally located vacation rental. It has everything, even Mama's Fish House next door (where guests get a 20% discount). The one-bedrooms are nestled in a tropical jungle, while the two-bedrooms face the beach. Both have terra-cotta floors, complete kitchens, sofa beds, and laundry facilities.

HAIKU
MODERATE

✪ **Maui Tradewinds.** Haiku, c/o Hawaii's Best Bed & Breakfasts, P.O. Box 563, Kamuela, HI 96743. ☎ **800/262-9912** or 808/885-4550. Fax 808/885-0559. www.bestbnb.com. 1 unit. TV TEL. $125 double. 2-night minimum. Extra person $10. DISC.

No expense was spared in the construction of this 1,000-square-foot studio apartment, located on the lower level of a custom-built home in the rolling hills of Haiku. Maui Tradewinds distinguishes itself from other accommodations with its floor-to-ceiling windows that capture the ocean view, blonde wood floors, recessed lighting, bamboo furniture, laundry facilities, top-of-the-line kitchen equipment, outdoor Jacuzzi, and full bathroom with dry/steam sauna. With the sofa bed, the unit sleeps up to four adults.

✪ **Pilialoha B&B Cottage.** 2512 Kaupakalua Rd. (0.7 mi. from Kokomo intersection), Haiku, HI 96708. ☎ **808/572-1440.** Fax 808/572-4612. www.pilialoha.com. 1 cottage. TV TEL. $100 double. 3-night minimum. Rates include continental breakfast. Extra person $20. No credit cards.

The minute you arrive at this split-level country cottage, located on 2 acres of eucalyptus trees, you'll see owner Machiko Heyde's artistry at work. Just in front of the cottage is a garden blooming with some 200 varieties of roses. You'll find more of Machiko's handiwork inside the quaint cottage, which is great for couples but can sleep up to five: There's a queen bed in the master bedroom, a twin bed in a small adjoining room, and a queen sleeper sofa in the living room. A large lanai extends from the master bedroom. You'll find a great movie collection for rainy days or cool country nights, a washer/dryer, beach paraphernalia (including snorkel equipment), and a garage. Machiko delivers breakfast daily; if you plan on an early morning ride to the top of Haleakala, she'll make sure you go with a thermos of coffee and her homemade bread.

INEXPENSIVE

Maui Dream Cottages. 265 W. Kuiaha Rd. (1 block from Pauwela Cafe), Haiku, HI 96708. ☎ **808/575-9079.** Fax 808/575-9477. www. planet-hawaii.com/haiku. 2 cottages (with showers only). TV. $70 for up to 4. 7-night minimum. MC, V.

Essentially a vacation rental, this 2-acre country estate is located atop a hill overlooking the ocean. The grounds are dotted with fruit trees (bananas, papayas, and avocados, all free for the picking), and the front lawn is comfortably equipped with a double hammock, chaise longues, and table and chairs. One cottage has two bedrooms, one bathroom, full kitchen, washer/dryer, and entertainment center. The other is basically the same, but with only one bedroom (plus a sofa bed in the living room). They're both very well maintained, comfortably outfitted with furniture that's not only attractive but also casual enough for families with kids. The Haiku location is quiet and restful and offers the opportunity to see how real islanders live.

However, you'll have to drive a good 20 to 25 minutes to restaurants in Makawao or Paia for dinner. Hookipa Beach is about a 20-minute drive, and Baldwin Beach (good swimming) is about 25 minutes away.

TWIN FALLS
INEXPENSIVE

✪ **Maluhia Hale.** P.O. Box 687 (off Hana Hwy., nearly a mile past Twin Falls bridge), Haiku, HI 96708. ☎ **808/572-2959.** Fax 808/572-2959. www.maui.net/~djg/index.html. 2 units. TV. $95 cottage double, $110 suite double. 2-night minimum. Rates include continental breakfast. Extra person $20. No credit cards.

Diane and Robert Garrett design and build homes that are works of art. Here, they've created a private country cottage that has the feeling of a gracious old Hawaiian plantation home. A sense of peace reigns in the cottage: You enter through an open and airy screened veranda, which leads to a glassed-in sitting room, a bed in lacy white linen, and a kitchenette. Hand-selected antiques fill the cottage, and Diane's exquisite flower arrangements add splashes of color. A traditional Hawaiian bathhouse is adjacent, with an old claw-foot tub and separate shower. In the main house is a romantic suite complete with a small kitchenette and screened porch. Diane does light housekeeping daily; no matter which accommodation you choose, at the end of the day, you'll return to a softly lit place filled with sweet-smelling tropical flowers. A simply wonderful place.

HUELO
MODERATE

✪ **Huelo Point Flower Farm.** Off Hana Hwy., between mile markers 3 and 4. P.O. Box 1195, Paia, HI 96779. ☎ **808/572-1850.** www.maui.net/~huelopt. 4 units. $120 cottage double, $140 carriage house double, $240 guest house double (rates include continental breakfast). $2,200 per week for main house for 6. Extra person $15. 2-night minimum, except for 7-night minimum in main house. No credit cards.

Here's a little Eden by the sea on a spectacular, remote 300-foot sea cliff near a waterfall stream: a 2-acre estate overlooking Waipio Bay with two guest cottages, a guest house, and a main house available for rent. The studio-sized Gazebo Cottage has a glass-walled ocean front, a koa-wood captain's bed, TV, stereo, kitchenette, private ocean-side patio, private hot tub, and a half-bathroom with outdoor shower. The new 900-square-foot Carriage House apartment sleeps four and has glass walls facing the mountain and sea, plus a kitchen, den, decks, and a loft bedroom. The two-bedroom main house contains an exercise room, fireplace, sunken Roman bathtub, cathedral ceilings, and other extras. There's a natural pool with awaterfall and an oceanfront hot tub. You're welcome to pick fruit, vegetables, and flowers from the extensive garden. Homemade scones, tree-ripened papayas, and fresh-roasted coffee start youday. Despite its seclusion, off the crooked road to Hana, it's justa half hour to Kahului, or about 20 minutes to Paia's shops and restaurants.

✪ **Huelo Point Lookout B&B.** Off Hana Hwy. (between mile markers 3 and 4), c/o Hawaii's Best Bed & Breakfasts, P.O. Box 563, Kamuela, HI 96743. ☎ **800/262-9912** or 808/885-4550. Fax 808/885-0559. www.bestbnb,com. 3 cottages. TV TEL. $95–$275 cottage double. 3-night minimum. Rates include a welcome breakfast on arrival. Extra person $20. DISC.

About a quarter mile from the 300-foot cliffs of Waipio Bay is this lovely B&B, situated on 2 acres of tropical jungle with a hot tub, 40-foot freeform swimming pool, and a view all the way down the coastline to Hana. The main house has pentagonal glass walls that offer sweeping views of the ocean and up the side of Haleakala. It has two private entrances, a large bedroom with king bed, a kitchenette, a big bathroom with a tub for two, and a lotus pond and waterfall outside on the private deck. The Honeymoon Cottage is a totally renovated old fisherman's residence, with an upstairs bedroom, a full kitchen, a sitting room, and a solarium with lots of windows, skylights, and a deck. The bathroom has a Victorian tub and glass all around, with views of Haleakala on one side and the ocean on the other. The Halekala Cottage is smaller but full of amenities, including a full kitchen, king bed, and tiled bathroom that extends outside into the garden so that you can actually take a hot shower under the stars, surrounded by white lattice and tropical flowers. The newest cottage, Rainbow, located next to the swimming pool, features 25-foot-high glass walls with nothing but views. Other unique amenities include a private indoor hot tub, glass-ceilinged bathroom, and work-of-art wooden staircase.

6 At the End of the Road in East Maui: Hana

MODERATE

✪ **Ekena.** Off Hana Hwy., above Hana Airport (P.O. Box 728), Hana, HI 96713. ☎ **808/248-7047.** Fax 808/248-7047. www.maui.net/~ekena. 2 two-bedroom units. TV TEL. $150 double, $190–$275 for 4. 3-night minimum. Extra person $15. No credit cards.

Just one glance at the 360° view, and you can see why hosts Robin and Gaylord gave up their careers on the mainland and moved here.

This 8¹/₂-acre piece of paradise in rural Hana boasts ocean rain-forest views; the floor-to-ceiling sliding-glass doors in the sp. cious Hawaiian-style pole house bring the outside in. The elegant two-story home is exquisitely furnished, from the comfortable U-shaped couch that invites you to relax and take in the view to the top-of-the-line mattress on the king bed. The kitchen is fully equipped with every high-tech convenience you can imagine (guests have made complete holiday meals here). Only one floor (and one two-bedroom unit) is rented at any one time to ensure privacy. The grounds are impeccably groomed with tropical plants and fruit trees. Hiking trails into the rain forest start right on the property, and the beaches and waterfalls are just minutes away. Robin places fresh flowers in every room and makes sure you're comfortable; after that, she's available to answer questions about what Hana has to offer, but she also respects your privacy and lets you enjoy your vacation in peace.

✪ **Hamoa Bay Bungalow.** P.O. Box 773, Hana, HI 96713. ☎ **808/ 248-7884.** Fax 808/248-8642. E-mail: jody@maui.net. 1 cottage. TV TEL. $160 double. 2-night minimum. No credit cards.

Down a country lane guarded by two Balinese statues stands a little bit of Indonesia in Hawaii: a carefully crafted bungalow overlooking Hamoa Bay. Only 2 miles beyond Hasegawa's General Store on the way to Kipahulu, this enchanting retreat sits on 4 verdant acres within walking distance of black-sand Hamoa Beach (which James Michener considered one of the most beautiful in the Pacific). The romantic, 600-square-foot Balinese-style cottage is distinctly tropical, with giant Elephant bamboo furniture from Indonesia, batik prints, a king bed, a full kitchen, and a screened porch with hot tub and shower. Host Jody Baldwin, a lifelong Mauian who lives on the estate, loves to share the secrets of Hana, including the great mountain hiking trail nearby.

Hana Hale Malamalama. Across from the Mormon Church in Hana, c/o Hawaii's Best Bed & Breakfasts, P.O. Box 563, Kamuela, HI 96743. ☎ **800/ 262-9912** or 808/885-4550. Fax 808/885-0559. www.bestbnb.com. 5 units. TV TEL. $120–$175 double, $250 cottage double. 2-night minimum. Continental breakfast is served to guests at Bamboo Inn. Extra person $15. DISC.

Located on a historic site with ancient fish ponds and a cave mentioned in ancient chants, this place definitely exudes the spirit of old Hawaii. Host John takes excellent care of the ponds (he feeds the fish at 5pm every day, to the delight of his guests) and is fiercely protective of the hidden cave ("it's not a tourist attraction,

. There's access to a nearby rocky beach, which
_____ming but makes a wonderful place to watch the
_____ accommodations include fully equipped kitchens,
bathrooms, bedrooms, living/dining areas, and private lanais. The
main three-bedroom house is an architectural masterpiece, built
entirely of Philippine mahogany with 4-foot-wide skylights the
entire length of the house. Entry to the house is down stone steps,
so this is not a place for small children or anyone who has trouble
climbing steep steps.

The two-level Tree House cottage, nestled between a kamani tree
and a coconut palm, contains a Jacuzzi tub for two, a Balinese
bamboo bed, a small kitchen/living area, and a small deck. The
Pondside Bungalow is a quaint cottage, with full kitchen, living area,
and separate bedroom. We strongly recommend staying in the newest building, the Bamboo Inn, where guests are served continental
breakfast in the open courtyard. You'll never forget its coconut
floors, Indonesian decor, and ocean view from the lanai.

✪ **Heavenly Hana Inn.** P.O. Box 790, Hana, HI 96713. ☎ and fax **808/
248-8442.** www.placestogo.com. 4 units. TV TEL. $100 studio double,
$175–$250 suite. 2-night minimum. Rates include a full gourmet breakfast.
AE, DISC, JCB, MC, V. Located off Hana Hwy., just a stone's throw from the
center of Hana town. Children under 15 not accepted.

Owners Robert Filippi and Sheryl Murray understatedly describe
their B&B as a "Japanese-style inn at secluded and beautiful Hana."
That's a little like saying a Four Seasons hotel is a big building with
rooms. This impeccably thought-out accommodation is a little bit
of heaven, where no detail has been overlooked. The suites each have
a sitting room with a futon and couch, polished hardwood floors,
and a separate bedroom with a raised platform bed (with an excellent, firm mattress). The black-marble bathrooms contain huge tubs
and separate glassed-in showers. Flowers are everywhere, ceiling fans
keep the rooms cool, and the daily gourmet breakfast (a fruit course
and a main entree plus homemade breads and pastries) is not only
delicious, but also served in a setting filled with art, including the
hand-crafted dining table and matching chairs. The 2 acres of
grounds are done in Japanese style with a bamboo fence, tiny bridges
over a meandering stream, and Japanese gardens.

Papalani. Star Route 27 (4 mi. past Hasegawa's General Store), Hana, HI
96713. ☎ **808/248-7204.** Fax 808/248-7285. 2 units. TEL. $150 double.
3-night minimum. Extra person $25. No credit cards. No children under
8 accepted.

These luxurious, romantic accommodations are hidden from the road, offering privacy and quiet in a first-class setting. There is only one tiny drawback: mosquitoes—swarms of them, in fact. A stream runs through the property, and although hostess Cybil has done everything possible to eliminate this nuisance (like providing screened-in lanais so that you can enjoy the outdoors without experiencing these biting pests), bring your insect repellent.

Otherwise, Papalani lives up to its name, which means "heaven and all the spiritual powers." The apartment and the cottage, both professionally decorated, have white leather couches, wood floors, and expensive artwork. Everything is first-class, from the appliances in the kitchen to the faucets in the bathroom. The apartment has a kitchenette with minifridge, blender, and coffeemaker, while the separate cottage has a full kitchen. Both units have their own laundry facilities and private hot tubs. This is a TV-free environment, so you can really get in touch with nature. The great location means you're just a 5-minute walk to Waioka Stream (where there's good swimming in the pools), a mile from beautiful Hamoa Beach, and 5 minutes from Hana. Cybil asks that guests not smoke on the property and that meat be cooked on a barbecue outside.

INEXPENSIVE

If you'd like your own cottage, consider the simple but adequately furnished **Aloha Cottages,** 83 Keawa Place, P.O. Box 205, Hana, HI 96713 (☎ **808/248-8420**), which go for $60 to $92 double.

✪ **Tradewinds Cottage.** 135 Alalele Place (P.O. Box 385), Hana, HI 96713. ☎ **800/327-8097** or 808/248-8980. Fax 808/248-7735. www. maui.net/~twt/cottage.html. 2 cottages. TV TEL. $100 studio cottage double, $125 2-bedroom cottage double. 2-night minimum. Extra person $10. MC, V.

Nestled among the ginger and heliconias on a 5-acre flower farm are these two separate cottages, each with complete kitchen, carport, barbecue, hot tub, TV, ceiling fan, and sleeper sofa. The studio cottage sleeps up to four; a bamboo shoji blind separates the sleeping area (with queen bed) from the sofa bed in the living room. The Tradewinds cottage has two bedrooms (with queen bed in one room and two twins in the other), one bathroom (with shower only), sleeper sofa, and huge front porch. The atmosphere is quiet and relaxing, and hosts Mike and Rebecca Buckley, who have been in business for a decade, welcome families (they have two children, a cat, and a very sweet golden retriever). You can use their laundry facilities at no extra charge.

Waianapanapa State Park Cabins. Off Hana Hwy., c/o State Parks Division, 54 S. High St., Rm. 101, Wailuku, HI 96793. ☎ **808/984-8109.** 12 cabins. $45 for 4 (sleeps up to 6). Extra person $5. 5-night maximum. No credit cards.

These 12 rustic cabins are the best lodging deal on Maui. Everyone knows it, too—so make your reservations early (up to 6 months in advance). The cabins are warm and dry and come complete with kitchen, living room, bedroom, and bathroom with hot shower; furnishings include bedding, linen, towels, dishes, and very basic cooking and eating utensils. Don't expect luxury—this is a step above camping, albeit in a beautiful tropical jungle setting unlike any other in the islands. The key attraction at this 120-acre state beach park is the unusual horseshoe-shaped black-sand beach on Pailoa Bay, popular for shore fishing, snorkeling, and swimming. There's a caretaker on-site, along with rest rooms, showers, picnic tables, shoreline hiking trails, and historic sites. But bring mosquito protection—this *is* the jungle.

Dining

by Jocelyn Fujii

*I*n the past decade, with the ascension of Hawaii Regional Cuisine into national prominence, and with Maui as Hawaii's visitor-industry success story, the islands' best chefs have opened their Maui doors and turned this island into a culinary nexus.

But some things haven't changed: You can still dine well at Lahaina's open-air waterfront watering holes, where the view counts for 50% of the dining experience. There are budget eateries here, but not many; Maui's old-fashioned, multigenerational mom-and-pop diners are disappearing by attrition, eclipsed by the flashy newcomers, or clinging to the edge of existence in the older neighborhoods of central Maui. Although you'll have to work harder to find them in the resort areas, you won't have to go far to find creative cuisine, pleasing style, and stellar views in upcountry, south, and west Maui.

1 Central Maui

EXPENSIVE

Sam Choy's Kahului. Kaahumanu Center, 275 Kaahumanu Ave. (5 min. from Kahului Airport on Hwy. 32), Kahului. ☎ **808/893-0366.** Reservations recommended. Main courses $4–$10 breakfast, $7–$12 lunch, $25–$30 dinner. AE, DC, DISC, JCB, MC, V. Mon–Thurs 8am–9pm, Fri–Sun 7am–9:15pm. LOCAL/HAWAII REGIONAL.

Sam Choy's cooking, which the *Wall Street Journal* calls "blue-collar chow," has spread from Hawaii to Tokyo, loco moco, poke, and all. But Choy's plans to open a restaurant upstairs in the Kaahumanu Center, where the Sharktooth brewery used to be, haven't yet materialized, keeping his eatery on the first floor of the mall at front row center. It's still poke paradise: His seared poke salad remains a lunchtime staple (vastly overrated, in our opinion), and his seafood laulau, macadamia-nut-crusted ono, and rib-eye steak are some of the evening attractions. At breakfast, locals gather for poke omelets, spinach and shiitake mushroom omelets, the morning's fresh catch, taro cakes, and other regional favorites.

MODERATE

Marco's Grill & Deli. 444 Hana Hwy., Kahului. ☎ **808/877-4446.** Main courses $12.95–$19.95. AE, DC, DISC, JCB, MC, V. Daily 7:30am–10pm (hot entrees from 10am). ITALIAN.

Located in the elbow of central Maui, where the roads to upcountry, west, and south Maui converge, Marco's is popular for its home-made Italian fare and friendly informality. This is one of those comfortable neighborhood fixtures favored by all generations, who stop here for breakfast, lunch, and dinner, before and after movies, on the way to and from baseball games and concerts, and for business lunches. The antipasto salad, vegetarian lasagna, and roasted peppers with garlic, provolone cheese, and anchovies are taste treats, but don't ignore the meatballs and Italian sausage: homemade and robust, they're served on French bread with all the trimmings.

✪ **A Saigon Cafe.** 1792 Main St., Wailuku. ☎ **808/243-9560.** Main courses $6.50–$16.95. DC, MC, V. Mon–Sat 10am–9:30pm, Sun 10am–8:30pm. VIETNAMESE.

How's this for attitude: There's no sign. But Jennifer Nguyen can afford to be elusive, because as difficult as this restaurant is to find, it's always bustling. The menu runs the gamut, from a dozen different soups to cold and hot noodles (including the popular beef noodle soup called *pho*) and chicken and shrimp cooked in a clay pot. Wok-cooked Vietnamese specialties—sautéed with spicy lemongrass and sweet-and-sour sauces—highlight the produce of the season, and the fresh catch (ono, opakapaka) comes whole and crisp or steamed with ginger and garlic. You can create your own Vietnamese "burritos" from a platter of tofu, noodles, and vegetables that you wrap in rice paper and dip in garlic sauce. The Nhung Dam, the Vietnamese version of fondue—a hearty spread of basil, cucumbers, mint, romaine, bean sprouts, pickled carrots, turnips, and vermicelli, wrapped in rice paper and dipped in a legendary sauce— is cooked at your table.

INEXPENSIVE

Class Act. At Maui Community College, 310 Kaahumanu Ave., Wailuku. ☎ **808/984-3480.** Reservations recommended. 5-course lunch $15. No credit cards. Wed and Fri 11am–12:15pm (last seating). Cuisine changes weekly.

Part of a program run by the distinguished Food Service Department of Maui Community College, this restaurant has a growing following. Student chefs show their stuff with a flourish in their "classroom," where they pull out all the stops as if it were their own place. Linen, china, servers in ties and white shirts, and a five-course lunch make this a five-star value. The appetizer, soup, salad, and dessert are set, but you can choose between the regular entree and a heart-healthy entree prepared in the culinary tradition of the week. The filet mignon of French week is popular, and so are the Thai curries; Chinese stir-fries; pastas; and Japanese, Austrian, Moroccan, and other international menus served throughout the months. Tea and soft drinks are offered—and they can get pretty fancy, with fresh fruit and spritzers—but otherwise it's BYOB.

Ichiban. Kahului Shopping Center, 47 Kaahumanu Ave., Kahului. ☎ **808/ 871-6977.** Main courses $4.25–$5.25 breakfast, from $4.25 lunch (combination plates $8.50), $4.95–$26.95 dinner (combination dinner $11.95, dinner specials from $8.95). DC, MC, V. Mon–Fri 6:30am–2pm and 5–9pm, Sat 10:30am–2pm and 5–9pm. JAPANESE/SUSHI.

What a find: an informal neighborhood restaurant that serves inexpensive, home-cooked Japanese food *and* good sushi at realistic prices. Local residents consider Ichiban a staple for breakfast, lunch, or dinner and a haven of comforts: egg-white omelets, great saimin, chicken yakitori, sushi (everything from unagi and scallop to California rolls), and combination plates—teriyaki chicken, teriyaki meat, *tonkatsu* (pork cutlet), rice, and pickled cabbage. The sushi may not be inexpensive, but like the specials, such as steamed opakapaka for $18.75, it's a good value. *Tip:* We love the tempura, miso soup, and spicy ahi hand roll.

✪ **Maui Bake Shop.** 2092 Vineyard St., Wailuku. ☎ **808/242-0064.** Most items under $5. AE, CB, DISC, MC, V. Mon–Fri 7am–4pm, Sat 7am–2pm. BAKERY/DELI.

Maui native Claire Fujii-Krall and her husband, baker José Krall (who trained in the south of France and throughout Europe), turn out buttery brioches, healthy nine-grain and two-tone rye breads, focaccia, strudels, sumptuous fresh-fruit gâteaux, puff pastries, and dozens of other baked goods and confections. The front window displays the more than 100 bakery and deli items, among them salads, a popular eggplant marinara focaccia, homemade quiches, and a moist, inexpensive calzone with chicken-pesto-mushroom-cheese filling.

Restaurant Matsu. Maui Mall, 70 E. Kaahumanu Ave., Kahului. ☎ **808/ 871-0822.** Most items less than $6. No credit cards. Mon–Thurs 9am–6pm, Fri 9am–9pm, Sat 9am–5:30pm, Sun 10am–4pm. JAPANESE/LOCAL.

Customers have come from Hana (more than 50 mi. away) just for Matsu's California rolls, while regulars line up for the cold saimin (julienned cucumber, egg, Chinese-style sweet pork, and red ginger on noodles) and the bento plates, various assemblages of chicken, teriyaki beef, fish, and rice, which make great take-out lunches for working folks and picnickers. We love the tempura udon and the saimin, steaming mounds of wide and fine noodles swimming in homemade broths and topped with condiments. The daily specials are a changing lineup of home-cooked classics: ox-tail soup, roast pork with gravy, teriyaki ahi, and breaded mahimahi.

Wei Wei BBQ and Noodle House. Millyard Plaza, 210 Imi Kala St., Wailuku. ☎ 808/242-7928. Combination plates $4.95–$6.95, main courses $3–$8.50. No credit cards. Daily 10am–9pm. CHINESE/NOODLES.

Wei Wei is the darling of the on-the-go, no-nonsense, noodle-loving Maui crowd. You order at the counter, fast-food style, from a menu that includes Chinese classics: saimin with roast duck, shrimp-vegetable chow mein, dim sum, and the extremely popular house fried noodles. American favorites—hamburger, teriyaki chicken burger, turkey sandwich, and the popular chicken katsu burger—are winning fans, too.

2 West Maui

LAHAINA
EXPENSIVE

The Chart House. 1450 Front St., at Honoapiilani Hwy. (Hwy. 30). ☎ 808/661-0937. Main courses $16.95–$36.95. AE, CB, DC, DISC, MC, V. Daily 5–10pm, lounge until midnight. AMERICAN.

The Chart House restaurants have a knack for finding locations with drop-dead-gorgeous views, and Lahaina has one of the best. Location is its strongest suit: Perched at the north end of Front Street, removed from congested Lahaina proper and elevated for optimal view, the restaurant offers a singular look at Lanai, Molokai, the ocean, and the sunset. At this writing renovations are planned, as well as menu changes (most welcome) to include more Hawaii regional flavors and presentations. Otherwise, expect the formula fare that marks all Chart Houses: prime rib; East-West prawns and garlic steak; and an assortment of fresh fish in teriyaki, garlic-herb, and mayonnaise sauces. Especially indulgent is the mud pie, a weighty dessert of Kona coffee ice cream, Oreo cookie crust, fudge, almonds, and whipped cream.

Other Chart House locations are at 100 Wailea Ike Dr. in Wailea (☎ 808/637-8005), and 500 N. Puunene in Kahului (☎ 808/877-2476).

Lahaina & Kaanapali Dining

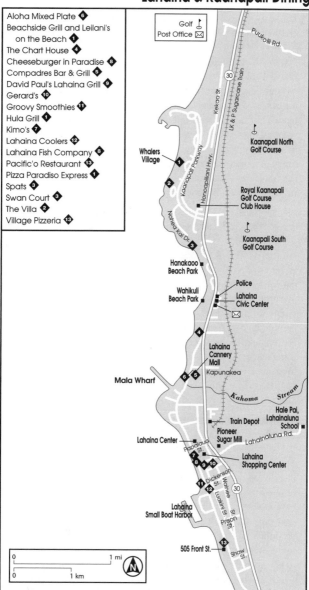

Aloha Mixed Plate 6
Beachside Grill and Leilani's
   on the Beach 1
The Chart House 4
Cheeseburger in Paradise 8
Compadres Bar & Grill 5
David Paul's Lahaina Grill 9
Gerard's 10
Groovy Smoothies 11
Hula Grill 1
Kimo's 7
Lahaina Coolers 12
Lahaina Fish Company 8
Pacific'o Restaurant 13
Pizza Paradiso Express 1
Spats 3
Swan Court 3
The Villa 2
Village Pizzeria 13

Golf
Post Office

Puukolii Rd.

Kekaa St.

Honoapiilani Hwy

LK & P Sugarcane Train

Kaanapali North
Golf Course

Whalers
Village

Kaanapali Parkway

Nohea Kai Dr.

Royal Kaanapali
Golf Course
Club House

Kaanapali South
Golf Course

Hanakaoo
Beach Park

Police

Wahikuli
Beach Park

Lahaina
Civic Center

Lahaina
Cannery
Mall

Kapunakea

Mala Wharf

Kahoma Stream

Hale Pai,
Lahainaluna
School

Train Depot

Pioneer
Sugar Mill

Lahainaluna Rd.

Lahaina Center

Papalaua St.

Lahaina
Shopping Center

Dickenson St.

Wainee St.

Luakini St.

Prison St.

Lahaina
Small Boat Harbor

505 Front St.

Shaw St.

0   1 mi

0   1 km

✪ **David Paul's Lahaina Grill.** 127 Lahainaluna Rd. ☎ **808/667-5117.** Reservations required. Main courses $19–$38. AE, CB, DC, DISC, MC, V. Daily 5:30–10pm. Bar daily 5:30pm–midnight. NEW AMERICAN.

Nationally applauded and a recipient of numerous culinary awards, David Paul's is most people's favorite Maui restaurant. A special custom-designed chef's table can be arranged with 48-hour notice for parties of six to eight, but the daily menu is enticement enough: tequila shrimp with firecracker rice, Kona lobster-crab cakes in a sesame-Dijon sauce, Kona coffee–roasted rack of lamb, kalua duck in a plum wine reduction, seared ahi encrusted in Maui onion, and many other seductions. The bar is the busiest spot in Lahaina, and the ambience—black-and-white tile floors, pressed tin ceilings, eclectic 1890s decor—is a good match for the cuisine.

Gerard's. Plantation Inn, 174 Lahainaluna Rd. ☎ **808/661-8939.** Reservations recommended. Main courses $26.50–$32.50. AE, CB, DC, DISC, JCB, MC, V. Daily 6–10pm. FRENCH.

Winner of the *Wine Spectator* Award of Excellence for 1997, Gerard's offers Gallic fare that scores high in this competitive culinary atmosphere. The rave-drawing starters: the oyster and shiitake mushroom appetizer, savory and steaming in puff pastry, and the ahi tartare with taro chips, followed by Gerard's famous roasted Hawaiian snapper in a spicy orange and ginger-butter sauce. Gerard Reversade specializes in fresh seafood, which he buys daily from the fishermen at the harbor, then transforms into haute cuisine. Choices for game lovers include duck confit with garlic petals, venison with peppered sauce and ohelo-berry compote, and a legendary grilled rack of lamb with mint crust and poached garlic.

Pacific'o Restaurant. 505 Front St. ☎ **808/667-4341.** Reservations recommended. Main courses $9–$14 lunch, $19–$26 dinner. AE, CB, DC, MC, V. Daily 11am–4pm and 5:30–10pm. PACIFIC RIM/CONTEMPORARY PACIFIC.

You can't get any closer to the ocean than the tables here, which are literally on the beach. With good food complementing this sensational setting, plus live jazz in the evenings, foodies and aesthetes have little to complain about. The split-level dining starts at the top, near the entrance, with a long, cordial bar (where you can also order lunch or dinner) and a few tables along the railing. Steps lead to the outdoor tables, where the award-winning seafood dishes come to you with the backdrop of Lanai across the channel. We love the Asian gravlax, a marvel of house-cured salmon on sweet potato applejack, topped with wasabi-chive sour cream and caviar. The shrimp and basil wontons, and the ahi and ono tempura wrapped in nori and fried tempura style, are winners as well. Fresh fish comes grilled, steamed in bamboo, and bathed in exotic Asian spices.

MODERATE

Compadres Bar & Grill. Lahaina Cannery Mall, 1221 Honoapiilani Hwy. ☎ **808/661-7189.** Main courses $12–$18.50. DC, JCB, MC, V. Daily 8am–11:30pm. MEXICAN.

Despite its concrete floor and high industrial ceilings, Compadres exudes an upbeat spirit and good cheer. The food is classic Tex-Mex, good any time of the day, beginning with huevos rancheros, egg burritos, hotcakes, and omelets (the Acapulco is heroic) and progressing to enchiladas and appetizers for the margarita-happy crowd. Stay spare (vegetable enchilada in fresh spinach tortilla) or get hefty (Texas T-bone and enchiladas); it's a carefree place with a large capacity for merrymaking.

✪ **Kimo's.** 845 Front St. ☎ **808/661-4811.** Reservations recommended for dinner. Main courses $5.95–$10.95 lunch, $12.95–$23.95 dinner. AE, DC, DISC, MC, V. Daily 11am–3pm and 5–10:30pm. STEAK/SEAFOOD.

Kimo's works not only because of its oceanfront patio and upstairs dining room, but because, for the price, there are some satisfying choices. It's always crowded, buzzing with people having fun on a deck that takes in Molokai, Lanai, and Kahoolawe. Burgers and sandwiches are affordable and reliable, and the fresh catch in garlic-lemon and a sweet-basil glaze is a top seller, rivaling the hefty prime rib complete with salad, carrot muffins, herb rolls, and herb rice. The waistline-defying hula pie—macadamia-nut ice cream in a chocolate-wafer crust with fudge and whipped cream—originated here.

Lahaina Fish Company. 831 Front St. ☎ **808/661-3472.** Main courses $7.95–$22.95. AE, JCB, MC, V. Daily 11am–midnight. SEAFOOD.

The open-air dining room is literally over the water, with flickering torches after sunset and an affordable menu that covers the seafood-pasta basics. Before 3pm, head to an ocean-side table and order a cheeseburger, chickenburger, fishburger, a generous basket of peel-and-eat shrimp, or sashimi; lingering is highly recommended. From noon to 5pm, cocktails are reduced and the big attraction is the appetizer-happy menu. Nightly specials range from island fish-and-chips to several pastas; standard steak-and-seafood combos; and four types of fresh island fish prepared in Asian, American, and European styles.

INEXPENSIVE

Aloha Mixed Plate. 1285 Front St. ☎ **808/661-3322.** Main courses $3.50–$9.95. MC, V. Daily 7:30am–10pm, Thurs–Sat 10:30am–1am. PLATE LUNCHES/BEACHSIDE GRILL.

The operators of the Old Lahaina Luau have moved north in a big way. Recently, they opened this eatery in a charming, freestanding, plantation-style building directly across from the Lahaina Cannery Mall, next to the site of the luau. You can sit on an open deck under umbrellas and tuck into inexpensive mahimahi, kalua pig and cabbage, shoyu chicken, teriyaki beef, and other local plate-lunch specials, all at budget-friendly prices. Gardenburgers and hamburgers cost even less. In pricey Lahaina, a find.

Cheeseburger in Paradise. 811 Front St. ☎ **808/661-4855.** Main courses $5.95–$9.95. AE, DISC, MC, V. Daily 8am–11pm. AMERICAN.

Wildly successful, always crowded, and very noisy with its live music in the evenings, Cheeseburger is a shrine to the American classic. The home of three-napkin cheeseburgers with attitude, this is burger country, tropical style, with everything from tofu and gardenburgers to the biggest, juiciest beef and chicken burgers, served on whole-wheat and sesame buns baked fresh daily. There are good reasons why the two-story green-and-white building next to the seawall is always packed: good value, good grinds, and a great ocean view. Onion rings, chili-cheese fries, and cold beer complete the carefree fantasy.

Groovy Smoothies. 708 Front St. ☎ **808/661-8219.** Smoothies under $4.50. No credit cards. Daily 9am–9:30pm. SMOOTHIES.

This closet-size takeout stand makes the best smoothies in Lahaina. But if they're too pure for you, there's always muffins, espresso, and Danishes. We love the mango-and-banana smoothie, but others may pine for the piña colada, the Elvis Peachly, or any of the berry delights.

Lahaina Coolers. 180 Dickenson St. ☎ **808/661-7082.** Main courses $7.50–$9.95 lunch, $9.50–$18.95 dinner. AE, DC, DISC, MC, V. Daily 8am–midnight, bar until 2am. ECLECTIC.

The newly renovated Coolers has shed its rubber zoris for a more upscale menu and look—wood floors, teak chairs, tablecloths, umbrellas, a new bar that looks like a surfboard—but it's still casual in the true Maui way. A huge marlin still hangs above the bar, a big TV shows continuous surf videos, and open windows on three sides create a cordial, cheerful atmosphere. Hot tips: steak or skillet-roasted clams with garlic, served sizzling hot on a cast-iron skillet;

house-made pasta, a special touch for a place more Beach Boys than Puccini; and fresh fish dinner specials at $18.95. The cuisine's gone international with peel-and-eat shrimp, artichoke hearts on pizza or crostini, burgers, fresh fish tacos, shrimp tempura, and Moroccan chicken. The Evil Jungle Pizza, grilled chicken in a spicy Thai peanut sauce, and the Evil Jungle Pasta are menu staples. A big plus: Everything can be prepared vegetarian upon request.

Village Pizzeria. 505 Front St. ☎ **808/661-8112.** Salad and pizza $3.95, main courses and special pizzas $6.95–$24.50. AE, DC, DISC, MC, V. Daily 11am–9:30pm. PIZZA.

With thin or thick crust, more than a dozen toppings, and the signature clam-and-garlic pizza that you can smell from around the corner, this pizzeria is a corner landmark at the 505 Front St. shopping complex. Appetizers, sandwiches, and pasta round out the offerings.

KAANAPALI
EXPENSIVE

Spats. Hyatt Regency Maui, 200 Nohea Kai Dr. ☎ **808/661-1234.** Reservations recommended. Main courses $20–$30. AE, DISC, MC, V. Daily 6–10pm. ITALIAN.

Descend the stairs to the Italianate entrance and behold the chandeliers, Titian reds, and sensory stimuli straight out of a Coppola film. When we visited, the dining room was filled with the aroma of garlic and tomato and an Italian aria floated through the sound system. The Spats salad was notable, a celebration of simplicity and freshness. We also loved the puttanesca and the tiramisu, lighter and cakier than most, and delicious without being frothy.

Swan Court. Hyatt Regency Maui, 200 Nohea Kai Dr. ☎ **808/661-1234.** Reservations recommended for dinner. Main courses $28–$38. AE, DC, DISC, JCB, MC, V. Daily 6:30–11:30am and 6–10pm. CONTINENTAL.

Even as a resort restaurant, Swan Court is hard to resist. Recent refurbishments have added a dance floor and new furnishings to this romantic restaurant. Come here as a splurge or on a bottomless expense account, and enjoy the continental menu in incomparable surroundings. The combination of waterfalls, ocean view, Japanese gardens, and swans and flamingos serenely gliding by is irresistible, especially with alfresco dining and appropriately extravagant fare. The menu changes frequently, but some basics remain: fresh opakapaka with ginger-citrus vinaigrette, broiled rack of lamb with Maui onion marmalade, basil-scented prawns with pepper-seared bison.

The Villa. Westin Maui, 2365 Kaanapali Pkwy. ☎ **808/667-2525**. Reservations recommended. Main courses $18–$32, fixed-price menu $28. AE, DC, DISC, JCB, MC. V. Daily 6–9pm. HAWAII REGIONAL.

The Westin's signature restaurant offers a romantic ambience with tables encircling a man-made lagoon near waterfalls and a large banyan tree. The dining room is surrounded by water, and even with its soaring ceilings and enormous visual scale, it's an informal, comfortable place, with dishes that range from good to excellent. The fixed-price menu might offer black turtle bean soup or smoked ahi risotto; grilled marinated chicken and wild-mushroom pasta; and the pièce de résistance, the ahi poke martini. Served in a martini glass, the fresh, finely cubed ahi comes topped with seaweed, shiso (a savory flat leaf used as an accompaniment in sushi), tobiko (flying-fish roe), finely cubed cucumber, green onions, and a daringly spicy garlic sauce.

MODERATE

Beachside Grill and Leilani's on the Beach. Whalers Village, 2435 Kaanapali Pkwy. ☎ **808/661-4495**. Reservations suggested for dinner. Lunch and dinner (Beachside Grill) $5.95–$9.95; dinner (Leilani's) from $14.95. AE, DC, DISC, MC, V. Beachside Grill daily 11am–11pm (bar daily until 12:30am); Leilani's daily 5–10pm. STEAK/SEAFOOD.

The Beachside Grill is the informal, less expensive room downstairs on the beach, where folks wander in off the sand for a frothy beer and a beachside burger. Leilani's is the dinner-only room, with more expensive but still not outrageously priced steak and seafood offerings. At Leilani's, you can order everything from affordable spinach, cheese, and mushroom ravioli to lobster and steak at the higher market price. Still, children can order a quarter-pound hamburger for under $5 or a broiled chicken breast for a couple dollars more—a value for sure. Pasta, rack of lamb, filet mignon, and Alaskan king crab at market price are among the temptations in the upstairs room. Although the steak-and-lobster combinations can be pricey, the good thing about Leilani's is the strong middle range of entree prices, especially the fresh fish for around $20. All of this, of course, comes with an ocean view. There's live Hawaiian music every afternoon except Friday, when the rock 'n' roll Aloha Friday set gets those decibels climbing. Free concerts are usually offered on a stage outside the restaurant from 2pm to sunset on the last Sunday of the month. The popular program, Music on the Beach, is always a big draw—and another big reason to love Leilani's.

⭘ **Hula Grill.** Whalers Village, 2435 Kaanapali Pkwy. ☎ **808/667-6636.**
Reservations recommended for dinner. Lunch and Barefoot Bar menus
$5.95–$11.95, dinner main courses from $12.95. AE, CB, DC, DISC, MC, V.
Daily 11am–12:30am. HAWAII REGIONAL/SEAFOOD.

Who wouldn't want to tuck into poisson cru, crab and corn cakes,
or ahi poke rolls under a thatched umbrella, with a sand floor and
palm trees at arm's length and a view of Lanai across the channel?
What a cheerful place this is, a Kaanapali magnet, *the* place to dine
while watching swimmers and catamarans bobbing in the sea.
Peter Merriman, a culinary guru and one of the originators of
Hawaii Regional Cuisine, segued seamlessly from his smallish, Big
Island upcountry enclave to this large, high-volume dining room on
the beach. He has redefined chain-restaurant cuisine with this
300-seat, open-air restaurant in the style of a 1930s kamaaina beach
house.

Hula Grill is one of those dining rooms with a wide range of
prices and choices; although it can be expensive, it doesn't have to
be. The superb menu includes Merriman's signature wok-charred
ahi; seafood pot stickers; and several different fresh-fish preparations, including his famous ahi poke rolls, lightly sautéed rare ahi
wrapped in rice paper with Maui onions. Lunchtime burgers are
de rigueur, or order gourmet appetizers from the Barefoot Bar
menu (sandwiches, crab wontons, fresh fish-and-chips, pizza,
smoked-turkey sandwiches). There's happy-hour entertainment
and Hawaiian music daily.

INEXPENSIVE

Pizza Paradiso Express. Whalers Village, 2435 Kaanapali Pkwy. ☎ **808/
667-0333.** Gourmet pizza $3.35–$3.95 (by the slice), whole pizzas $16.95–$22.95.
No credit cards. Daily 11am–10pm. PIZZA.

Word's out that the pastas are selling as fast as the pizzas. From the
Veg Wedge to the Maui Wowie (with ham and Maui pineapple),
the Jimmy Hoffa (pepperoni and mozzarella), and the God Father
(roasted chicken, artichoke hearts, sun-dried tomatoes, the works),
these pizzas are always described in superlatives, even by jaded New
Yorkers. Pizza Paradiso has hit upon a simple but effective formula:
good crust, uncompromising sauces, and toppings loyal to tradition
but with an edge for those who want it. Create your own pizza with
a long menu of possibilities, and enjoy it in this mallish fast-food
atmosphere—or take it to Kaanapali Beach, just a few steps away.

The new **Pizza Paradiso** location in Honokowai is also garner-
ing rave reviews (see below).

HONOKOWAI, KAHANA & NAPILI
EXPENSIVE

A Pacific Cafe Honokowai. Honokowai Marketplace, 3350 Lower Honoapiilani Rd. ☎ **808/669-2724.** Reservations recommended. Main courses $19–$30. AE, DC, JCB, MC, V. Daily 5–10pm. HAWAII REGIONAL.

How does Jean-Marie Josselin do it? A large rotisserie with an open, U-shaped kitchen, a 1,000-square-foot lanai, and a menu that has earned him star status among Maui foodies. The offerings change daily, but you can count on fresh island ingredients: innovative soups, such as the "creamless" asparagus soup with seared sea scallops and white truffle oil; grilled items (ahi steak au poivre, Mongolian rack of lamb); house specialties (wok-charred mahimahi with sesame-garlic crust, pan-seared ono with soba noodles), and meats and pizzas baked in the tandoor oven.

✪ **Roy's Kahana Bar & Grill/Roy's Nicolina Restaurant.** Kahana Gateway, 4405 Honoapiilani Hwy. ☎ **808/669-6999.** Reservations strongly recommended. Main courses $13–$26. AE, CB, DC, DISC, JCB, MC, V. Roy's Kahana daily 5:30–10pm; Roy's Nicolina, daily 5:30–10pm. EUROASIAN.

These two sibling restaurants are next door to each other, have the same menu, and are busy, busy, busy. They bustle with young, hip servers impeccably trained to deliver blackened ahi or perfectly seared lemongrass shutome (broadbill swordfish) hot to your table, in rooms that sizzle with cross-cultural tastings. Both are known for their rack of lamb and fresh seafood (usually eight or nine choices), and for the large, open kitchens that turn out everything from pizza to sake-grilled New York steak and roasted half chickens in garlic and orange, glistening in cabernet sauce. If pot stickers are on the menu, don't resist.

Sea House Restaurant. Napili Kai Beach Club, 5900 Honoapiilani Hwy. ☎ **808/669-1500.** Reservations required for dinner. Main courses $15–$26, appetizers $4–$13. AE, MC, V. Sat–Thurs 8–11am, noon–2pm (pupu menu 2–9pm), and 5:30–9pm (6–9pm in summer); Fri Polynesian Show 6–9pm. STEAK/SEAFOOD.

The Sea House is not glamorous, famous, or hip, and its food is not always terrific, but it's worth mentioning for its view of Napili Bay, one of the two most gorgeous in West Maui. The Napili Kai Beach Club, where Sea House is located, is a charming throwback to the days when hotels blended in with their surroundings, had lush tropical foliage, and were sprawling rather than vertical. Dinner entrees come complete with soup or salad, vegetables, and rice or potato. The lighter appetizer menu is a delight—more than a dozen choices range from sautéed or blackened crab cake to crisp

Pacific Rim sushi of ahi wrapped in nori and cooked tempura style. The top attraction here, however, is the million-dollar view. On Friday nights, a Polynesian dinner show features the children of the Napili Kai Foundation, an organization devoted to supporting Hawaiian culture.

MODERATE

Fish & Game Brewing Co. & Rotisserie. Kahana Gateway, 4405 Honoapiilani Hwy. ☎ **808/669-3474.** Reservations recommended for dinner. Main courses $6.95–$12.95 lunch, $13.95–$25.95 dinner. AE, CB, DC, DISC, JCB, MC, V. Daily 11am–3pm, happy hour 3–5:30pm, dinner 6–10pm, late-night menu 10:30pm–2am. SEAFOOD.

Large microbrew vats have been installed to one side of what used to be Fish & Game Sports Grill, a popular spot in Kahana notable for its overabundance of testosterone and ubiquitous TVs. The restaurant consists of an oyster bar, deli counter and retail section, and tables. The small retail section sells fresh seafood, while the sit-down menu covers basic tastes: salads (Caesar, Oriental chicken with wontons), fish-and-chips, fresh fish sandwiches ($10.95), cheeseburgers ($7.95), and beer—lots of it. At dinner, count on heavier meats and the fresh catch of the day (ahi, mahimahi, ono), with rotisserie items such as grilled chicken, steaks, and duck. The special late-night menu offers shrimp, cheese fries, quesadillas, and other lighter fare.

INEXPENSIVE

Hawaiian Moons Community Market & Deli. Honokowai Marketplace, 3636 Lower Honoapiilani Rd. ☎ **808/665-1339.** Menu items $5.50–$14.95. AE, DC, JCB, MC, V. Mon–Sat 7am–5pm (health-food store until 9pm), Sun 7am–6pm; hot foods served Mon–Sat 10:30am–5pm, Sun 10:30am–6pm. NATURAL FOODS.

Our favorite south Maui health-food store has set out its shingle in west Maui with this natural-foods deli that also offers fresh fish specials, chili, soups, sushi, a salad bar, and sandwiches (not to mention an ATM!). The ingredients are wholesome: eggless mayonnaise, grain mustard, free-range turkey, "mock chicken" made of seasoned tofu, gardenburgers, whole-wheat bread, and a gourmet tuna sandwich with capers, red peppers, fresh dill, celery, and seasonings. This is an all-purpose natural-foods market and deli with a large selection of Maui products and produce; area health foodies are rejoicing.

Maui Tacos. Napili Plaza, 5095 Napili Hau St. ☎ **808/665-0222.** Most items under $6.95. No credit cards. Mon–Sat 9:30am–9pm, Sun 9:30am–8pm. MEXICAN.

Mark Ellman's Maui Tacos chain is growing faster than you can say "Haleakala." Ellman put gourmet Mexican on paper plates and on the island's culinary map. Barely more than a take-out counter with a few tables, this and the other three Maui Tacos on the island are all the rage among hungry surfers, discerning diners, burrito buffs, and Hollywood glitterati, like Sharon Stone, whose picture adorns a wall or two. We like the excellent fresh-fish tacos, chimichangas, searing salsas, and mouth-breaking compositions such as the Hookipa, a "surf burrito" of fresh fish, black beans, and salsa. Hard tacos, soft tacos, vegetarian burritos, regular burritos, quesadillas, nachos, enchiladas—no chihuahua's asking for Taco Bell.

Additional locations are in Kaahumanu Center, Kahului (☎ 808/871-7726); Lahaina Square, Lahaina (☎ 808/661-8883); and Kamaole Beach Center, Kihei (☎ 808/665-0222).

Pizza Paradiso Italian Caffe. Honokowai Marketplace, 3350 Lower Honoapiilani Rd. ☎ **808/667-2929.** Pizzas $11.95–$22.95, pastas $5.95–$8.95. MC, V. Daily 7:30am–10pm. PIZZA/ITALIAN.

Owner Paris Nabavi had such success with his Pizza Paradiso in Whalers Village that he opened up in the new marketplace—and keeps expanding to keep up with demand. The pastas—marinara, pescatore, Alfredo, Florentine, and pesto, with options and add-ons on top of that—are selling as fast as the pizzas and panini sandwiches. Take-out or dine in, this is a hot spot in the neighborhood, with free delivery.

KAPALUA
EXPENSIVE

The Bay Club. Kapalua Bay Hotel & Villas, 1 Bay Dr. ☎ **808/669-5656.** Reservations recommended for dinner. Dress code at dinner: evening resort wear for women, long slacks for men. Main courses $24–$38. AE, CB, JCB, MC, V. Daily 11:30am–2pm and 6–9:30pm. SEAFOOD.

Tried and true, the Bay Club is one of Maui's lasting pleasures. The classic enjoyments—a stellar view, beatific sunsets, attentive service from bow-tied servers—are matched by a seafood menu that has lost none of its luster with the years. The Caesar salad is still tossed tableside, the seafood is fresh, the peppered steak just so, the vegetarian dishes quite elegant. A perfect lunch: onion leek soup ($7.50) and the seafood Cobb ($14), a peerless untossed salad of shrimp, scallops, calamari, vegetables, and walnuts. (The grilled ahi on poi bread looked enticing, too.) Duck, rack of lamb, bouillabaisse, salads, fresh catches, sandwiches and pasta for lunch, and a host of simple delights can be relished in this open-air dining room. The view changes as the sun moves south, eventually to set behind Lanai in the winter months.

Plantation House. 200 Plantation Club Dr. (at Kapalua Plantation Golf Course). ☎ **808/669-6299.** Reservations recommended. Main courses $18–$24. AE, MC, V. Daily 8am–3pm and 5:30–10pm. SEAFOOD/ISLAND REGIONAL.

With its teak tables, fireplace, and open sides, Plantation House gets high marks for ambience: the 360° view from high among the resort's pine-studded hills takes in Molokai and Lanai, the ocean, the rolling fairways and greens, the northwestern flanks of the West Maui Mountains, and the daily sunset spectacular. Readers of the *Maui News* have deemed this the island's "Best Ambience"—a big honor on this island of ubiquitous views. Choices include fresh fish prepared seven ways—among them, Mediterranean (seared), Upcountry (sautéed with Maui onions and vegetable stew), Island (pan-seared in sweet sake and chile-sesame sauce), Asian Pacific (charred with Asian mushrooms and sake sauce), and Rich Forest (with roasted wild mushrooms), the top seller.

MODERATE

Jameson's Grill & Bar at Kapalua. 200 Kapalua Dr. (at the 18th hole of the Kapalua Golf Course). ☎ **808/669-5653.** Reservations recommended for dinner. Lunch $5.95–$11.95; cafe menu (3–10pm) $6.95–$12.95; dinner main courses $15.95–$39.95. AE, DC, DISC, JCB, MC, V. Daily 8am–10pm. AMERICAN.

This is the quintessential country-club restaurant, open-air with mountain and ocean views. The glass-enclosed room is across the hall from the Kapalua pro shop, a short lob from the tennis courts and golf course. The familiar Jameson's mix of fresh fish (sautéed, wok-seared, or grilled), stuffed shrimp, prawns, rack of lamb, ahi steak, and other basic surf-and turf selections prevail at dinner. At lunch, for duffers dashing to make tee time, inexpensive "golf sandwiches" (roast beef, turkey, tuna salad) are a pleasing alternative if you're not in the mood for the other, richer, choices: fish-and-chips, patty melt, crab cakes, and an affordable cafe menu of gourmet appetizers. A swell start to a Kapalua day: eggs Benedict, eggs Elizabeth (marlin on a muffin with all the trimmings), or eggs Kapalua (crab cakes topped with poached egg and wild-mushroom sauce), for just under $10. With the view of Lanai across the channel and the charming bonsai on every table, it's hard to beat.

✪ **Sansei Seafood Restaurant and Sushi Bar.** Kapalua Shops, 115 Bay Dr. ☎ **808/669-6286.** Reservations recommended. Main courses $15–$19.75. AE, DC, DISC, MC, V. Sat–Wed 5:30–10pm, sushi bar until 11pm; Thurs–Fri 5:30pm–1am. PACIFIC RIM.

People drive from central Maui to dine here, and that's a long drive. Why do they come? Furiously fusion, part Hawaii Regional Cuisine, and all parts sushi, Sansei is tirelessly creative, with a menu that scores higher with the adventurous than the purists. Maki is the mantra here: Paia maki, asparagus maki, and so on, and if you don't like cilantro, watch out for those complex spicy crab rolls. Also on the menu: panko-crusted ahi sashimi, ahi carpaccio, udon and ramen, lobster tail, traditional shrimp and vegetable tempura, Asian rock-shrimp cake in ginger-lime chili butter and cilantro pesto. But there's simpler fare as well, such as pasta and wok-tossed upcountry vegetables.

3 South Maui

MAALAEA & KIHEI
EXPENSIVE

✪ **A Pacific Cafe Maui.** Azeka Place II, 1279 S. Kihei Rd. ☎ **808/879-0069.** Reservations recommended. Main courses $24.75–$32. AE, CB, DC, CB, MC, V. Daily 5:30–10pm. HAWAII REGIONAL.

This restaurant is busy every night of the week, so make your reservations as early as possible. You'll dine on rattan chairs at hammered-copper tables under very high ceilings, in a room bordered with windows overlooking the parking lot (but you'll be so busy enjoying the food, you won't notice the lack of view). From the open kitchen and a menu that changes daily comes a stream of marvels: the signature tiger-eye ahi sushi tempura, light and delectable; garlic-sesame, pan-seared mahimahi, a Pacific Cafe staple; salmon firecracker rolls; pan-seared sea scallops; and the recently introduced hormone-free, Hawaii-grown specialty meats—lamb, elk, veal, and Kobe beef.

Carelli's on the Beach. 2980 S. Kihei Rd. ☎ **808/875-0001.** Reservations recommended. Main courses $22–$38. MC, V. Daily 6–10pm, bar until 11pm. ITALIAN/SEAFOOD.

Kihei's well-tanned, chicly attired trendies come here for pasta, seafood, and the view. It is stupendous: With its prime on-the-sand location at Keawakapu Beach, you can watch the sunset in ravishing surroundings over cioppino (the most popular item, at a pricey $36), fresh fish specials, seafood ravioli, carpaccio, rack of lamb in Asiago cheese crust with truffle sauce, and other Italian favorites. The wood-burning brick oven turns out great pizzas, and the food is top-drawer. To sit at a table on the dining floor, though, a $25 minimum order is required—a policy that lacks aloha.

Five Palms. Mana Kai Maui Resort, 2960 S. Kihei Rd. ☎ **808/879-2607.**
Reservations recommended for dinner. Main courses $17.95–$49. AE, DC, JCB,
MC, V. Daily 8am–2:30pm and 5–9pm. ECLECTIC.

This is the best lunch spot in Kihei—open-air, with tables a few feet
from Keawakapu Beach and million-dollar views of Kahoolawe and
Molokini. The white-sand beach with lava outcroppings is Kihei's
finest feature, and this unpretentious dining room is the front-row
seat for diners. At lunch, the hot items include Kula greens, burgers,
sandwiches on homemade focaccia, a perfectly grilled vegetable platter, and capellini with shiitake mushrooms, sun-dried tomatoes, and
white-wine sauce. At dinner, with the torches lit on the beach and
the main dining room open, the ambience shifts to evening romantic, but it's still casual.

Steve Amaral's Cucina Pacifica. Upstairs in the Rainbow Mall, 2439 S. Kihei
Rd., no. 201A. ☎ **808/875-7831.** Reservations recommended. Main courses
$19–$32. AE, DC, DISC, MC, V. Sun–Thurs 5:30–10pm, Fri–Sat 5:30pm–1am.
MEDITERRANEAN/SEAFOOD.

If you're willing to pay these prices for dinner in a room without
a view—in Kihei, no less—then Cucina may appeal to you. The
menu features Mediterranean culinary traditions and fresh Maui
seafood and vegetables; the restaurant has an air of pretension, but
there's no doubting Amaral's culinary skill. The menu changes
seasonally to highlight fresh seasonal produce. What you might
find during winter: Italian winter truffle and potato soup; wild-
mushroom risotto; spanakopita of pan-seared diver scallops; and
a Spanish stew of clams, meaty mussels, whole shrimp, and scallops. In the spring: seared ahi Genovese, in an herb crust with
Maui basil pesto; skillet-crisped snapper with watercress and
caramelized Maui onions; and Maui onion and tiger prawn risotto.
There's live music Wednesday, Friday, and Saturday evenings,
with dancing into the wee hours.

The Waterfront at Maalaea. Maalaea Harbor, 50 Hauoli St. ☎ **808/
244-9028.** Reservations recommended. Main courses $18–$38. AE, DC, DISC,
JCB, MC, V. Daily 5–8:30pm (last seating). SEAFOOD.

The Waterfront has won awards for wine excellence, service,
and seafood. Loyal diners rave about the friendly staff and seafood,
served in simple surroundings with a bay and harbor view. You
have nine choices of preparations for the several varieties of fresh
Hawaiian fish, ranging from en papillote (baked in buttered parch-
ment) to light cuisine (broiled or poached, then topped with
steamed, fresh vegetables). Other choices: Kula onion soup, an

excellent Caesar salad, lobster chowder, and grilled eggplant layered with Maui onions, tomatoes, and spinach, served with red-pepper coulis and Big Island goat cheese.

MODERATE

Buzz's Wharf. Maalaea Harbor, 50 Hauoli St. ☎ **808/244-5426.** Reservations suggested. Main courses $10.95–$24.95. AE, CB, DC, DISC, JCB, MC, V. Daily 11am–10pm. AMERICAN.

Buzz's is another formula restaurant that offers a superb view, substantial sandwiches, meaty french fries, and surf-and-turf fare—in a word, satisfying but not sensational. Still, this bright, airy dining room is a fine way station for whale watching over a cold beer and a fresh mahimahi sandwich with fries. Some diners opt for several appetizers (stuffed mushrooms, steamer clams, clam chowder, onion soup) and a salad (there are three different types of Caesar), then splurge on dessert. Buzz's prize-winning Tahitian Baked Papaya is a warm, fragrant melding of fresh papaya with vanilla and coconut—the pride of the house.

The Greek Bistro. 2511 S. Kihei Rd. ☎ **808/879-9330.** Reservations recommended. Combination and family style dinners $14.95–$21.95 per person; family style platter $35 for 2. Children's portions also available for considerably less. AE, DC, CB, JCB, MC, V. Daily 5–10pm. GREEK.

The banana trees, yellow ginger, and hibiscus that surround the tile-floored terrace add a lot of character to the dining experience at this indoor/outdoor bistro, especially in chaotic Kihei. Homemade pita bread, quality feta and spices, classic spanakopita and chicken and lamb souvlaki (the Greek version of shish kebab) are some of the authentic and popular Mediterranean offerings. The family-style combination platters include lamb souvlaki and the fresh fish of the day.

Hapa's Brew Haus & Restaurant. Lipoa Shopping Center, 41 E. Lipoa St. ☎ **808/879-9001.** Reservations recommended. Main courses $8–$18.95. AE, DISC, JCB, MC, V. Daily 4pm–2am. BREW HOUSE/INTERNATIONAL.

Food, beer, and music are the primary offerings here, but the best news is the weekly Wednesday night appearance of guitarist and singer nonpareil Willie K. Besides being a nightclub, Hapa's is also a microbrewery with lagers to accompany the chicken wings, poke, spring rolls, baked artichoke hearts, nachos, Caesar salad, sandwiches, pizzas, plate lunches, and noodles. From 4 to 6pm daily, pupus are reduced to half price and draft beer goes for $2. The pizzas come heaped with grilled chicken, pesto shrimp, clams, garlic sauce, vegetables, and any number of combinations, on thin or thick crust. On Sundays from 2 to 6pm, members of the Maui Symphony Orchestra Band (MSO) take over the stage and play swing music—and after that, the teen disco starts spinning.

La Pastaria. Lipoa Shopping Center, 41 E. Lipoa St. ☎ **808/891-1555.** Reservations recommended. Main courses $9–$26. AE, DISC, MC, V. Mon–Sat 5–10pm. ITALIAN/SEAFOOD.

La Pastaria was a Kihei fixture that disappeared when the owners opened Hapa's instead. But La Pastaria is back, a tiny bistro with only 32 seats and every dish made to order, resurrected where Hapa's pool tables used to be. On the menu: frutti di mare, mushroom penne (with portobello and shiitake), linguine carbonara, filet mignon, double breast of chicken in rosemary, and fresh catch sautéed or grilled, served in one of four sauces. Diners at La Pastaria can duck next door to Hapa's for late-night entertainment without a cover charge.

Stella Blues Cafe & Deli. Long's Center, 1215 S. Kihei Rd. ☎ **808/874-3779.** Main courses $9.95–$17.95. DISC, MC, V. Daily 8am–9pm. AMERICAN.

Stella Blues gets going at breakfast and continues through to dinner with something for everyone—vegetarians, children, pasta and sandwich lovers, hefty steak eaters, and sensible diners who'll spring for the inexpensive fresh Kula green salad. Grateful Dead posters line the walls, and a covey of gleaming motorcycles is invariably parked outside. It's loud and lively, casual, irreverent, and unpretentious. Sandwiches are the highlight, two dozen selections ranging from Tofu Extraordinaire to Mom's egg salad on croissant to gardenburgers and grilled chicken. Tofu wraps and the mountain-size Cobb salads are popular, and for the carefree, large coffee shakes with mounds of whipped cream. Daily specials include fresh seafood and other surprises—all home-style cooking, made from scratch, down to the pesto mayonnaise and homemade herb bread. At dinner, selections are geared toward good-value family dining, from affordable full dinners to pastas and burgers.

INEXPENSIVE

○ **Alexander's Fish & Chicken & Chips.** 1913 S. Kihei Rd. ☎ **808/874-0788.** Fish-and-chips $6.75–$9.50. MC, V. Daily 11am–9pm. FISH- AND-CHIPS/SEAFOOD.

Look for the ocean mural in front, Kalama Park across the street, and a marketplace next door: This is Alexander's, a friendly neighborhood take-out stand with patio seating outside and a very busy kitchen (beachwear is welcome here). Fresh ono, mahimahi, and ahi, broiled or fried, fly out of the kitchen with baskets of french fries or rice. Equally popular are the 13-piece shrimp, chicken, oyster, calamari, rib, or fish baskets for $16.50 to $19.95. This may be the most popular restaurant on the south shore—and they use canola oil.

The Coffee Store. Azeka Place II, 1279 Kihei Rd. ☎ **808/875-4244.** All items under $8.50. AE, CB, DC, DISC, MC, V. Sun–Thurs 6am–10pm, Fri–Sat 6am–11pm. COFFEEHOUSE.

This simple, classic coffeehouse for caffeine connoisseurs serves two dozen different types of coffee and coffee drinks. Breakfast items include smoothies, lox and bagels, quiches, granola, and assorted pastries. Pizza, salads, vegetarian lasagna, veggie-and-shrimp quesadillas, and sandwiches (gardenburger, tuna, turkey, ham, grilled veggie panini) also move briskly from the take-out counter. If that's too tame, the turkey and veggie tortilla-wrapped sandwiches are a local legend. There are only a few small tables and they fill up fast, often with musicians and artists who spent the previous evening entertaining at the Wailea and Kihei resorts.

Peggy Sue's. Azeka Place II, 1279 S. Kihei Rd. ☎ **808/875-8944.** Burgers $6–$11, plate lunches $5–$10. DC, MC, V. Sun–Thurs 11am–9pm, Fri–Sat 11am–10pm. AMERICAN.

Just for a moment, forget that diet and take a leap. Peggy Sue's, a 1950s-style diner with oodles of charm, is a swell place to spring for a chocolate malt and french fries. You'll find the best malt on the island here, as well as sodas, shakes, floats, and egg creams. Old-fashioned soda-shop stools, an Elvis Presley Boulevard sign, and jukeboxes on every Formica table serve as backdrop for the famous burgers, brushed with teriyaki sauce and served with all the goodies, as well as plate lunches and gardenburgers.

Shaka Sandwich & Pizza. 1295 S. Kihei Rd. ☎ **808/874-0331.** Sandwiches $3.75–$8, pizzas up to $25.95. Sun–Thurs 10:30am–9pm, Fri–Sat 10:30am–10pm (deliveries daily 10:30am–9pm). PIZZA.

How many "best pizzas" are there on Maui? It depends on which shore you're on, the west or the south. At this south-shore old-timer, award-winning pizzas share the limelight with New York–style hoagies and Philly cheese steaks, calzones and salads, homemade garlic bread, and homemade meatball sandwiches. Shaka uses fresh Maui produce, homemade sauces, and homemade Italian bread.

Choose thin or Sicilian thick crust with gourmet toppings: Maui onions, spinach, anchovies, jalapeño peppers, and a spate of other vegetables. Clam-and-garlic pizza, spinach pizza (with olive oil, spinach, garlic, and mozzarella), and the Shaka Supreme (with at least 10 toppings!) will satisfy even the insatiable.

WAILEA
EXPENSIVE

Joe's Bar & Grill. Wailea Tennis Club, 131 Wailea Ike Place. ☎ **808/ 875-7767.** Reservations recommended. Main courses $17–$30. AE, DC, MC, V. Daily 5:30–10:30pm. AMERICAN GRILL.

Beverly Gannon's style of American home-cooking with a regional twist is inspiring and inimitable, with hearty staples you're not likely to forget: Molokai mashed potatoes, perhaps the best you'll have on Maui; slipper lobster and filet mignon; and our favorite, an appetizer of ahi tartare in a sesame-caper sauce. We also recommend the crisp calamari with spicy Thai fish sauce and the ahi with farfalle in basil, garlic, and tomato. Whatever you order, save room for the chocolate cake. The 360° view spans the golf course, tennis courts, ocean, and Haleakala. At night, the interior theater lighting highlights the 43-foot copper bar, high ceilings, plank floors, and informal ambience.

✪ **Nick's Fishmarket Maui.** Kea Lani Hotel, 4100 Wailea Alanui Dr. ☎ **808/ 879-7224.** Reservations recommended. Main courses $23.95–$38. AE, CB, DC, DISC, JCB, MC, V. Daily 5:30–10pm, bar until 11pm. SEAFOOD.

What a dining room! The private space with attractive murals seats 50, and the round bar, where you can sit facing the ocean, is highlighted by unobtrusive, minimalist, dangling amber lights that are one of the friendliest touches in the hotel. Stefanotis vines are rapidly creating shade on the terrace, where the sunset views reveal the best of Wailea. We love the onion vichyssoise with taro swirl and a hint of tobiko (flying-fish roe); Maui Wowie Greek salad with hearts of palm, Kula tomatoes, avocados, feta cheese, Maui onions, and rock shrimp; and the mahimahi, done to perfection. Bow-tied waiters and almond-scented cold towels add an extra touch to this ocean-side phenomenon—not to mention the torch lighting at sunset and the lavish wine list.

MODERATE

Caffé Ciao. Kea Lani Hotel, 4100 Wailea Alanui Dr. ☎ **808/875-4100.** Reservations recommended. Main courses $14.95–29.95, pizzas $15–$21. AE, CB, DC, DISC, JCB, MC, V. Daily 11am–10pm, bar until 11pm. ITALIAN.

There are two parts to this charming trattoria: the deli/take-out section and the tables under the trees, next to the bar. Rare and wonderful wines are sold in the deli, along with ultraluxe rose soaps and other bath products, assorted pastas, roasted potatoes, vegetable panini, vegetable lasagna, abundant salads, and an appealing selection of microwavable and take-out goodies for those nights when room service or going out won't do. A standout: chef Massimo's special Italian salsa, made with premium tomatoes and olive oil. On the terrace under the trees, the tables are cheerfully accented with Italian herbs growing in cachepots; there's friendly service to go with the pizzas and pastas.

SeaWatch. 100 Wailea Golf Club Dr. ☎ **808/875-8080.** Reservations required for dinner. Main courses $4.50–$12 lunch, from $21 dinner. AE, DC, MC, V. Daily 8am–10pm. ISLAND.

SeaWatch's use of fresh Maui produce, Big Island goat cheese, and island fish in ethnic preparations sets it apart from most other upscale clubhouse restaurants, and it's one of the more affordable stops in tony Wailea. Lunchtime sandwiches, pastas, salads, crab cakes, and soups are moderately priced, and you get 360° views to go with them. You'll dine on the terrace or in a high-ceilinged room, on a menu that carries the tee-off-to-19th-hole crowd with ease. Smoked salmon Benedict, Pacific crab cakes, and the fresh-catch sandwich are some of the breakfast and lunchtime stars. At dinner, the nightly fresh catch, which can be ordered in one of three preparations, is a SeaWatch staple. Save room for the warm chocolate soufflé and cinnamon ice cream.

MAKENA
EXPENSIVE

✪ **Hakone.** Maui Prince Hotel, 5400 Makena Alanui. ☎ **808/874-1111.** Reservations recommended. Complete dinners $22–$42; Mon night buffet $38, Sun sushi buffet $45; Kaiseki (multicourse Kyoto-style dinners, requiring 24-hr. advance notice) $85. AE, JCB, MC, V. Sun 6–9pm, Mon–Sat 6–9:30pm. JAPANESE.

The Prince Hotels know Japanese cuisine and spared no effort to create a slice of Kyoto in Makena, complete with sandalwood walls and pillars assembled by Japanese craftsmen. Hakone offers Japanese fare, very haute-Kyoto, gorgeously presented, and pricey. The popular Sunday-night sushi buffet and Monday-night Japanese dinner buffet offer a sampling of this elegant cuisine. The Japanese dinner buffet includes sushi, broiled miso butterfish, shrimp tempura, and several salads, as well as pupus, miso soup, and rice. Sashimi, tempura, broiled fish, and other traditional Japanese delicacies are offered on the regular menu.

✪ **Prince Court.** Maui Prince Hotel, 5400 Makena Alanui. ☎ **808/ 874-1111.** Reservations recommended. Main courses $27–29, Sun brunch $34. AE, JCB, MC, V. Sun 9:30am–1pm, Thurs–Mon 6–9:30pm. HAWAII REGIONAL.

Half of the Sunday brunch experience is the head-turning view of Makena Beach, the crescent-shaped islet called Molokini, and Kahoolawe island. The other half is the lavish buffet, spread over several tables: pasta, omelets, cheeses, pastries, sashimi, crab legs, smoked salmon, fresh Maui produce, and a smashing array of ethnic and continental foods. The dinner menu changes regularly, and although we miss the guava-glazed baby back ribs, the chef's special, which changes weekly, could offer up some pleasant surprises. Chef Greg Gaspar and assistant Eric Leterc are a formidable team, having fun with their Pacific Rim offerings with Mediterranean flavors. If the seafood risotto with poi is on the menu, don't miss it.

4 Upcountry Maui

MAKAWAO
MODERATE

Casanova Italian Restaurant. 1188 Makawao Ave. ☎ **808/572-0220.** Reservations recommended for dinner. Main courses $8–$23, 12-inch pizzas from $10. DC, MC, V. Mon–Sat 11:30am–2pm and 5:30–9pm, Sun 5:30–9pm. Lounge daily 5:30pm–12:30am or 1am. Deli daily 8am–6:30pm. ITALIAN.

Look for the tiny veranda with a few stools, always full, in front of a deli at Makawao's busiest intersection—that's the most visible part of Casanova's restaurant and lounge. Makawao's center of nightlife consists of a stage and dance floor, restaurant, and bar in the split-level dining room next to the deli. This is pasta heaven: spaghetti fra diavolo (seafood in a caper, Greek olive, and tomato sauce), spinach gnocchi in a fresh tomato-Gorgonzola sauce; a huge pizza selection; grilled lamb chops in balsamic vinegar; several types of fresh fish; and luscious desserts. Our personal picks on a stellar menu: garlic spinach topped with Parmesan and pine nuts, polenta with radicchio (the mushrooms and cream sauce are fabulous!), and tiramisu, the best on the island.

Polli's Mexican Restaurant. 1202 Makawao Ave. ☎ **808/572-7808.** Main courses $6–$15. AE, DC, DISC, MC, V. Daily from about 9am (call to see if they're open) to 10pm. MEXICAN.

Sizzling fajitas are the house special, featuring fish, shrimp, chicken, tofu, or steak in a dramatic entrance, on a crackling hot platter with vegetables and spices, six flour tortillas, sour cream, and guacamole—a gargantuan group endeavor. Expect the usual south-of-the-border favorites, from tamales, tacos, and burritos to cheese-, mushroom-, and Mexi-burgers, laced with jalapeños and pepper Jack cheese.

INEXPENSIVE

✪ **Café 'O Lei.** Paniolo Courtyard, 3673 Baldwin Ave. ☎ **808/573-9065.** Sandwiches and salads $4.50–$5.95. No credit cards. Mon–Sat 11am–4pm. AMERICAN/ISLAND.

Dana Pastula managed restaurants at Lanai's Manele Bay Hotel and the Four Seasons Resort Wailea before opening her tiny, charming outdoor cafe in this sunlit sliver of Makawao. And the alfresco dining is just part of it: From the sandwiches (roast chicken breast, turkey breast, prosciutto) and salads to the soup of the day, the offerings are homemade and excellent. The chic Makawao shopkeepers lunch here daily and never tire of the quinoa salad, the ginger chicken soup, the roasted-beet-and-potato soup, and the talk of the town—a towering Asian salad of Oriental vegetables, tofu, and baby greens, tossed in a sesame vinaigrette with fresh mint, ginger, and lemongrass, and served over Chinese noodles.

HALIIMAILE & PUKALANI

✪ **Haliimaile General Store.** Haliimaile Rd., Haliimaile. ☎ **808/572-2666.** Reservations recommended. Lunch $6–$14, dinner $14–$28. DC, MC, V. Mon–Fri 11am–2:30pm and 5:30–9:30pm, Sat 5:30–9:30pm, Sun 10am–2:30pm (brunch) and 5:30–9:30pm. AMERICAN.

Ten years after opening her foodie haven in the pineapple fields, Bev Gannon, one of the 12 original Hawaii Regional Cuisine chefs, is still going strong. You'll dine at tables set on old wood floors under high ceilings (sound ricochets fiercely here), in a peach-colored room emblazoned with works by local artists. The food, a blend of eclectic American with ethnic touches, manages to avoid the usual pitfalls of Hawaii Regional Cuisine: the same-old, same-old, I'm-bored-with-seared-ahi syndrome. Even the fresh-catch sandwich on the lunch menu is anything but prosaic. The house salad, island greens with Mandarin oranges, onions, toasted walnuts, and blue cheese, is a touch of genius, and the sashimi napoleon (crisp wonton layered with smoked salmon, ahi tartare, and sashimi, served with wasabi vinaigrette) is every bit as delicious as it sounds. Dinner splurges include the Szechuan salmon, Bev's Boboli topped with crab dip, and her famous paniolo ribs in tangy barbecue sauce.

Upcountry Cafe. Andrade Building, 7–2 Aewa Place (just off Haleakala Hwy.), Pukalani. ☎ **808/572-2395.** Lunch $5.95–$8.95, most dinner items under $14.95. MC, V. Mon 6:30am–3pm, Wed–Thurs 6:30am–3pm and 5:30–8:30pm, Fri–Sat 6:30am–3pm and 5:30–9pm, Sun 6:30am–1pm. AMERICAN/LOCAL.

Pukalani's inexpensive, casual, and very popular cafe features cows everywhere: on the walls, chairs, menus, aprons, even the exterior. But the food is the draw: simple, home-cooked comfort food such as meat loaf, roast pork, and humongous hamburgers, plus home-baked bread, oven-fresh muffins, and local faves such as saimin and Chinese chicken salad. Soups and salads (homemade cream of mushroom, Cobb and Caesar salads) and shrimp scampi with bow-tie pasta are among the cafe's other pleasures. The signature dessert is the cow pie, a naughty pile of chocolate cream cheese with macadamia nuts in a cookie crust, shaped like you-know-what.

KULA
EXPENSIVE

Kula Lodge. Haleakala Hwy. (Hwy. 377). ☎ **808/878-2517.** Reservations recommended for dinner. Main courses $7.25–$14 lunch, $18–$26 dinner. MC, V. Daily 6:30am–9pm. HAWAII REGIONAL/AMERICAN.

Don't let the dinner prices scare you, because the Kula Lodge is equally enjoyable, if not more so, for breakfast and lunch, when the prices are lower and the views through the picture windows have an eye-popping intensity. The outdoor dining area with its wood-burning oven is a recent addition, open from 11am daily for as long as the weather permits. The million-dollar view through the large picture windows spans the flanks of Haleakala, rolling 3,200 feet down to central Maui, the ocean, and the West Maui Mountains. If possible, go for sunset cocktails and watch the colors change. When darkness descends, a roaring fire and lodge atmosphere turn the attention to the coziness of the room. At breakfast, the lodge is famous for its banana–macadamia nut pancakes. For lunch, choices include smoked-turkey sandwiches, garden- and mahimahi burgers, soups, salads, seared ahi, and pizza.

INEXPENSIVE

Cafe 808. Lower Kula Rd., past Holy Ghost Church, across Morihara St. ☎ **808/878-6874.** Burgers from $3.50, main courses $4.50–$7.50. No credit cards. Daily 6am–8pm. AMERICAN/LOCAL.

The owners of the popular Upcountry Cafe opened this Formica-table haven on a quiet road in Kula, and word spread quickly. Despite its out-of-the-way location (or perhaps because of it), Cafe 808 has become the universal favorite among residents of all ages for its tasty, straightforward home-style cooking: chicken lasagna, smoked-salmon omelet, taro burger, beef burrito, roast pork, and a huge selection of local-style specials. Regulars rave about the roast pork, chicken katsu, saimin, and beef stew.

Grandma's Coffee House. At the end of Hwy. 37, Keokea. ☎ **808/ 878-2140.** Most items under $8.95. MC, V. Daily 7am–5pm. COFFEEHOUSE/ AMERICAN.

Alfred Franco's grandmother started what is now a fifth-generation coffee business back in 1918, when she was 16 years old. Today, the tiny wooden coffeehouse he named after her, still fueled by homegrown Haleakala coffee beans, is the quintessential roadside oasis. About 6 miles before the Tedeschi Vineyards in Ulupalakua, Grandma's is a gathering place for hot and cold espresso drinks, home-baked pastries, inexpensive pasta, sandwiches, homemade soups, fresh juices, and local plate-lunch specials. Aside from the coffee cake, muffins, and cinnamon rolls (all baked fresh daily), rotating specials include Hawaiian beef stew, ginger chicken, saimin, lentil soup, and sandwiches piled high with Kula vegetables.

Kula Sandalwoods Restaurant. Haleakala Hwy. (Hwy. 377). ☎ **808/ 878-3523.** Most items under $8.75. DISC, MC, V. Mon–Sat 6:30–2pm, Sun 6:30am–noon (brunch). AMERICAN.

The chef, Eleanor Loui, a graduate of the Culinary Institute of America, makes hollandaise sauce every morning from fresh upcountry egg yolks, sweet butter, and Myers lemons, which her family grows in the yard above the restaurant. This is Kula cuisine, with produce from the backyard and everything made from scratch: French toast with home-baked Portuguese sweetbread, crab cakes, hotcakes or Belgian waffles with fresh fruit, French baguettes, grilled teriyaki chicken breast, and an outstanding veggie burger. The Kula Sandalwoods salad features grilled chicken breast with crimson Kula tomatoes and onions and, when the garden allows, just-picked red-oak, curly green, and red-leaf lettuces. The Kula Sandalwoods omelet is an open-faced marvel with cheddar and Jack cheeses, tomatoes, and green onions, served with cottage potatoes—a gourmet treat. You'll dine in one of two separate rooms, in the gazebo, or on the terrace, with dazzling views in all directions, including, in the spring, a yard dusted with lavender jacaranda flowers and a hillside ablaze with fields of orange akulikuli blossoms.

5 East Maui: On the Road to Hana

KUAU & PAIA

EXPENSIVE

✪ **Mama's Fish House.** 799 Poho Place (off the Hana Hwy.), Kuau. ☎ **808/579-8488**. Reservations recommended. Main courses $22.95–$45. AE, CB, DC, JCB, MC, V. Daily 11am–9:30pm.

The restaurant's entrance, a cove with windsurfers, tide pools, white sand, and a canoe resting under palm trees, is a South Seas fantasy reminiscent of Gauguin. The menu and interior complement the setting splendidly, with curved lauhala-lined ceilings, split bamboo on the walls, lavish arrangements of tropical blooms, and picture windows to capture the view. Waiters in ultracool aloha shirts and waitresses with flowers behind their ears serve mai tais and seafood in a sea of pareu prints; for a moment, it feels like Tahiti. But it's Hawaii, which means mahimahi laulau with Kula spinach, baked in ti leaves, with kalua pig and lemongrass rice; mahimahi baked in roasted macadamia nuts, stuffed with shrimp and crab; and several types of fresh catch (monchong, onaga, ahi), offered in four preparations. Sashimi comes in several forms and is an appropriate start to the fish feast. *Hint:* We loved fisherman Mark Hobson's onaga, baked in a mustard crust with Maui onion and herbs.

MODERATE

Jacques Bistro. 89 Hana Hwy. ☎ **808/579-6255**. Reservations recommended. Main courses $8–$19. MC, V. Daily 5–10pm, bar until later. FRENCH/AMERICAN/ISLAND.

Fresh local seafood with a French touch, served in Paia by a chef named Jacques in a room with a 42-foot monkeypod bar and arches, columns, and a garden lanai lush with palms, bromeliads, and towering banyan trees—that's Paia's newest bistro. The owners transformed this site with fresh ideas and a likable chef who whips up diverse, affordable delights: catch of the day (from Paia fishermen), ahi poke, bouillabaisse, sashimi, seviche, steak, duck, and special touches such as seasoned purple potatoes and lightly steamed Kula vegetables. (For light eaters, the gargantuan Greek salad and perfect seviche are starters that equal an entree.) With this setting and menu, they could have jacked up the prices and injected some attitude—but they haven't. When lit up at night, Jacques is an oasis of serenity at Paia's busiest corner.

INEXPENSIVE

Milagros Food Company. Hana Hwy. and Baldwin Ave. ☎ **808/579-8755.** Breakfast about $7, lunch $3–$8, dinner $7–$16. DC, DISC, MC, V. Daily 8am–9:30pm. SOUTHWESTERN/SEAFOOD.

Milagros has gained a following with its great food, upbeat atmosphere, and highly touted margaritas. Although there are fabulous fish tacos, this is much more than Mexican food. Regulars anticipate the fresh ahi creation of the evening, a combination of Southwestern and Pacific Rim styles and flavors accompanied by fresh veggies and Kula greens. Blackened ahi taquitos and pepper-crusted ono pasta are among the new offerings at this Paia hot spot. The bountiful chile rellenos plate comes with grilled ahi, beans, rice, and Kula greens—a sensation, and generous. The daily happy hour features $2.50 margaritas ($12 for a pitcher) from 3 to 6pm. Outdoor seating at this nexus of Paia makes this a great spot for people watching, too.

Paia Fish Market. 110 Hana Hwy. ☎ **808/579-8030.** Lunch and dinner plates $6.95–$18.95. DC, MC, V. Daily 11am–9:30pm. SEAFOOD.

This really is a fish market, with fresh fish to take home and cooked seafood, salads, pastas, fajitas, and quesadillas to take out or enjoy at the few picnic tables inside the restaurant. It's an appealing and budget-friendly selection: Cajun-style fresh catch, fresh fish specials (ahi, salmon), fish tacos and quesadillas, and seafood and chicken pastas. You can also order hamburgers, cheeseburgers, and fish-and-chips (shrimp-and-chips, too), and wonderful lunch and dinner plates, cheap and tasty. Peppering the walls are photos of the number-one sport here, windsurfing.

Pic-nics. 30 Baldwin Ave. ☎ **808/579-8021.** Most items under $6.95. JCB, MC, V. Daily 7am–7pm. SANDWICHES/PICNIC LUNCHES.

Breakfast is terrific here—omelets, eggs to order, Maui Portuguese sausage, Hawaiian pancakes—and so is lunch. Pic-nics is famous for many things, among them the spinach-nut burger, an ingenious vegetarian blend topped with vegetables and cheddar cheese. Stop here to fill your picnic basket for the drive to Hana or upcountry Maui. These are gourmet sandwiches (Kula vegetables, home-baked breast of turkey, Cajun fish) worthy of the most idyllic picnic spot. The rosemary herb–roasted chicken can be ordered as a plate lunch (two scoops of rice and Haiku greens) or as part of the Hana Bay picnic, which includes sandwiches, meats, Maui-style chips, and home-baked cookies and muffins. You can also order old-fashioned fish-and-chips, shrimp-and-chips, or pastries baked fresh daily. Fresh breads from the Maui Bake Shop add to the appeal, and several coffee drinks made with Maui-blend coffee may give you the jolt you need for the drive ahead.

Raw Experience. 42 Baldwin Ave. ☎ **808/579-9729.** Main courses $5.95– $10. MC, V. Mon–Thurs 10am–6pm, Fri–Sun 10am–8pm. VEGAN/JUICE BAR.

Raw Experience gets top marks in our book. This juice bar/ restaurant has dispelled most myths about raw food, organic food, and raw organic food—that it's healthful but boring—with a tire-lessly creative menu and food that's good for you, visually appeal-ing, and exciting to the palate. You don't have to be a tofu addict to love the hummus made of sprouted chickpeas and herbs, angel-hair pasta made of carrots and beets with a sun-dried tomato–vegetable marinara, and soups ranging from spicy Thai coconut to creamy carrot-ginger broth. For sushi lovers: carrot-almond pâté and sunflower-seed cheese rolled with vegetables and avocado in sun-dried nori. The salads—mounds of fresh and marinated veg-etables with zesty dressings—include sprouts, seaweeds, and exotic fruit. Besides the usual roster of fresh-squeezed juices, they also serve exotic fruit in season, whipped up into creamy smoothies.

The Vegan. 115 Baldwin Ave. ☎ **808/579-9144.** Main courses $4.95–$8.95. MC, V. Daily noon–9pm. GOURMET VEGETARIAN/VEGAN.

Wholesome foods with ingenious soy substitutes and satisfying flavors appear on a menu that dares you to feel deprived. Not here! Pad Thai garlic noodles are the best-selling item, cooked in a creamy coconut sauce and generously seasoned with garlic and spices. Cur-ries, grilled polenta, pepper steak made of seitan (a meat substitute), and organic hummus are among the items that draw vegetarians from around the island. Proving that desserts are justly deserved, the Vegan offers a carob cake and coconut milk–flavored tapioca pud-ding that hints of Thailand yet doesn't contain dairy milk.

HAIKU

✪ **Pauwela Cafe.** 375 W. Kuiaha Rd. ☎ **808/575-9242.** Most items under $6. No credit cards. Mon–Sat 7am–3pm, Sun 8am–2pm. INTERNATIONAL.

It's a long drive from anywhere, but the kalua turkey sandwich is reason enough for the journey. For many reasons, the tiny cafe with concrete floors and six tables has a strong local following. Becky Speere, a gifted chef, and her husband, Chris, a food-service instructor at Maui Community College and a former sous chef at the Maui Prince Hotel, infuse every sandwich, salad, and muffin with a high degree of culinary finesse. We never dreamed we could dine so well with such pleasing informality. The scene-stealing kalua turkey is one success layered upon another: warm, smoky, moist shredded turkey, served with cheese on home-baked French bread and covered with a green-chile and cilantro sauce. It gets our vote as the best sandwich on the island. The salads, too, are fresh and uncomplicated, served with homemade dressings. For breakfast, eggs chilaquile are a good starter, with layers of corn tortillas, pinto beans, chiles, cheese, and herbs, topped with egg custard and served hot with salsa and sour cream—the works, for an unbelievable $5.50. All the breads are baked on the premises—French baguette, Scottish oat, whole wheat, English muffins—and served in broke-the-mouth sandwiches, such as the roasted eggplant with aged provolone.

6 At the End of the Road in East Maui: Hana

Hana Ranch Restaurant. Hana Hwy. ☎ **808/248-8255.** Reservations required Fri–Sat. Main courses $16.95–$34.95. AE, DC, DISC, JCB, MC, V. Restaurant daily 7am–10am and 11am–3pm, Fri–Sat 6–8pm. Take-out counter daily 6:30am–10am and 11am–4pm. AMERICAN.

Part of the Hotel Hana-Maui operation, the Hana Ranch Restaurant is the informal alternative to the hotel's dining room. In fact, it's the only other dining room in Hana. Dinner choices include New York steak; prawns and pasta; and a few Pacific Rim options, such as spicy shrimp wontons and the predictable fresh-fish poke. Aside from the weekly, warmly received Wednesday Pizza Night, the luncheon buffet is a more affordable prospect: baked mahimahi, pocket pita sandwiches ($7.95 to $10.95), chicken stir-fry, club and fresh catch sandwiches, and cheeseburgers. It's not an inspired menu, and the service can be nonexistent—especially when the tour buses descend during the lunch rush. There are indoor tables as well as two outdoor pavilions that offer ocean views. At the take-out stand adjoining the restaurant, the fast-food classics prevail: teriyaki plate lunch, mahimahi sandwich, cheeseburgers, hot dogs, and ice cream.

5

Fun in the Surf & Sun

by Jeanette Foster

This is why you have come to Maui—the sun, the sand, the surf. In this chapter, we'll tell you about the best beaches, from where to go to soak up the rays to the best place to plunge beneath the waves for a fish's-eye view of the underwater world. We've covered a range of ocean activities on Maui, including our favorite places and operators for these marine adventures, as well as the greatest golf courses.

1 Beaches

Maui has more than 80 accessible beaches of every conceivable description, from rocky black-sand beaches to powdery golden sands; there's even a rare red-sand beach. What follows is a selection of the finest of Maui's beaches, carefully chosen to suit a variety of needs, tastes, and interests.

For beach toys and equipment, contact **Rental Warehouse,** in Lahaina at 578 Front St., near Prison Street (☎ **808/661-1970**), or in Kihei at Azeka Place II, on the mountain side of Kihei Road near Lipoa Street (☎ **808/875-4050**). Beach chairs rent for $2 a day, coolers (with ice!) for $2 a day, and a host of toys (Frisbees, volleyballs, and more) for $1 a day.

WEST MAUI
✪ D. T. FLEMING BEACH PARK

This quiet, out-of-the-way beach cove, named after the man who started the commercial growing of pineapple on the Valley Isle, is a great place to take the family. The crescent-shaped beach, located north of the Ritz-Carlton Hotel, starts at the 16th hole of the Kapalua golf course (Makaluapuna Point) and rolls around to the sea cliffs at the other side. Ironwood trees provide shade on the land side. Offshore, a shallow sandbar extends to the edge of the surf. The waters are generally good for swimming and snorkeling; sometimes, off on the right side near the sea cliffs, the waves build enough for bodyboarders and surfers to get a few good rides in. This park has lots of facilities: rest rooms, showers, picnic tables, barbecue grills, and a paved parking lot.

✪ KAPALUA BEACH

The beach cove that fronts the Kapalua Bay Hotel is the stuff of dreams: a golden crescent bordered by two palm-studded points. The sandy bottom slopes gently to deep water at the bay mouth; the water is so clear that you can see where the gold sands turn to green, and then deep blue. Protected from strong winds and currents by the lava-rock promontories, Kapalua's calm waters are great for snorkelers and swimmers of all ages and abilities, and the bay is big enough to paddle a kayak around without getting into the more challenging channel that separates Maui from Molokai. Waves come in just right for riding. Fish hang out by the rocks, making it great for snorkeling. The beach is accessible from the hotel on one end, which provides sun chairs with shades and a beach-activities center for its guests, and a public access way on the other. It isn't so wide that you'll burn your feet getting in or out of the water, and the inland side is edged by a shady path and cool lawns. Outdoor showers are stationed at both ends. Parking is limited to about 30 spaces in a small lot off Lower Honoapiilani Road, by Napili Kai Beach Club, so arrive early; next door is a nice but somewhat pricey oceanfront restaurant, Kapalua's Bay Club (see chapter 4 for a review). Facilities include showers, rest rooms, lifeguards, rental shack, and plenty of shade.

✪ KAANAPALI BEACH

Four-mile-long Kaanapali is one of Maui's best beaches, with grainy gold sand as far as the eye can see. The beach parallels the sea channel through most of its length, and a paved beach walk links hotels and condos, open-air restaurants, and Whalers Village shopping center. Because Kaanapali is so long and most hotels have adjacent swimming pools, the beach is crowded only in pockets—there's plenty of room to find seclusion. Summertime swimming is excellent. The best snorkeling is around Black Rock, in front of the Sheraton; the water is clear, calm, and populated with clouds of tropical fish. Facilities include outdoor showers; you can use the rest rooms at the hotel pools. Various beach-activity vendors line up in front of the hotels, offering nearly every type of water activity and equipment. Parking is a problem, though. There are two public entrances: At the south end, turn off Honoapiilani Highway into the Kaanapali Resort, and pay for parking there; or continue on Honoapiilani Highway, turn off at the last Kaanapali exit at the stoplight near the Maui Kaanapali Villas, and park next to the beach signs indicating public access.

WAHIKULI COUNTY WAYSIDE PARK

This small stretch of beach, adjacent to Honoapiilani Highway between Lahaina and Kaanapali, is one of Lahaina's most popular beach parks. It's packed on weekends, but during the week it's a great place for swimming, snorkeling, sunbathing, and picnics. Offshore, the bottom is composed of rocks and sand, gradually sloping down to deeper water. Facilities include paved parking, rest rooms, showers, and small covered pavilions with picnic tables and barbecue grills.

LAUNIUPOKO COUNTY WAYSIDE PARK

Families with children will love this small park off Honoapiilani Highway, just south of Lahaina. A large artificial wading pool for kids fronts the shady park, with giant boulders protecting the wading area from the surf outside. Just to the left is a small sandy beach with good swimming when conditions are right. Offshore, the waves are occasionally big enough for surfing. The view from the park is one of the best: You can see the islands of Kahoolawe, Lanai, and Molokai in the distance. Facilities include paved parking lot, rest rooms, showers, picnic tables, and barbecue grills. It's crowded on weekends.

SOUTH MAUI
KAMAOLE III BEACH PARK

Three beach parks—Kamaole I, II, and III—stand like golden jewels in the front yard of the funky seaside town of Kihei, which all of a sudden is sprawling like suburban blight. The beaches are the best thing about Kihei (if you don't count A Pacific Cafe Maui—see chapter 4 for a review). All three are popular with local residents and visitors because they're easily accessible. On weekends they're jam-packed with fishers, picnickers, swimmers, and snorkelers. The most popular is Kamaole III, or "Kam-3," as locals say. The biggest of the three beaches, with wide pockets of golden sand, it's the only one with a playground for children and a grassy lawn that meets the sand. Swimming is safe here, but scattered lava rocks are toe stubbers at the water line, and parents should watch to make sure that kids don't venture too far out, because the bottom slopes off quickly. Both the north and south shores are rocky fingers with a surge big enough to attract fish and snorkelers, and the winter waves attract bodysurfers. Kam-3 is also a wonderful place to watch the sunset.

Using Activity Desks to Book Your Island Fun

If you want to go with an outfitter or a guide and you'd like to save some money, consider booking your activity through a discount activities center or activities desk. These agents—whose sole business it is to act as a clearinghouse for activities, much like a consolidator functions as a discount clearinghouse for airline tickets—can often get you a better price than you'd get by booking an activity directly with the outfitter.

Discount activities centers will, in effect, split their commission with you, giving themselves a smaller commission to get your business—and passing, on average, a 10% discount on to you. In addition to saving you money, good activity centers should be able to help you find, say, the snorkel cruise that's right for you, or the luau that's most suitable for both you *and* the kids. But it's in the activities agent's best interest to sign you up with outfitters from which they earn the most commission; some agents have no qualms about booking you into any activity if it means an extra buck for them. If an agent tries to push a particular outfitter or activity too hard, be skeptical. Conversely, they'll try to steer you away from outfitters that don't offer big commissions. For example, Trilogy, the company that offers Maui's most popular snorkel cruises to Lanai (and the only one with rights to land at Lanai's Hulupoe Beach), offers only minimal commissions to agents and does not allow agents to offer

Facilities include rest rooms, showers, picnic tables, barbecue grills, and lifeguards. There's also plenty of parking on South Kihei Road, across from the Maui Parkshore condos.

✪ WAILEA BEACH

Wailea, which means "water of Lea," the Hawaiian goddess of canoe makers, is the best golden-sand crescent on Maui's sunbaked southwestern coast. One of five beaches within Wailea Resort, Wailea is big, wide, and protected on both sides by black lava points. It's the front yard of the Four Seasons Wailea and the Grand Wailea Resort Hotel and Spa, respectively Maui's most elegant and outrageous beach hotels. From the beach, the view out to sea is magnificent, framed by neighboring Kahoolawe and Lanai and the tiny crescent of Molokini, probably the most popular snorkel spot in these parts. The clear waters tumble to shore in waves just the any discounts at all; as a result, most activities desks you speak to on Maui will automatically try to steer you away from Trilogy even if you say you want to book with it.

Another important word of warning: Be careful to avoid those activities centers offering discounts as fronts for time-share sales presentations. Using a free snorkel cruise or luau tickets as bait, they'll suck you into a 90-minute presentation—and try to get you to buy into a Maui time-share in the process. Not only will they try to sell you a big white elephant you never wanted in the first place, but—since their business is time-shares, not activities—they also won't be as interested, or as knowledgeable, about which activities might be right for you. These shady deals seem to be particularly rampant on Maui. Just do yourself a favor and avoid them altogether.

We recommend **Tom Barefoot's Cashback Tours** (e-mail: barefoot@maui.net), at Dolphin Shopping Center, 2395 S. Kihei Rd., Kihei (☎ **808/879-4100**), and at 834 Front St., Lahaina (☎ **808/661-8889**). Tom offers a 10% discount on all tours, activities, and adventures when you pay in cash or with traveler's checks. If you pay with a credit card or personal check, he'll give you a 7% discount. The two showrooms are loaded with pictures and maps of all the activities the company books. We found Tom's to be very reliable and honest.

right size for gentle riding, with or without a board. From shore, you can see Pacific humpback whales in season (December through April), and unreal sunsets nightly. Facilities include rest rooms, outdoor showers, and limited free parking at the blue SHORELINE ACCESS sign, on Wailea Alanui Drive, the main drag of this resort. Wailea Resort's beaches might seem off-limits, hidden from plain view by an intimidating wall of luxury resorts, but they're all open to the public.

ULUA BEACH

One of the most popular beaches in Wailea, Ulua is a long, wide, crescent-shaped gold-sand beach between two rocky points. When the ocean is calm, Ulua offers Wailea's best snorkeling; when it's rough, the waves are excellent for bodysurfers. The ocean bottom is shallow and gently slopes down to deeper waters, making swimming generally safe. The beach is usually occupied by guests of nearby resorts; in high season (from Christmas to March and June to August), it's carpeted with beach towels, and packed with sunbathers like sardines in cocoa butter. Facilities include showers and rest rooms. A variety of equipment is available for rent at the nearby Wailea Ocean Activity Center. To find Ulua, look for the new blue SHORELINE ACCESS sign on South Kihei Road, near Stouffer Wailea Beach Resort. A tiny parking lot is nearby.

☉ MALUAKA BEACH (MAKENA BEACH)

On the southern end of Maui's resort coast, development falls off dramatically, leaving a wild, dry countryside of green kiawe trees. The Maui Prince sits in isolated splendor, sharing Makena Resort's 1,800 acres with only a couple of first-rate golf courses and a necklace of perfect beaches. The strand nearest the hotel is Maluaka Beach, often called Makena, notable for its beauty and its views of Molokini Crater, the offshore islet, and Kahoolawe, the so-called "target" island. It's a short, wide, palm-fringed crescent of golden, grainy sand set between two black-lava points and bounded by big sand dunes topped by a grassy knoll. Swimming in this mostly calm bay is considered the best on Makena Bay, which is bordered on the south by Puu Olai cinder cone and historic Keawala'i Congregational Church. Facilities include rest rooms, showers, a landscaped park, lifeguards, and roadside parking. Along Makena Alanui, look for the SHORELINE ACCESS sign near the hotel, turn right, and head down to the shore.

ONELOA BEACH (BIG BEACH)

Oneloa, which means "long sand" in Hawaiian, is one of the most popular beaches on Maui. Locals call it Big Beach—it's 3,300 feet long and more than 100 feet wide. Mauians come here to swim, fish, sunbathe, surf, and enjoy the view of Kahoolawe and Lanai. Snorkeling is good around the north end at the foot of Puu Olai, a 360-foot cinder cone. During storms, however, big waves lash the shore and a strong rip current sweeps the sharp drop-off, posing a danger for inexperienced open-ocean swimmers. There are no facilities except portable toilets, but there's plenty of parking. To get here, drive past the Maui Prince Hotel to the second dirt road, which leads through a kiawe thicket to the beach.

On the other side of Puu Olai is **Little Beach,** a small pocket beach where assorted nudists work on their all-over tans, to the chagrin of uptight authorities who take a dim view of public nudity. You can get a real nasty sunburn and a lewd-conduct ticket, too.

EAST MAUI
BALDWIN PARK

Located off the Hana Highway between Sprecklesville and Paia, this popular beach park is well used by Maui residents, especially bodyboard enthusiasts. Named after Harry Baldwin, who was a delegate to Congress, the park was originally developed for the employees of Hawaiian Commercial & Sugar Co., who lived in the nearby area. In 1963, the company turned the park over to the county. It's easy to see why this place is so popular: The surf breaks along the entire length of the white-sand beach, creating perfect conditions for bodyboarding. On occasion, the waves get big enough for surfing. A couple of swimming areas are safe enough for children: one in the lee of the beach rocks near the large pavilion, and another at the opposite end of the beach, where beach rocks protect a small swimming area. There's a large pavilion with picnic tables and kitchen facilities, barbecue grills, additional picnic tables on the grassy area, rest rooms, showers, a semipaved parking area, a baseball diamond, and a soccer field. The park is well used on weekends; weekdays are much quieter.

HOOKIPA BEACH PARK

Two miles past Paia, on the Hana Highway, you'll find one of the most famous windsurfing sites in the world. Due to constant wind and endless waves, Hookipa attracts top windsurfers and wave jumpers from around the globe. Surfers and fishermen also enjoy this small, gold-sand beach at the foot of a grassy cliff, which provides a natural amphitheater for spectators. Except when international competitions are being held, weekdays are the best time to watch the daredevils fly over the waves. When the water is flat, snorkelers and divers explore the reef. Facilities include rest rooms, showers, pavilions, picnic tables, barbecue grills, and a parking lot.

✪ WAIANAPANAPA STATE PARK

Four miles before Hana, off the Hana Highway, is this beach park, which takes its name from the legend of the Waianapanapa Cave, where Chief Kaakea, a jealous and cruel man, suspected his wife, Popoalaea, of having an affair. Popoalaea left her husband and hid herself in a chamber of the Waianapanapa Cave. She and her attendant ventured out only at night, for food. Nevertheless, a few days later, Kaakea was passing by the area and saw the shadow of the servant. Knowing he had found his wife's hiding place, Kaakea entered the cave and killed her. During certain times of the year, the water in the tide pool turns red as a tribute to Popoalaea, commemorating her death. Scientists claim, however, that the change in color is due to the presence of small red shrimp.

Waianapanapa State Park's 120 acres have 12 cabins, a caretaker's residence, a beach park, picnic tables, barbecue grills, rest rooms, showers, a parking lot, a shoreline hiking trail, and a black-sand beach (it's actually small black pebbles). This is a wonderful area for both shoreline hikes (bring insect repellent, as the mosquitoes are plentiful) and picnicking. Swimming is generally unsafe, though, due to powerful rip currents and strong waves breaking offshore, which roll into the beach unchecked. Because Waianapanapa is crowded on weekends with local residents and their families, as well as tourists, weekdays are generally a better bet.

✪ HAMOA BEACH

This half moon–shaped, gray-sand beach (a mix of coral and lava) in a truly tropical setting is a favorite among sunbathers seeking rest and refuge. The Hotel Hana-Maui maintains the beach and acts as though it's private, which it isn't—so just march down those lava-rock steps and grab a spot on the sand. James Michener said of Hamoa, "Paradoxically, the only beach I have ever seen that looks like the South Pacific was in the North Pacific—Hamoa Beach . . . a beach so perfectly formed that I wonder at its comparative obscurity." The 100-foot-wide beach is three football fields long and sits below 30-foot black-lava sea cliffs. An unprotected beach open to the ocean, Hamoa is often swept by powerful rip currents. Surf breaks offshore and rolls ashore, making this a popular surfing and bodysurfing area. The calm left side is best for snorkeling in summer. The hotel has numerous facilities for guests; there's an outdoor shower and rest rooms for nonguests. Parking is limited. Look for the Hamoa Beach turnoff from Hana Highway.

2 Hitting the Water

BOATING & SAILING

For fishing charters, see "Sportfishing," below. For trips that combine snorkeling with whale watching, see "Whale-Watching Cruises," below.

You can experience the thrill of competition sailing with **World Class Yacht Charters,** 107 Kahului Heliport, Kahului, HI 96732 (☎ **800/600-0959** or 808/667-7733). There's nothing like it, especially when all you have to do is hold on and cheer. *World Class,* a 65-foot custom yacht designed for Maui waters, takes 24 passengers for a variety of sailing adventures: 2-hour whale-watching tours for $25; 4-hour morning snorkel sails for $59; high-performance sails for $35; and a 2-hour trade-winds sunset sail for $45. The 2pm high-performance sailing tour is the most exciting. Be prepared to get wet: The captain and crews of this cutter-rigged, high-tech yacht are serious about sailing. All trips leave from Kaanapali Beach.

You can also take a ride on **America II,** Lahaina Harbor, slip 5 (☎ **888/667-2133** or 808/667-2195), a U.S. contender in the America's Cup. It's a true racing boat: no snorkeling, just the thrill of racing the wind. Trips include a morning whale-watching sail, an afternoon sail, and a sunset sail. Each trip lasts 2 hours and costs $29.95 to $32.95 for adults, $14.95 to $16.48 for children ages 6 to 12; free for children 5 and under.

SNORKEL CRUISES TO MOLOKINI

If you'd like to take a snorkel boat to Molokini (see "Snorkeling," below), call the **Ocean Activities Center,** 1847 S. Kihei Rd., Kihei (☎ **800/798-0652** or 808/879-4485), which also operates out of a number of hotels and condos. The best deal is the Maka Kai cruise, which includes continental breakfast, deli lunch, snorkel gear, and instruction; it's $55 for adults, $35 for children ages 3 to 12. The 5-hour cruise departs from Maalaea Harbor, slip 62, at 7am.

You can also try **Maui Classic Charters** (☎ **800/736-5740** or 808/879-8188; www.mauicharters.com). Its snorkel-sail cruises on the 63-foot *Lavengro* leave Maalaea, slip 80, at 7am for a 6-hour journey that includes continental breakfast and deli lunch; it costs $59 for adults and $40 for children under 12. This outfitter also has a new boat, *Four Winds II,* a 55-foot glass-bottom catamaran, which offers both 5-hour snorkel trips ($69 for adults, $45 for children ages 3 to 12) and 3 1/2-hour trips ($40 for adults, $30 for children) with a naturalist on board during whale season.

For an action-packed snorkel-sail experience, check out **Pride of Maui,** which operates out of Maalaea Harbor (☎ **808/875-0955**). The 5 1/2-hour cruises not only go to Molokini, but also stop at Turtle Bay, off the cost of the Maui Prince Hotel, and in Makena, for more snorkeling. Continental breakfast, barbecue lunch, gear, and instruction are included in the price: $76 for adults, $69 for kids 13 to 17, $49 for kids 3 to 12, and free for kids under 3.

DAY CRUISES TO MOLOKAI

The **Lahaina Princess**, Lahaina Harbor, slip 3 (☎ **800/275-6969** or 808/667-6165; fax 808/661-5792; www.maui.net/~ismarine), a

65-foot, 149-passenger yacht, sails from Lahaina to Kaunakakai, Molokai, offering visitors four different options: the Walking Tour (boat passage only), the Cruise Drive Tour (boat passage and rental car), the Alii Tour (boat passage, guided van tour, and lunch), and the Overnight Trip (boat passage and overnight stay at Kaluakoi Resort). Prices range from $73 for the Walking Tour ($37 for children ages 3 to 12) to $169 per person for the Overnight Trip, double occupancy. Trips are offered on Tuesday and Thursday from April to mid-December, and on Saturday only from mid-December to April.

DAY CRUISES TO LANAI

Hop aboard ✪ **Trilogy Excursions'** 50-foot catamaran for a 90-minute sail to Lanai and a fun-filled day of sailing, snorkeling, swimming, and whale watching. This is the only cruise that offers a personalized ground tour of the island. Breakfast (homemade cinnamon buns and freshly brewed Kona coffee) and lunch (a Hawaiian barbecue) are included. The trip is $159 for adults, $79.50 for children ages 3 to 12, and free for children under 3—we think it's worth every penny. Call ☎ **800/874-2666** or 808/661-4743, or point your browser to www.sailtrilogy.com.

The ✪ **Expeditions Lahaina/Lanai Passenger Ferry** (☎ **808/661-3756**) will take you from Maui to Lanai and back for $50 round-trip. The ferry services run daily, five times a day. Before you go, contact **Red Rover** (☎ **87-RED ROVER or** 808/565-7722; www.onlanai.com/rover.htm) or **Lanai City Service** (☎ **800/800-4000** or 808/565-7227) to arrange vehicle and equipment rentals or rides.

A day with **Club Lanai** (☎ **808/871-1144**) consists of a catamaran trip departing from Lahaina Harbor, slip 4, at 7:30am to Lanai's eastern shore, where you can spend the day snorkeling, kayaking, bicycling, and relaxing in a hammock at an 8-acre beachfront estate. An all-you-can-eat buffet lunch and an open bar are included in the cost: $89 for adults, $69 for children ages 13 to 20, $29 for children ages 4 to 12, and free for children 3 and under.

Scotch Mist (☎ **808/661-0386**), a 50-foot Santa Cruz sailboat anchored in Lahaina Harbor, slip 9, offers half-day sail-snorkel cruises to Lanai; you won't actually set foot on Lanai, but you'll swim with the fish in its sparkling offshore waters. The price—$70 for adults, $49 for children ages 5 to 11, and free for kids under 4—includes snorkel gear, fruit juice, fresh pineapple spears, Maui chips, beer, wine, and soda.

For an amazingly smooth, stable, and swift ride, call *Maui Nui Explorer* (☎ 800/852-4183 or 808/873-3475). This 48-foot, 49-passenger adventure craft leaves Lahaina Harbor for a 4-hour journey along the coast of Lanai, where you'll be able to swim and snorkel in remote coves and bays. Coffee, juice, and a deli-style lunch (sandwiches, Maui chips, fresh fruit, and cookies) are included, along with snacks, snorkel gear, and whale watching (in season). There's always a Hawaiian cultural specialist/marine-life expert on board to answer questions about the islands and their surrounding waters. The cost is $65 for adults and $45.50 for children ages 5 to 11.

BODYBOARDING (BOOGIE BOARDING) & BODYSURFING

Bodysurfing—riding the waves without a board, becoming one with the rolling water—is a way of life in Hawaii. Some bodysurfers just rely on their outstretched hands (or hands at their sides) to ride the waves; others use handboards (flat, paddlelike gloves).

For additional maneuverability, try a boogie or bodyboard (also known as belly boards or *paipo* boards). These 3-foot-long vehicles, which support the upper part of your body, are easy to carry and very maneuverable in the water. Both bodysurfing and bodyboarding require a pair of open-heeled swim fins to help propel you through the water. Both kinds of wave riding are very popular in the islands because the equipment is inexpensive and easy to carry, and both sports can be practiced in the small, gentle waves.

You can rent boogie boards and fins for $6.50 a day or $26 a week from **Snorkel Bob's** (www.snorkelbob.com), open from 8am to 5pm daily at two locations: Napili Village Hotel, 5425 Lower Honoapiilani Rd., Napili (☎ 808/669-9603); and 161 Lahainaluna Rd., Lahaina (☎ 808/661-4421). They're also available for rent from **West Hawaii Surfing Academy,** 658 Front St. (in front of the Wharf Cinema Center and across the street from the Banyan Tree), Lahaina (☎ 808/667-5399), for $5 for 2 hours. The cheapest place to rent boogie boards is **Rental Warehouse,** in Lahaina at 578 Front St., near Prison Street (☎ 808/661-1970), or in Kihei at Azeka Place II, on the mountain side of Kihei Road, near Lipoa Street (☎ 808/875-4050), where they go for as little as $2 a day.

Baldwin Beach, just outside Paia, has great bodysurfing waves nearly year-round. In winter, Maui's best bodysurfing spot is **Mokuleia Beach,** known locally as Slaughterhouse because of the cattle slaughterhouse that once stood here, not because of the waves—although they are definitely for expert bodysurfers only. To get to Mokuleia, take Honoapiilani Highway just past Kapalua Bay Resort; various hiking trails will take you down to the pocket beach.

Storms from the south bring fair bodysurfing conditions and great boogie boarding to the lee side of Maui: **Oneloa** (Big Beach) in Makena, **Ulua** and **Kamaole III** in Kihei, and **Kapalua** beaches are all good choices.

OCEAN KAYAKING

One of Maui's best kayak routes is along the Kihei Coast, where there's easy access to calm water. Mornings are always best, because the wind comes up around 11am, making seas choppy and paddling difficult.

Kayak rentals are available for $15 per hour from **West Hawaii Surfing Academy,** 658 Front St. (in front of the Wharf Cinema Center and across the street from the Banyan Tree), Lahaina (☎ **808/ 667-5399**). The island's cheapest kayak rentals are at **Rental Warehouse,** in Lahaina at 578 Front St., near Prison Street (☎ **808/ 661-1970**), or in Kihei at Azeka Place II, on the mountain side of Kihei Road, near Lipoa Street (☎ **808/875-4050**), where one-person kayaks are $10 a day and two-person kayaks are $15 a day.

For the uninitiated, our favorite kayak-tour operator is **Makena Kayak Tours** (☎ **808/879-8426**). Professional guide Dino leads the 2½-hour tour from Makena Landing and loves taking first-time kayakers over the secluded coral reefs and into remote coves. His wonderful tour will be the highlight of your trip; it costs $55 per person, including refreshments and snorkel and kayak equipment.

Gordon Godfrey, Suzanne Simmons, and the expert guides of **South Pacific Kayaks,** 2439 S. Kihei Rd., Kihei, HI 96753 (☎ **800/776-2326** or 808/875-4848; fax 808/875-4691; www.maui.net/~kayak), are Maui's oldest kayak-tour company. They offer ocean kayak tours that include lessons, a guided tour, and snorkeling. Tours run from 2½ to 5 hours and range in price from $59 to $89. Kayak rentals start at $20 a day.

In Hana, **Hana Bay Kayak and Snorkel Tours** (☎ **808/ 248-7711**) runs 2½-hour tours of Hana's coastline on wide, stable "no roll" kayaks (plus snorkeling) for $59 per person. You can also spend a day learning how to kayak-surf with an instructor for $79 for 7 hours—or rent your own kayak for $27.50 per hour.

SCUBA DIVING

Some people come to Maui for the sole purpose of plunging into the tropical Pacific and exploring the underwater world. You can see the great variety of tropical marine life (more than 100 endemic species found nowhere else on the planet), explore sea caves, and swim with sea turtles and monk seals in the clear tropical waters off the island.

We recommend going early in the morning. Trade winds often rough up the seas in the afternoon, so most dive operators schedule early morning dives that end at noon, and then take the rest of the day off.

Everyone dives **Molokini,** a marine-life park and one of Hawaii's top dive spots. This crescent-shaped crater has three tiers of diving: a 35-foot plateau inside the crater basin (used by beginning divers and snorkelers), a wall sloping to 70 feet just beyond the inside plateau, and a sheer wall on the outside and backside of the crater that plunges 350 feet. This underwater park is very popular thanks to calm, clear, protected waters and an abundance of marine life, from manta rays to clouds of yellow butterfly fish.

If you're interested in the marine environment and natural history, call **Mike Severns Diving,** P.O. Box 627, Kihei (☎ **808/ 879-6596;** www.severns.maui.hi.us), for small (12-person maximum, divided into two groups of six people each), personal diving tours on his 38-foot Munson/Hammerhead boat with freshwater shower. Mike and his wife, Pauline Fiene-Severns, are both biologists who make diving not only fun, but also educational (they have a spectacular underwater photography book called *Molokini Island*). In their 20-plus years of operation, they have been accident-free. Two-tank dives are $100 without equipment ($109 with equipment).

If the Severns are booked, contact **Ed Robinson's Diving Adventures** (☎ **800/635-1273** or 808/879-3584; fax 808/874-1939; www.mauiscuba.com), another great dive operator. Ed is a widely published underwater photographer who offers specialized charters for small groups. Most of his business comes from repeat customers. Ed offers two-tank dives for $104 ($10 extra for equipment); his dive boats depart from Kihei boat ramp.

Maui's largest diving retailer, with everything from rentals to scuba-diving instruction to dive-boat charters, is **Maui Dive Shop** (www.mauidiveshop.com or www.scubasales.com), which can be found all over the island: in Kihei at Azeka Place II Shopping Center (☎ **808/879-1919**), Kamaole Shopping Center (☎ **808/ 879-1533**), and 1455 S. Kihei Rd. (☎ **808/879-3388**); in Lahaina at Lahaina Cannery Mall (☎ **808/661-5388**); and in the Honokowai Market Place (☎ **808/661-6166**). Other locations include Wailea Shopping Village (☎ **808/879-3166**); Whalers

Village, Kaanapali (☎ **808/661-5117**); and Kahana Gateway, Kahana (☎ **808/669-3800**).

SNORKELING

Some snorkel tips: Always go with a buddy. Look up every once in a while to see where you are, how far offshore you are, and whether there's any boat traffic. Don't touch anything; not only can you damage coral, but camouflaged fish and shells with poisonous spines might surprise you. Always check with a dive shop, lifeguards, and others on the beach about the area in which you plan to snorkel: Are there any dangerous conditions you should know about? What are the current surf, tide, and weather conditions?

Snorkel Bob's (www.snorkelbob.com) can rent everything you need at their three Maui locations: 161 Lahainaluna Rd., Lahaina (☎ **808/661-4421**); Napili Village, 5425-C Lower Honapiilani Hwy., Napili (☎ **808/669-9603**); and Kihei Market Place, 34 Keala St. (just off S. Kihei Road), Kihei (☎ **808/879-7449**). Snorkel gear (fins, mask, and snorkel) rent for $2.50 to $6.50 a day, or $9 to $39 a week.

Rental Warehouse, in Lahaina at 578 Front St., near Prison Street (☎ **808/661-1970**), and in Kihei at Azeka Place II, on the mountain side of Kihei Road, near Lipoa Street (☎ **808/ 875-4050**), also has everything you need to experience the underwater world. The snorkel sets include mask, fins, snorkel, gear bag, map of great snorkeling areas, no-fog lotion (for your mask), and fish identification chart—just add water and you're ready to go.

Maui's best snorkeling beaches include **Kapalua Beach; Black Rock,** at Kaanapali Beach; along the Kihei coastline, especially at **Kamaole III Beach Park;** and along the Wailea coastline, particularly at **Ulua Beach.** Mornings are best, because local winds don't kick in until around noon. If you'd like to head over to Lanai for a pristine day of snorkeling, see "Day Cruises to Lanai" under "Boating & Sailing," above.

Two truly terrific places require more effort to get to but are worth it, because they're home to Maui's tropical marine life at its best:

✪ **MOLOKINI** Like a crescent moon fallen from the sky, this sunken crater sits almost midway between Maui and the uninhabited island of Kahoolawe. Tilted so that only the thin rim of its southern side shows above water in a perfect semicircle, Molokini stands like a scoop against the tide, and it serves, on its concave side, as a natural sanctuary for tropical fish and snorkelers, who commute daily in a fleet of dive boats to this marine-life preserve. See "Snorkel Cruises to Molokini" under "Boating & Sailing," above, for details on getting here.

AHIHI-KINAU NATURAL PRESERVE   You can't miss in Ahihi Bay, a 2,000-acre state natural area reserve in the lee of Cape Kinau, on Maui's rugged south coast, where Haleakala spilled red-hot lava that ran to the sea in 1790. Fishing is strictly *kapu* here, and the fish know it; they're everywhere in this series of rocky coves and black-lava tide pools. The black, barren, lunar-like land stands in stark contrast to the green-blue water. After snorkeling, check out La Pérouse Bay on the south side of Cape Kinau, where the French admiral La Pérouse became the first European to set foot on Maui. A lava-rock pyramid known as Pérouse Monument marks the spot. To get here, drive south of Makena past Puu Olai to Ahihi Bay, where the road turns to gravel and sometimes seems like it'll disappear under the waves. At Cape Kinau, there are three four-wheel-drive trails that lead across the lava flow; take the shortest one, nearest La Pérouse Bay.

SPORTFISHING

The largest blue marlin taken on a rod and reel in the waters around Maui tipped the scale at more than 1,200 pounds. Marlin, tuna, ono, and mahimahi await the baited hook in Maui's coastal and channel waters. No license is required; just book a sportfishing vessel out of Lahaina or Maalaea harbors. Most charter boats that troll for big-game fish carry a maximum of six passengers. You can walk the docks, inspecting boats and talking to captains and crews, or book through an activities desk or one of the outfitters recommended below.

Shop around: Prices vary widely according to the boat, the crowd, and the captain. A shared boat for a half-day of fishing starts at $100; a shared full day of fishing starts at around $140. A half-day exclusive (you get the entire boat) is around $300 to $535; a full-day exclusive boat can range from $450 to $900. Also, many boat captains tag and release marlin or keep the fish for themselves (sorry, that's Hawaii style). If you want to eat your mahimahi for dinner or have your marlin mounted, tell the captain before you go.

If you want to fish out of Maalaea, you can spend the day with **Capt. Joe Yurkanin** and **Capt. Ermin Fergerstrom** on their 37-foot Tollycraft, the **No Ka Oi III** (☎ 800/798-0652 or 808/879-4485). For other ideas, try the **Maalaea Activities** desk at the harbor (☎ 808/242-6982).

At Lahaina Harbor, go for one of the following charter companies: **Hinatea Sportfishing,** slip 27 (☎ 808/667-7548); **Lucky Strike Charters,** slips 50 and 51 (☎ 808/661-4606); or **Aerial Sportfishing Charters,** slip 2 (☎ 808/667-9089).

SURFING

Always wanted to learn to surf, but didn't know who to ask? Contact the **Nancy Emerson School of Surfing,** P.O. Box 463, Lahaina, HI 96767 (☎ **808/244-SURF** or 808/874-1183; fax 808/874-2581; www.maui.net/~ncesurf/ncesurf.html). Nancy has been surfing since 1961—she was a stunt performer for various movies, including *Waterworld.* She has pioneered a new instructional technique called "Learn to Surf in One Lesson." It's $70 per person for 2 hours with a group; private classes run $115 for 2 hours.

Even if you've never seen a surfboard before, Andrea Thomas claims she can teach you the art of riding the waves. She has instructed thousands at **Maui Surfing School,** P.O. Box 424, Puunene, HI 96784 (☎ **800/851-0543** or 808/875-0625; www.mauisurf.com), including students as young as 3 and as "chronologically gifted" as 70. She backs her classes with a guarantee that she'll get you surfing, or you'll get 110% of your money back. Two-hour lessons are $60, available by appointment.

Steve and Ava McNanie, owners of the **West Maui Surfing Academy,** 658 Front St. (in front of the Wharf Cinema Center, across the street from the Banyan Tree), Lahaina (☎ **808/667-5399**), offer 2¹/₂-hour lessons for $65; surfboards are $10 for 2 hours. Surfboards are also available for rent from **Hunt Hawaii Surf and Sail** in Paia (☎ **808/575-2300**), starting at $20 a day.

Surfers on a budget will find the lowest rates on rental boards at **Rental Warehouse,** in Lahaina at 578 Front St., near Prison Street (☎ **808/661-1970**), and in Kihei at Azeka Place II, on the mountain side of Kihei Road, near Lipoa Street (☎ **808/875-4050**). "Goober's" boards rent for $10 a day and "shredder's" boards go for $19 a day.

Expert surfers visit Maui in winter when the surf's really up. The best surfing beaches include **Honolua Bay, Lahaina Harbor** (in summer, there'll be waves just off the channel entrance with a south swell), **Maalaea** (a clean, world-class left), and **Hookipa Beach,** where surfers get the waves until noon; after that—in a carefully worked-out compromise to share this prized surf spot—the windsurfers take over.

WHALE WATCHING

Every winter, pods of Pacific humpback whales make the 3,000-mile swim from the chilly waters of Alaska to bask in Maui's summery shallows, fluking, spy hopping, spouting, and having an all-around swell time. The whale-watching season usually begins in January and lasts, sometimes, until May. About 1,500 to 3,000 humpback whales appear in Hawaii waters each year.

Humpbacks are one of the world's oldest, most impressive inhabitants. Adults grow to be about 45 feet long and weigh a hefty 40 tons; when they splash, it looks as though a 747 has hit the drink.

WHALE WATCHING FROM SHORE

The best time to whale watch is between mid-December and April: Just look out to sea. There's no best time of day for whale watching, but the whales seem to appear when the sea is glassy and the wind calm. Once you see one, keep watching in the same vicinity; they might stay down for 20 minutes. Bring a book—and binoculars, if you can. You can rent binoculars for $2 a day at **Rental Warehouse,** in Lahaina at 578 Front St., near Prison Street (☎ **808/661-1970**), and in Kihei at Azeka Place II, on the mountain side of Kihei Road, near Lipoa Street (☎ **808/875-4050**).

Some good whale-watching points on Maui are:

McGregor Point   On the way to Lahaina, there's a scenic lookout at mile marker 9 (just before you get to the Lahaina Tunnel); it's a good viewpoint to scan for whales.

Outrigger Wailea Resort   On the Wailea coastal walk, stop at this resort (formerly the Aston Wailea Resort) to look for whales through the telescope installed as a public service by the Hawaiian Island Humpback Whale National Marine Sanctuary.

Olowalu Reef   Along the straight part of Honoapiilani Highway, between McGregor Point and Olowalu, you'll see whales leap out of the water. Sometimes, their appearance brings traffic to a screeching halt: People abandon their cars and run down to the sea to watch, causing a major traffic jam. If you stop, pull off the road so that others can pass.

Puu Olai   It's a tough climb up this coastal landmark near the Maui Prince Hotel, but you're likely to be well rewarded: This is the island's best spot for offshore whale watching. On the 360-foot cinder cone overlooking Makena Beach, you'll be at the right elevation to see Pacific humpbacks as they dodge Molokini and

Keep Your Distance!

In your excitement at seeing a whale or a school of dolphins, don't get too close—both are protected under the Marine Mammals Protection Act. Swimmers, kayakers, and windsurfers must stay at least 100 yards away from all whales, dolphins, and other marine mammals. And yes, they have prosecuted visitors for swimming with dolphins! If you have any questions, call the **National Marine Fisheries Service** (☎ **808/541-2727**) or the **Hawaiian Islands Humpback Whale National Marine Sanctuary** (☎ **800/ 831-4888**).

cruise up Alalakeiki Channel between Maui and Kahoolawe. If you don't see one, you'll at least have a whale of a view.

WHALE-WATCHING CRUISES

For a closer look, take a whale-watching cruise. The **Pacific Whale Foundation,** 101 N. Kihei Rd., Kihei, HI 96753 (☎ **800/ 942-5311** or 808/879-8811; www.pacificwhale.org), is a nonprofit foundation in Kihei that supports its whale research by offering cruises and snorkel tours, some to Molokini and Lanai. They operate a 65-foot power catamaran called *Ocean Spirit,* a 50-foot sailing catamaran called *Manute'a,* and a sea kayak. They have 15 daily trips to choose from, and their rates for a 2-hour whale-watch cruise would make Moby Dick smile (starting at $19.80 for adults, $14.90 for children). Cruises are offered from December through May, out of both Lahaina and Maalaea harbors.

The **Ocean Activities Center** (☎ **800/798-0652** or 808/ 879-4485) runs three 2-hour whale-watching cruises on its spacious 65-foot catamaran, which leaves out of Maalaea Harbor; trips are $30 for adults and $18 for children 3 to 12. Bring a towel and your swimsuit; everything else—fins, mask, snorkel, and usually whales—is provided.

WHALE WATCHING BY KAYAK & RAFT

Seeing a humpback whale from an ocean kayak or raft is awesome. The best budget deal for rafting is **Capt. Steve's Rafting Excursions,** P.O. Box 12492, Lahaina, HI 96761 (☎ **808/667-5565**), which offers 2-hour whale-watching excursions out of Lahaina Harbor. Take the early bird trip at 7:30am and spot some whales for only $35 per person (regular rates are $55 for adults, $35 for children 12 and under).

Kayakers should call **South Pacific Kayaks,** 2439 S. Kihei Rd., Kihei (☎ **800/776-2326** or 808/875-4848; www.maui.net/ ~kayak), which leads small groups on 3-hour trips in the calm waters off Maui for $59 per person.

WINDSURFING

Maui has Hawaii's best windsurfing beaches. In winter, windsurfers from around the world flock to the town of **Paia** to ride the waves. **Hookipa Beach,** known all over the globe for its brisk winds and excellent waves, is the site of several world-championship contests. **Kanaha,** west of Kahului Airport, also has dependable winds; when conditions are right, it's packed with colorful butterfly-like sails. When the winds turn northerly, **Kihei** is the spot to be; some days, you can spot whales in the distance behind the windsurfers.

Hawaiian Island Surf and Sport, 415 Dairy Rd., Kahului (☎ **800/231-6958** or 808/871-4981; fax 808/871-4624; www.hawaiianisland.com), offers lessons, rentals, and repairs. Other shops offering rentals and lessons are **Hawaiian Sailboarding Techniques,** 444 Hana Hwy., Kahului (☎ **808/871-5423**); and **Maui Windsurf Co.,** 520 Keolani Place, Kahului (☎ **800/872-0999** or 808/877-4816). Complete equipment rental (board, sail, rig harness, and roof rack) is available from $45 a day and $295 a week. Lessons, from beginner to advanced, range in price from $50 to $75 for 2 hours.

3 Great Golf

In some circles, Maui is synonymous with golf. The island's world-famous golf courses start at the very northern tip of the island and roll right around to Kaanapali, jumping down to Kihei and Wailea in the south. There are also some lesser-known municipal courses that offer challenging play for less than $100. Golfers new to Maui should know that it's windy here, especially between 10am and 2pm, when winds of 10 to 15 m.p.h. are the norm. Play two to three clubs up or down to compensate for the wind factor. We also recommend bringing extra balls—the rough is thicker here and the wind will pick your ball up and drop it in very unappealing places (like water hazards). If your heart is set on playing on a resort course, book at least a week in advance. For the ardent golfer on a tight budget: Play in the afternoon, when discounted twilight rates are in effect. There's no guarantee you'll get 18 holes in, especially in winter when it's dark by 6pm, but you'll have an opportunity to experience these world-famous courses at half the usual fee.

If you don't bring your own, rent clubs from **Rental Warehouse,** in Lahaina at 578 Front St., near Prison Street (☎ **808/661-1970**), or in Kihei at Azeka Place II, on the mountain side of Kihei Road, near Lipoa Street (☎ **808/875-4050**), where top-quality clubs go for $15 a day, not-so-top-quality for $10 a day. **Golf Club Rentals** (☎ **808/665-0800;** www.maui.net/~rentgolf) offers custom-built clubs for men, women, and juniors in both right- and left-handed versions. Their rates are just $15 a day and they offer delivery islandwide.

For last-minute and discount tee times, call **Stand-by Golf** (☎ **888/645-BOOK** in Hawaii, or 808/874-0600 from the mainland) between 7am and 11pm, Hawaii standard time. Stand-by offers discounted (by 10% to 40%) and guaranteed tee times for same-day or next-day golfing.

CENTRAL MAUI

Waiehu Municipal Golf Course. P.O. Box 507, Wailuku, HI 96793. ☎ **808/ 244-5934.** From the Kahului Airport, turn right on the Hana Hwy. (Hwy. 36), which becomes Kaahumanu Ave. (Hwy. 32). Turn right at the stoplight at the junction of Waiehu Beach Rd. (Hwy. 340). Go another 1½ miles, and you'll see the entrance on your right.

This public, ocean-side, par-72 golf course is like playing two different courses: The first nine holes, built in 1930, are set along the dramatic coastline, whereas the back nine holes, added in 1966, head toward the mountains. It's a fun playing course that probably won't challenge your handicap. The only hazard here is the wind, which can rip off the ocean and play havoc with your ball. Basically, this is a flat and straight course. The only hole that can raise your blood pressure is the 511-yard, par 5, 4th hole, which is very narrow and very long. To par here, you have to hit a long accurate drive, then another long and accurate fairway drive, and finally a perfect pitch over the hazards to the greens (yeah, right).

Facilities include a snack bar, driving range, practice greens, golf-club rental, and clubhouse. Since this is a public course, the greens fees are low—$25 Monday through Friday, $30 Saturday and Sunday—but getting a tee time is tough.

WEST MAUI

✪ **Kaanapali Courses.** Off Hwy. 30, Kaanapali. ☎ **808/661-3691.** At the first stoplight in Kaanapali, turn onto Kaanapali Pkwy.; the first building on your right is the clubhouse.

Both courses at the Kaanapali Resort offer a challenge to all golfers, from high handicappers to near-pros. The par-72, 6,305-yard **North Course** (originally called the Royal Lahaina Golf Course) is a true Robert Trent Jones design: an abundance of wide bunkers; several long, stretched-out tees; and the largest, most contoured greens on Maui. It has a tricky 18th hole (par 4; 435 yd.) with a water hazard on the approach to the green. The par-72, 6,250-yard **South Course** is an Arthur Jack Snyder design; although shorter than the North Course, it requires more accuracy on the narrow, hilly fairways. It, too, has a water hazard on its final hole, so don't tally up your score card until the final putt is sunk.

Facilities include a driving range, putting course, and clubhouse with dining. Greens fees are $130, $65 after 2pm (for resort guests, $105, $65 after 2pm); weekday tee times are best.

✪ **Kapalua Resort Courses.** Off Hwy. 30, Kapalua.

The views from these three championship courses are worth the greens fees alone. The first to open was the **Bay Course** (☎ 808/ 669-8044), a par-72, 6,761-yard course inaugurated in 1975. Designed by Arnold Palmer and Ed Seay, this course is a bit forgiving with its wide fairways; the greens, however, are difficult to read. The well-photographed 5th overlooks a small ocean cove; even the pros have trouble with this rocky par-3, 205-yard hole. The par-71, 6,632-yard **Village Course** (☎ 808/669-8044), another Palmer/ Seay design, is the most scenic of the three courses; the hole with the best vista is definitely the 6th, which overlooks a lake with the ocean in the distance. But don't get distracted by the view—the tee is between two rows of Cook pines.

The **Plantation Course** (☎ 808/669-8044), scene of the PGA Kapalua Mercedes Championship, was designed by Ben Crenshaw and Bill Coore. A 6,547-yard, par-73 course on a rolling hillside of the West Maui Mountains, this one is excellent for developing your low shots and precise chipping. Facilities for the three courses include locker rooms, a driving range, and an excellent restaurant. Greens fees are $140 ($70 after 2pm) at the Village and Bay courses, $150 at the Plantation Course (at all times). Weekdays are your best bet for tee times.

SOUTH MAUI

✪ **Makena Courses.** On Makena Alanui Dr., just past the Maui Prince Hotel. ☎ 808/879-3344.

Here you'll find 36 holes of "Mr. Hawaii Golf"—Robert Trent Jones Jr.—at its best. Add to that spectacular views: Molokini islet looms in the background, humpback whales gambol offshore in winter, and the tropical sunsets are spectacular. This is golf not to be missed; the par-72, 6,876-yard **South Course** has a couple of holes you'll never forget. The view from the par-4 15th hole, which shoots from an elevated tee 183 yards downhill to the Pacific, is magnificent. The 16th hole has a two-tiered green that's blind from the tee 383 yards away (that is, if you make it past the gully off the fairway). The par-72, 6,823-yard **North Course** is more difficult and more spectacular. The 13th hole, located partway up the mountain, has a view that makes most golfers stop and stare. The next hole is even more memorable: a 200-foot drop between tee and green.

Facilities include clubhouse, driving range, two putting greens, pro shop, lockers, and lessons. Beware of crowded conditions on weekends. Greens fees are $85 for Makena Resort guests, $140 for nonguests.

Silversword Golf Club. 1345 Piilani Hwy. (near the Lipoa St. turnoff), Kihei. ☎ 808/874-0777.

Sitting in the foothills of Haleakala, just high enough to afford spectacular ocean views from every hole, this course is for golfers who love the views as much as the fairways and greens. It's very forgiving, especially for duffers and high handicappers. Just one caveat: Go in the morning. Not only is it cooler, but, more important, it's less windy. In the afternoon, the winds really pick up, blustering down Haleakala with great gusto. Silversword is a fun course to play, with some challenging holes (the par-5 no. 2 is a virtual minefield of bunkers, and the par-5 no. 8 shoots over a swale and then up a hill).

Greens fees vary with the season; from April 1 to October 31, they're $59, with twilight rates of $42. The rest of the year, they're $70, with twilight rates of $48. You can play nine holes after 3:30pm, year-round, for $23.

✪ **Wailea Courses.** Wailea Alanui Dr. (off Wailea Iki Dr.), Wailea. ☎ **888/ 328-MAUI** or 808/879-2966.

There are three courses to choose from at Wailea. The **Blue Course,** a par-72, 6,700-yard flat, open course designed by Arthur Jack Snyder and dotted with bunkers and water hazards, is for duffers and pros alike. The wide fairways appeal to beginners, and the undulating terrain makes it a course everyone can enjoy. A little more difficult is the par-72, 7,073-yard championship **Gold Course,** with narrow fairways, several tricky dogleg holes, and the classic Robert Trent Jones Jr. challenges: natural hazards, like lava-rock walls, and native Hawaiian grasses. The **Emerald Course,** originally an Arthur Jack Snyder design, was renovated by Robert Trent Jones Jr. into a more challenging course.

With 54 holes to play, getting a tee time is slightly easier here on weekends than at other resorts, but weekdays are best (the Gold Course is usually the toughest to book). Facilities include a pro shop, a restaurant, locker rooms, and a complete golf training facility. Greens fees are $80 to $140, depending on the season and where you're staying. Twilight rates range from $60 to $75. Special deals are available April through December.

UPCOUNTRY MAUI

Pukalani Country Club. 360 Pukalani St., Pukalani. ☎ **808/572-1314.** Take the Hana Hwy. (Hwy. 36) to Haleakala Hwy. (Hwy. 37) to the Pukalani exit; turn right onto Pukalani St. and go 2 blocks.

This cool course at 1,100 feet offers a break from the resorts' high greens fees, and it's really fun to play. The par-72, 6,962-yard course has 19 greens. There's an extra green because the third hole offers golfers two different options: a tough iron shot from the tee (especially into the wind), across a gully (yuck!) to the green; or a shot down the side of the gully across a second green into sand traps below. (Most people choose to shoot down the side of the gully; it's actually easier than shooting across a ravine.) High handicappers will love this course; more experienced players can make it more challenging by playing from the back tees. Facilities include club and shoe rentals, practice areas, lockers, a pro shop, and a restaurant. Greens fees, which include the cart fee, are only $20.

6

Seeing the Sights

by Jeanette Foster

*T*here is far more to the Valley Isle than just sun, sand, and surf. Get out and see for yourself the other-worldly interior of a 10,000-foot volcanic crater; watch endangered sea turtles make their way to nesting sites in a wildlife sanctuary; wander back in time to the days when whalers and missionaries fought for the soul of Lahaina; and feel the energy of a thundering waterfall cascade into a serene mountain pool.

1 By Air, Land & Sea: Guided Island Adventures

Admittedly, the adventures below aren't cheap. However, each one offers such a wonderful opportunity to see Maui from a unique perspective that, depending on your interests, you might make one of them the highlight of your trip—it'll be worth every penny.

FLYING HIGH: HELICOPTER RIDES

Only a helicopter can bring you face-to-face with remote sites like Maui's little-known Wall of Tears, up near the summit of Puu Kukui in the West Maui Mountains. A helicopter ride on Maui isn't a wild ride; it's more like a gentle gee-whiz zip into a seldom-seen Eden. You'll glide through canyons etched with 1,000-foot waterfalls, and over dense rain forests; you'll climb to 10,000 feet, high enough to glimpse the summit of Haleakala, and fly by the dramatic vistas at Molokai.

Among the many helicopter-tour operators on Maui, the best is **Blue Hawaiian,** at Kahului Airport (☎ **800/745-BLUE** or 808/ 871-8844; www.bluehawaiian.com), which not only takes you on the ride of your life, but also entertains, educates, and leaves you with an experience you'll never forget. Flights vary from 45 minutes to a half-day affair and range from $130 to $220. A keepsake video of your flight is available for $19.95 (so your friends at home can ooh and aah).

If Blue Hawaiian is booked, try **Sunshine Helicopters** (☎ **800/ 544-2520** or 808/ 871-0722; www.sunshinehelicopters.com), which offers a variety of flights from short hops around the West Maui Mountains to island tours. Prices range from $99 to $179.

GOING UNDER: SUBMARINE RIDES

This is the stuff dreams are made of: Plunge 100 feet under the sea in a state-of-the-art, high-tech submarine and experience swarms of vibrant tropical fish up close and personal as they flutter through the deep blue waters off Lahaina. **۞ Atlantis Submarines,** 665 Front St., Lahaina, HI 96761 (☎ **800/548-6262** or 808/ 667-7816), offers trips out of Lahaina Harbor, every hour on the hour from 8am to 3pm. Tickets are $79. Allow 2 hours for your underwater adventure.

ECOTOURING

Venture into the lush West Maui Mountains with an experienced guide on one of the **Ritz-Carlton Kapalua's Eco-Tours** (☎ **808/ 669-6200**). After a continental breakfast, you'll hike by streams and waterfalls, through native trees and plants, and on to breathtaking vistas. The tour takes breaks for a picnic lunch, dips in secluded pools, and memorable photo opportunities. The 2- to 3-mile, 4-hour excursion is classified as "easy"; it's offered Saturday through Monday and costs $65. The 4- to 5-mile, 6-hour hike, classified as "easy-moderate," is offered Tuesday through Friday; it costs $110 for adults, $90 for children 13 to 18. Wear comfortable walking or hiking shoes and bring a swimsuit, sunscreen, and a camera. The tour company supplies the meals, a fanny pack with bottled water, and rain gear if necessary. No children under 13 are allowed.

About 1,500 years ago, the verdant Kahakuloa Valley was a thriving Hawaiian village. Today, only a few hundred people live in this secluded hamlet, but old Hawaii still lives on here. Explore the valley with **Ekahi Tours** (☎ **808/877-9775**). Your guide, a Kahakuloa resident and a Hawaiiana expert, walks you through a taro farm, explains the mystical legends of the valley, and gives you a peek into ancient Hawaii. The Kahakuloa Valley Tour is $60 for adults, $50 for children under 12. It starts at 7am daily and lasts 7^1/$_2$ hours. A snack, beverages, and hotel pickup are included in the price.

If you would like a knowledgeable guide to accompany you on a hike, contact **Maui Hiking Safaris,** P.O. Box 11198, Lahaina, HI 96761 (☎ **888/445-3963** or 808/573-0168; fax 808/572-3037; www.maui.net/~mhs). Owner Randy Warner takes visitors on half-day (4 to 5 hours) and full-day (8 to 10 hours) hikes into valleys, rain forests, and coastal areas. Randy has been hiking around Maui for more than 10 years and is wise in the ways of Hawaiian history, native flora and fauna, and volcanology. His rates are $49 for a half day, $89 for a full day (children 13 and under get 10% off on all hikes), and include day packs, rain parkas, snacks, water, and, on full-day hikes, sandwiches.

Maui's oldest hiking-guide company is **Hike Maui,** P.O. Box 330969, Kahului, HI 96733 (☎ **808/879-5270;** www. hikemaui.com), headed by Ken Schmitt, who pioneered guided hikes on the Valley Isle. Hike Maui offers five different hikes a day, ranging from an easy 3¹/₂-mile stroll through the rain forest to a waterfall ($75 for adults, $55 for children 15 and under) to a strenuous, full-day hike in the rain forest and along a mountain ridge ($115 for adults, $90 for children 15 and under). Rates include equipment and transportation.

An all-day hike to the lush rain forests and waterfall pools of the West Maui Mountains is offered exclusively by **Kapalua Nature Society** (☎ **800/KAPALUA** or 808/669-0244). Groups of up to nine can go on guided hiking tours, which include a picnic lunch and transportation to and from the trails. Two exclusive hikes are offered: the easy, 1³/₄-mile Maunalei Arboretum/Puu Kaeo Nature Walk, which starts at 1,200 feet above sea level and goes to the 1,635-foot summit of Puu Kaeo; and the breathtaking, 4-mile Manienie Ridge Hike, a more strenuous hike with moderate slope, some uneven footing, and close vegetation. Kapalua Nature Society is a not-for-profit organization dedicated to preserving the island's natural and cultural heritage. Proceeds go toward the preservation of Puu Kukui rain forest. The cost is $59; children must be 12 or older.

2 Central Maui

Central Maui isn't exactly tourist central; this is where real people live. You'll most likely land here and head directly to the beach. However, there are a few sights worth checking out if you need a respite from the sun 'n' surf.

WAILUKU

This historic gateway to Iao Valley (see below) is worth a visit, if only for a brief stop at the **Bailey House Museum,** 2375-A Main St. (☎ **808/244-3326;** fax 808/244-3920). Missionary and sugar planter Edward Bailey's 1833 home—an architectural hybrid of stones laid by Hawaiian craftsmen and timbers joined in a display of Yankee ingenuity—is a treasure trove of Hawaiiana. Inside, you'll find an eclectic collection, from precontact artifacts like scary temple images, dog-tooth necklaces, and a rare lei made of tree-snail shells to latter-day relics like Duke Kahanamoku's 1919 redwood surfboard and a koa-wood table given to President Ulysses S. Grant, who had to refuse it because he couldn't accept gifts from foreign countries. There's also a gallery devoted to a few of Bailey's landscapes, painted from 1866 to 1896, which capture on canvas a Maui we can only imagine today. Hours are daily from 10am to 4pm. Admission is $4 for adults, $3.50 for seniors, and $1 for children 6 to 12.

The historic town of Wailuku, which most visitors merely whiz by on their way to Iao Valley, has played a significant role in Maui's history over the past 200 years. One of Hawaii's bloodiest battles took place here in 1790, when Kamehameha I fought the Maui chiefs in his bid to unite the Hawaiian Islands. Wailuku, which means "bloody waters," took its name from that battle, in which the carnage was so intense that the 4-mile Iao Stream turned red from the slaughter.

Wailuku was also where the missionaries landed in the mid-1800s to "save" the natives and convert them to Christianity. You can still see the New England architectural influences they brought to this quaint community.

Sugar came to Wailuku in 1860, when the Wailuku Sugar Compaany housed its operations in the old town. The industry drew immigrants from China, Japan, Okinawa, Korea, the Philippines, and Europe, each contributing aspects of its culture to the local way of life.

In the 1970s, however, sugar lost its sweetness, and sugar planters began to cut back operations due to economic conditions. Wailuku began to shrink. As modern subdivisions popped up in nearby Kahului and retail shops moved to shopping centers there, Wailuku became frozen in history.

Today, visitors can experience the past 200 years of Maui's history by spending an hour wandering through Wailuku.

IAO VALLEY

A couple of miles north of Wailuku, past the Bailey House Museum where the little plantation houses stop and the road climbs ever higher, Maui's true nature begins to reveal itself. The transition between suburban sprawl and raw nature is so abrupt that most people who drive up into the valley don't realize they're suddenly in a rain forest. The walls of the canyon begin to close around them, and a 2,250-foot needle pricks gray clouds scudding across the blue sky. After the hot tropic sun, the air is moist and cool, and the shade a welcome comfort.

Iao ("Supreme Light") Valley, 10 miles long and encompassing 4,000 acres, is the eroded volcanic caldera of the West Maui Mountains. The head of the Iao Valley is a broad circular amphitheater where four major streams converge into Iao Stream. At the back of the amphitheater is rain-drenched Puu Kukui, the West Maui Mountains' highest point. No other Hawaiian valley lets you go from seacoast to rain forest so easily. This peaceful valley, full of tropical plants, rainbows, waterfalls, swimming holes, and hiking trails, is a place of solitude, reflection, and escape for residents and visitors alike.

The park is open daily from 7am to 7pm. Go early in the morning or late in the afternoon, when the sun's rays slant into the valley and create a mystical atmosphere. You can bring a picnic and spend the day, but be prepared at any time for a tropical cloudburst, which often soaks the valley and swells both waterfalls and streams. To enter from Wailuku, take Main Street, then turn right on Iao Valley Road to the entrance to the state park.

For information, contact **Iao Valley State Park,** State Parks and Recreation, 54 S. High St., Rm. 101, Wailuku, HI 96793 (☎ **808/ 984-8109;** fax 808/984-8111; www.hawaii.gov). The ✪ **Hawaii Nature Center,** 875 Iao Valley Rd. (☎ **808/244-6500**), home of the Iao Valley Nature Center, features hands-on, interactive exhibits and displays relating the story of Hawaiian natural history; it's an important stop for all who want to explore Iao Valley. Hours are daily from 10am to 4pm; admission is $5 for adults and $3 for children under 12.

Two paved walkways loop into the massive green amphitheater, across the bridge of Iao Valley Stream, and along the stream itself. The one-third–mile loop on a paved trail is Maui's easiest hike—you can even take your grandmother on this one. The leisurely walk will allow you to enjoy lovely views of the Iao Needle and the lush vegetation. Others often proceed beyond the state park border and take two trails deeper into the valley, but the trails enter private land, and NO TRESPASSING signs are posted.

The feature known as **Iao Needle** is an erosional remnant composed of basalt dikes. The phallic rock juts an impressive 2,250 feet above sea level. Youngsters play in **Iao Stream,** a peaceful brook that belies its bloody history. In 1790, King Kamehameha the Great and his men engaged in the bloody battle of Iao Valley to gain control of Maui. When the battle ended, so many bodies blocked Iao Stream that the battle site was named Kepaniwai, or "damning of the waters." An architectural heritage park of Hawaiian, Japanese, Chinese,

Filipino, and New England–style houses stands in harmony by Iao Stream at **Kepaniwai Heritage Garden.** This is a good picnic spot, as there are plenty of picnic tables and benches. You can see ferns, banana trees, and other native and exotic plants in the **Iao Valley Botanic Garden** along the stream.

3   Lahaina & West Maui

THE SCENIC ROUTE TO WEST MAUI: KAHEKILI HIGHWAY

The usual road to West Maui from Wailuku is the Honoapiilani Highway, which takes you across the isthmus to Maalaea and around to Lahaina, Kaapanali, and Kapalua. But those in search of a back-to-nature driving experience should go the other way, along the ✪ **Kahekili Highway** (Highway 340). ("Highway" is a bit of an euphemism for this paved but somewhat precarious narrow road; check your rental-car agreement before you head out.) It was named after the great chief Kahekili, who built houses from the skulls of his enemies.

On the way, stop at the **Halekii and Pihanakalani Heiau,** which most visitors rarely see. To get here from Wailuku, turn north from Main Street onto Market Street. Turn right onto Mill Street and follow it until it ends; then make a left on Lower Main Street. Follow Lower Main until it ends at Waiehu Beach Road (Highway 340), and turn left. Turn left on Kuhio Street and again at the first left onto Hea Place, and drive through the gates and look for the Hawaii Visitor's Bureau marker.

These two heiau, built in 1240 from stones carried up from the Iao Stream below, sit on a hill with a commanding view of central Maui and Haleakala. Kahekili, the last chief of Maui, lived here. After the bloody battle at Iao Stream, Kamehameha I reportedly came to the temple here to pay homage to the war god, Ku, with a human sacrifice. Halekii ("House of Images") is made of stone walls with a flat grassy top, whereas Pihanakalani ("gathering place of supernatural beings") is a pyramid-shaped mount of stones. If you sit quietly nearby (never walk on any heiau, because that's considered disrespectful), the view alone explains why this spot was chosen.

Go back to Waiehu Beach Road (Highway 340), turn left, head for the tiny town of Waiehu, and then on to the true wild nature of Maui: a narrow and winding road that weaves for 20 miles along an ancient Hawaiian coastal footpath.

Lahaina

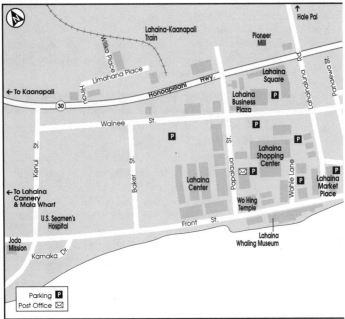

If you want views, these are photo opportunities from heaven: steep ravines, rolling pastoral hills, tumbling waterfalls, exploding blowholes, crashing surf, jagged lava coastlines, and a tiny Hawaiian village straight off a postcard.

Along the route, nestled in a crevice between two steep hills, is the picturesque village of **Kahakuloa** ("the tall hau tree"), with a dozen weather-worn houses, a church with a red-tile roof, and vivid green taro patches. From the northern side of the village, you can look back at the great view of Kahakuloa, the dark boulder beach, and the 636-foot Kahakuloa Head rising in the background.

A couple of miles down the road, just past the 16-mile marker, look for the **pohaku kani** sign, marking the huge, 6-foot-by-6-foot, bell-shaped stone. To "ring" the bell, look on the side facing Kahakuloa for the deep indentations, and strike the stone with another rock.

A little farther down the road (less than a half mile), you'll come to a wide turnoff providing a great photo op: a view of the jagged coastline down to the crashing surf.

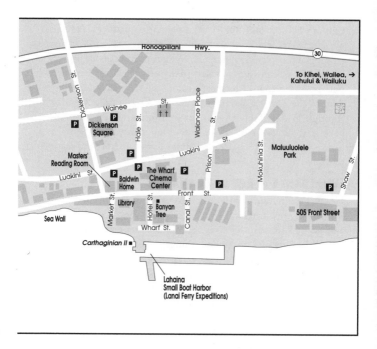

Just past the 20-mile mark, after a sharp turn in the road, look for a small turnoff on the mauka side of the road (just after the guardrail ends). Park here and walk across the road, and on your left you'll see a spouting **blow hole.** In winter, this is an excellent spot to look for whales.

As the road rounds the point, the island of Molokai comes into view. At Honokohau, the road becomes Honoapiilani Highway (Highway 30). At the next valley, you'll come to the twin bays, **Honolua** and **Mokuleia,** which have been designated as Marine Life Conservation Areas (the taking of fish, shells, or anything else is prohibited).

KAPALUA

If you're taking the Kahekili Highway (Highway 340), Kapalua is the first resort area you'll see in West Hawaii.

For generations, West Maui meant one thing: pineapple. Hawaii's only pineapple cannery today, **Maui Pineapple Co.,** offers tours of its pineapple plantation through the Kapalua Resort Activity

Center (☎ **808/669-8088**). Real plantation workers lead the 2^1/$_2$-hour tours, which feature the history of West Maui, facts about growing and harvesting pineapple, and lots of trivia about plantation life. Participants are even allowed to pick and harvest their own pineapple. The tours, which depart from the Kapalua Shops (next door to the Kapalua Bay Hotel), are given twice daily Monday through Friday; fees are $26 per person, and children must be at least 12 years old. Before or after the tour, you might want to take some time to wander through the Kapalua Resort (see chapters 3 and 5).

A WHALE OF A PLACE IN KAANAPALI

Heading south from Kapalua, the next resort area you'll come to is Kaanapali. If you haven't seen a real whale yet, go to **Whalers Village,** 2435 Kaanapali Pkwy., a shopping center that has adopted the whale as its mascot. You can't miss it: a huge, almost life-size metal sculpture of a mother whale and two nursing calves greets you. A few more steps, and you're met by the looming, bleached-white bony skeleton of a 40-foot sperm whale; it's pretty impressive.

On the second floor of the mall is the **Whale Center of the Pacific** (www.mauimapp.com/museums/whalecenter.htm), which features two museums. **Whalers Village Museum** (☎ **808/ 661-5992**) centers around the "Golden Era of Whaling" (1825–60) from the whaler's point of view, depicting the long voyages, the dangers of the hunt, and the whalers' constant longing for home. Harpoons and scrimshaw are on display, and the museum has even re-created the cramped quarters of a whaler's seagoing vessel.

Across the way, **Hale Kohola, House of the Whale** (☎ **808/ 661-6752**) tells the story from the whale's point of view, as it were. The museum houses exhibits on 70 species of whales and more whale lore than you could hope to absorb. Venture into the Bone Room, where volunteers scrape and identify the bones of marine mammals that wash ashore in Hawaiian waters to use in future exhibits. Pick up the free *Whale Watch Guide* that points you out the door and toward the ocean.

Both museums are open during mall hours, daily from 9:30am to 10pm; admission is free. For tips on seeing the real thing, see "Whale Watching" under "Hitting the Water," in chapter 5.

HISTORIC LAHAINA

Located between the waving green sugarcane blanketing the West Maui Mountains and the deep azure ocean offshore, Lahaina has managed to preserve its 19th-century heritage while still accommodating 20th-century guests.

In ancient times, powerful chiefs and kings ruled this hot, dry ocean-side village. At the turn of the 19th century, after King Kamehameha united the Hawaiian Islands, he made Lahaina the royal capital—which it remained until 1845, when Kamehameha III moved the capital to the larger port of Honolulu.

In the 1840s, the whaling industry was at its peak: Hundreds of ships called into Lahaina every year. The streets were filled with sailors 24 hours a day. Even Herman Melville, who later wrote *Moby Dick,* was among the throngs of whalers in Lahaina.

Just 20 years later, the whaling industry was waning, and sugar had taken over the town. The Pioneer Sugar Mill Co., which still exists today, reigned over Lahaina for the next 100 years.

Today, the drunken and derelict whalers who wandered through Lahaina's streets in search of bars, dance halls, and brothels have been replaced by hordes of tourists crowding into the small mile-long main section of town in search of boutiques, art galleries, and chic gourmet eateries. Lahaina's colorful past continues to have a profound influence today. This is no quiet seaside village, but a vibrant, cutting-edge kind of place, filled with a sense of history—but definitely with its mind on the future.

Baldwin Home Museum. 696 Front St. (at Dickenson St.). ☎ **808/ 661-3262.** Admission $3 adults, $2 seniors, $1 children, $5 family. Daily 10am–4:30pm.

The oldest house in Lahaina, this coral-and-rock structure was built in 1834 by Rev. Dwight Baldwin, a doctor with the fourth company of American missionaries to sail around the Horn to Hawaii. Like many missionaries, he came to Hawaii to do good—and did very well for himself. After 17 years of service, Baldwin was granted 2,600 acres for farming and grazing in Kapalua. His ranch manager experimented with what Hawaiians called *hala-kahiki,* or pineapple, on a 4-acre plot; the rest is history. Open for guided tours, the house looks as though Baldwin had just stepped out for a minute to tend a sick neighbor down the street.

Next door is the **Masters' Reading Room,** Maui's oldest building. This became visiting sea captains' favorite hangout once the missionaries closed down all of Lahaina's grog shops and banned prostitution; but by 1844, once hotels and bars started reopening, it lost its appeal. It's now the headquarters of the **Lahaina Restoration Foundation,** a plucky band of historians who try to keep this town alive and antique at the same time. Stop in and pick up a self-guided walking-tour map. You'll learn the stories of those who lived Lahaina's colorful past, from the missionary doctor who single-handedly kept a cholera epidemic from wiping out Maui's people to the boy king who lived on his very own island.

Banyan Tree. At the Courthouse Building, 649 Wharf St.

Of all the banyan trees in Hawaii, this is the biggest, most sheltering of all—so big that you can't get it in your camera's viewfinder. It was only 8 feet tall when it was planted in 1873 by Maui Sheriff William O. Smith to mark the 50th anniversary of Lahaina's first Christian mission; the big old banyan from India is now more than 50 feet tall, has 12 major trunks, and shades two-thirds of an acre in the courthouse square.

The Brig *Carthaginian II*. Lahaina Harbor. ☎ **808/661-8527.** Admission $3 adults, $2 seniors, $5 family. Daily 10am–4:30pm.

This authentically restored square-rigged brigantine is an authentic replica of a 19th-century whaling ship, the kind that brought the first missionaries to Hawaii. This floating museum features exhibits on whales and 19th-century whaling life. You won't believe how cramped the living quarters were—they make today's cruise-ship cabins look downright roomy.

Hale Pai. Lahainaluna High School Campus, 980 Lahainaluna Rd. (at the top of the mountain). ☎ **808/661-3262.** Free admission. Mon–Fri by appointment only.

When the missionaries arrived in Hawaii to spread the word of God, they found the Hawaiians had no written language. They quickly rectified the situation by converting the Hawaiian sounds into a written language. They then built the first printing press in order to print educational materials that would assist them on their mission. Hale Pai was the printing house for the Lahainaluna Seminary, the oldest American school west of the Rockies. Today Lahainaluna is the public high school for the children of West Maui.

Lahaina Jodo Mission. 12 Ala Moana St. (off Front St., near the Mala Wharf). ☎ **808/661-4304.** Free admission. Daily during daylight hours.

This site has long been held sacred. The Hawaiians called it Puunoa Point, which means "the hill freed from taboo." Japanese immigrants, who came to Hawaii in 1868 as laborers for the sugarcane plantations, loved to spend time in this peaceful place, which was once a small village named "Mala" ("garden"), and eventually built a small wooden temple to worship here. In 1968, on the 100th anniversary of the Japanese in Hawaii, a Great Buddha statue, the largest outside Japan (some 12 feet high and weighing $3^1/_2$ tons) was brought here from Japan. The immaculate grounds also contain a replica of the original wooden temple and 90-foot-tall pagoda.

Lahaina Whaling Museum. At Crazy Shirts, 865 Front St. (near Papalaua St.). ☎ **808/661-4775.** Free admission. Daily 9:30am–9pm.

Yankee whalers came to Lahaina to reprovision ships' stores, get drunk, and raise hell with "the girls of old Mowee." Everything was fine and dandy until 1819, when Congregational missionaries arrived and declared the port town "one of the breathing holes of hell." They tried to curb drinking and prostitution, but failed; Lahaina grew ever more lawless until the whaling era came to an end with the discovery of oil in Pennsylvania and the birth of the petroleum industry. That rambunctious era is recalled in this small museum full of art and relics from Lahaina's glory days.

Maluuluolele Park. Front and Shaw sts.

At first glance, this Front Street park appears to be only a hot, dry, dusty softball field. But under home plate is the edge of Mokuula, where a royal compound once stood more than 100 years ago, now buried under tons of red dirt and sand. Here, Prince Kauikeaolui, who ascended the throne as King Kamehameha III when he was only 10, lived with the love of his life, his sister Princess Nahienaena. Missionaries took a dim view of incest, which was acceptable to Hawaiian nobles in order to preserve the royal bloodlines. Torn between love for her brother and the new Christian morality, Nahienaena grew despondent and died at the age of 21. King Kamehameha III, who reigned for 29 years—longer than any other Hawaiian monarch—presided over Hawaii as it went from kingdom to constitutional monarchy, and absolute power over the islands began to transfer from island nobles to missionaries, merchants, and sugar planters. Kamehameha died in 1854 at the age of 39. In 1918, his royal compound, containing a mausoleum and artifacts of the kingdom, was demolished and covered with dirt to create a public park. The baseball team from Lahainaluna School now plays games on the site of this royal place, still considered sacred to many Hawaiians.

Wo Hing Temple. Front St. (between Wahie Lane and Papalaua St.). ☎ **808/661-3262.** Admission by donation. Daily 10am–4pm.

The Chinese were among the various immigrants brought to Hawaii to work in the sugarcane fields. In 1909, several Chinese workers formed the Wo Hing society, a chapter of the Chee Kun Tong society, which dates from the 17th century. In 1912, they built this social hall for the Chinese community. Completely restored, the Wo Hing Temple contains displays and artifacts on the history of the Chinese in Lahaina; next door in the old cookhouse is a theater with movies of Hawaii taken by Thomas Edison in 1898 and 1903.

OLOWALU

Most people drive right by ✪ **Olowalu,** 5 miles down Honoapiilani Highway from Lahaina; there's little to mark the spot but a small general store and Chez Paul, an expensive, but not very good, French restaurant. Olowalu ("many hills") was the scene of a bloody massacre in 1790. The Hawaiians, fascinated with iron nails and fittings, stole a skiff from the U.S. ship *Eleanora,* took it back to shore here, and burned it for the iron parts. The captain of the ship, Simon Metcalf, was furious and tricked the Hawaiians into sailing out in their canoes to trade with the ship. As the canoes approached, he mowed them down with his cannons, killing a hundred people and wounding many others.

Olowalu has great snorkeling around the 14-mile marker, where there is a turtle cleaning station about 50 to 75 yards out from shore. Turtles line up here to have cleaner wrasses pick small parasites off.

4 South Maui

MAALAEA

At the bend in the Honopiilani Highway (Highway 30), Maalaea Bay runs along the south side of the isthmus between the West Maui Mountains and Haleakala. This is the windiest area on Maui: Trade winds blowing between the two mountains are funneled across the isthmus, and by the time they reach Maalaea, gusts of 25 to 30 m.p.h. are not uncommon.

This creates ideal conditions for windsurfers out in Maalaea Bay. Surfers are also seen just outside the small boat harbor in Maalaea, which has one of the fastest breaks in the state.

✪ **Maui Ocean Center.** Maalaea Harbor Village, at the triangle between Honoapiilani Hwy. and Maalaea Rd. ☎ **808/875-1962.** www.coralworld.com/moc. Admission $17 adults, $12 children 3–12, free for children under 3. Daily 9am–5pm.

This 5-acre facility houses the largest aquarium in the state and features regional marine life, including one of Hawaii's largest predators: the tiger shark. As you walk past some three dozen tanks and countless exhibits, you'll slowly descend from the "beach" to the deepest part of the ocean, without ever getting wet. Start at the surge pool, where you'll see shallow-water creatures like spiny urchins and cauliflower coral, then move on to the reef tanks, turtle pool, "touch" pool (with starfish and sea urchins), and eagle-ray pool before reaching the star of the show: the 100-foot-long, 600,000-gallon main tank, featuring tiger, gray, and white-tip sharks, as well as tuna, surgeonfish, triggerfish, and numerous other tropicals. The most phenomenal thing about this tank is that the walkway goes right through it—so you'll be surrounded on three sides by marine creatures.

KIHEI

Capt. George Vancouver "discovered" Kihei in 1778, when it was only a collection of fishermen's grass shacks on the hot, dry, dusty coast (hard to believe, eh?). A **totem pole** stands today where he's believed to have landed, across from Aston Maui Lu Resort, 575 S. Kihei Rd. Vancouver sailed on to discover British Columbia, where a great international city and harbor now bear his name.

West of the junction of Piilani Highway (Highway 31) and Mokulele Highway (Highway 350) is **Kealia Pond National Wildlife Preserve** (☎ **808/875-1582**), a 700-acre U.S. Fish and Wildlife wetland preserve where endangered Hawaiian stilts, coots, and ducks hang out and splash. These ponds work two ways: as bird preserves and as sedimentation basins that keep the coral reefs from silting from runoff. You can take a self-guided tour along a boardwalk dotted with interpretive signs and shade shelters, through sand dunes, and around ponds to Maalaea Harbor. The boardwalk starts at the outlet of Kealia Pond on the ocean side of North Kihei Road (near mile marker 2 on Piilani Highway). Among the Hawaiian waterbirds seen here are the black-crowned high heron, Hawaiian coot, Hawaiian duck, and Hawaiian stilt. There are also shorebirds like sanderling, Pacific golden plover, ruddy turnstone, and wandering tattler. From July to December, the hawksbill turtle comes ashore here to lay her eggs.

If you're interested in going to one of the many beaches along Kihei's 6-mile coast, eating in one of the dozens of restaurants, or taking in some shopping, the South Kihei Road borders the ocean and goes through the heart of town. If you're bypassing Kihei, take the Piilani Highway (Highway 31), which parallels the South Kihei Road, and avoid the hassle of stoplights and traffic.

WAILEA

The dividing line between arid Kihei and artificially green Wailea is distinct. The manicured 1,450 acres of this affluent resort stand out like an oasis along the normally dry leeward coast.

The best way to explore this golden resort coast is to rise with the sun and head for Wailea's 1¹/₂-mile **coastal nature trail,** stretching between the Kea Lani Hotel and the kiawe thicket just beyond the Renaissance Wailea. It's a great morning walk on Maui, a serpentine path that meanders uphill and down past native plants, old Hawaiian habitats, and a billion dollars' worth of luxury hotels. You can pick up the trail at any of the resorts or from clearly marked SHORELINE ACCESS points along the coast. The best time to go is when you first wake up; by midmorning, the coastal trail is too often clogged with joggers, and it grows crowded with beachgoers as the day wears on. As the path crosses several bold black-lava points, it affords new vistas of islands and ocean; benches allow you to pause and contemplate the view across Alalakeiki Channel, which jumps with whales in season. Sunset is another good time to hit the trail.

5 House of the Sun: Haleakala National Park

At once forbidding and compelling, ✪ **Haleakala National Park** ("House of the Sun") is Maui's main natural attraction. More than 1.3 million people a year go up the 10,023-foot-high mountain to peer down into the crater of the world's largest dormant volcano. (Haleakala is officially considered to be "active, but not currently erupting," even though it has not rumbled or spewed lava since 1790.) That hole would hold Manhattan: 3,000 feet deep, 7¹/₂ miles long by 2¹/₂ miles wide, and encompassing 19 square miles.

But there's more to do here than simply stare in a big black hole: Just going up the mountain is an experience in itself. Where else on the planet can you climb from sea level to 10,000 feet in just 37 miles, or a 2-hour drive, without ever leaving the ground? The snaky road passes through big puffy cumulus clouds to offer magnificent views of the isthmus of Maui, the West Maui Mountains, and the Pacific Ocean.

The Hawaiians recognized the mountain as a sacred site. Ancient chants tell of Pele, the volcano goddess, and one of her siblings doing battle on the crater floor where Kawilinau ("Bottomless Pit") now stands. Commoners in ancient Hawaii didn't spend much time here, though. The only people allowed into this sacred area were the kahunas, who took their apprentices to live for periods of time in this intensely spiritual place.

Many drive up to the summit in predawn darkness to watch the sunrise over Haleakala. Others take a trail ride inside the bleak lunar landscape of the wilderness inside the crater, or coast down the 37-mile road from the summit on a bicycle with special brakes. Hardy adventurers hike and camp inside the crater's wilderness.

JUST THE FACTS

Haleakala National Park extends from the summit of Mount Haleakala into the crater, down the volcano's southeast flank to Maui's eastern coast, beyond Hana. There are actually two separate and distinct destinations within the park: **Haleakala Summit** and the **Kipahulu** coast (See "Just Beyond Hana" in section 8, below). The summit gets all the publicity, but Kipahulu draws crowds, too—it's lush, green, and tropical, and home to Oheo Gulch (also known as Seven Sacred Pools). No road links the summit and the coast; you have to approach them separately, and you need at least a day to see each place.

WHEN TO GO   At the 10,023-foot summit, weather changes fast. With wind chill, temperatures can be below freezing any time of year. Summer can be dry and warm, winters wet, windy, and cold. Before you go, get current weather conditions from the park (☎ **808/572-9306**) or the **National Weather Service** (☎ **808/ 871-5054**).

From sunrise to noon, the light is weak, but the view is usually free of clouds. The best time for photos is in the afternoon, when the sun lights the crater and clouds are few. Go on full-moon nights for spectacular viewing.

ACCESS POINTS   **Haleakala Summit** is 37 miles, or about a 2-hour drive, from Kahului. To get here, take Highway 37 to Highway 377 to Highway 378. For details on the drive, see "The Drive to the Summit," below. Pukalani is the last town for water, food, and gas.

The **Kipahulu** section of the national park is on Maui's east end near Hana, 60 miles from Kahului on Highway 36 (the Hana Highway). Due to traffic and rough road conditions, plan on 4 hours for the drive, one way (see "Driving the Road to Hana," below). Hana is the only nearby town for services, water, gas, food, and overnight lodging; some facilities may not be open after dark.

INFORMATION, VISITOR CENTERS & RANGER PROGRAMS   For information before you go, contact **Haleakala National Park,** Box 369, Makawao, HI 96768 (☎ **808/572-9306;** www.nps.gov.hale).

One mile from the park entrance, at 7,000 feet, is **Haleakala National Park Headquarters** (☎ 808/572-9306), open daily from 7am to 4pm. You can pick up information on park programs and activities, get camping permits, and, occasionally, see a Hawaiian nene (goose)—one or more are often here to greet visitors. Rest rooms, a pay phone, and drinking water are available.

The **Haleakala Visitor Center,** open daily from sunrise to 3pm, is near the summit, 11 miles from the park entrance. It offers a panoramic view of the volcanic landscape, with photos identifying the various features, and exhibits that explain its history, ecology, geology, and volcanology. Park staff members are often handy to answer questions. The only facilities are rest rooms and water.

THE DRIVE TO THE SUMMIT

If you look on a Maui map, almost in the middle of the part that resembles a torso, there's a black wiggly line that looks like this: WWWWW. That's **Highway 378,** also known as **Haleakala Crater Road**—one of the few roads in the world that climbs from sea level to 10,000 feet in just 37 miles. This grand corniche has at least 33 switchbacks; passes through numerous climate zones; goes under, in, and out of clouds; takes you past rare silversword plants and endangered Hawaiian geese sailing through the clear, thin air; and offers a view that extends for more than 100 miles.

Going to the summit takes about 2 hours from Kahului. No matter where you start out, you'll follow Highway 37 (Haleakala Highway) to Pukalani, where you'll pick up Highway 377 (which is also Haleakala Highway), which you'll take to Highway 378. Along the way, expect fog, rain, and wind. You might encounter stray cattle and downhill bicyclists. Fill up your gas tank before you go—the only gas available is 27 miles below the summit at Pukalani. There are no facilities beyond the ranger stations. Bring your own food and water.

Remember, you're entering a high-altitude wilderness area. Some people get dizzy due to the lack of oxygen; you might also suffer lightheadedness, shortness of breath, nausea, or worse: severe headaches, flatulence, and dehydration. People with asthma, pregnant women, heavy smokers, and those with heart conditions should be especially careful in the rarefied air. Bring water and a jacket or a blanket, especially if you go up for sunrise. Or you might want to go up to the summit for sunset instead.

At the **park entrance,** you'll pay an entrance fee of $10 per car (or $2 for a bicycle). About a mile from the entrance is **Park Headquarters,** where an endangered **nene,** or Hawaiian goose, might greet you with its unique call. With its black face, buff cheeks, and partially webbed feet, the gray-brown bird looks like a small Canada goose with zebra stripes; it brays out "nay-nay" (thus its name), doesn't migrate, and prefers lava beds to lakes. The unusual goose clings to a precarious existence on these alpine slopes. Vast populations of more than 25,000 once inhabited Hawaii, By 1951, there were only 30 left. Now protected as Hawaii's state bird, the wild nene on Haleakala numbers fewer than 250—and the species remains endangered.

Beyond headquarters are **two scenic overlooks** on the way to the summit. Stop at Leleiwi on the way up and Kalahaku on the way back down, if only to get out, stretch, and get accustomed to the heights. Take a deep breath, look around, and pop your ears. If you feel dizzy or drowsy, or get a sudden headache, consider turning around and going back down.

Leleiwi Overlook is just beyond mile marker 17. From the parking area, a short trail leads you to a panoramic view of the lunar-like crater. When the clouds are low and the sun is in the right place, usually around sunset, you can experience a phenomenon known as the "Specter of the Brocken"—you can see a reflection of your shadow, ringed by a rainbow, in the clouds below.

Two miles farther along is **Kalahaku Overlook,** the best place to see a rare **silversword.** You can turn into this overlook only when you are descending from the top. The silversword is the punker of the plant world, its silvery bayonets displaying tiny purple bouquets—like a spacey artichoke with attitude. This botanical wonder proved irresistible to humans, who gathered them in gunnysacks for Chinese potions, for British specimen collections, and just for the sheer thrill of having something so rare. Silverswords grow only in Hawaii, take from 4 to 50 years to bloom, and then, usually between May and October, send up a 1- to 6-foot stalk with a purple bouquet of sunflower-like blooms. They're now very rare, so don't even think about taking one home.

Continue on, and you'll quickly reach the **Haleakala Visitor Center,** which offers spectacular views. You'll feel as if you're at the edge of the earth. But don't turn around here; the actual summit's a little farther on, at **Puu Ulaula Overlook** (also known as Red Hill), the volcano's highest point, where you'll find a mysterious cluster of buildings officially known as Haleakala Observatories, but unofficially called **Science City.** If you do go up for sunrise, the building at Puu Ulaula Overlook, a triangle of glass that serves as a windbreak, is the best viewing spot. After the daily miracle of sunrise—the sun seems to rise out of the vast crater (hence the name "House of the Sun")—you can see all the way across Alenuihaha Channel to the often snowcapped summit of Mauna Kea on the Big Island.

MAKING YOUR DESCENT   Put your car in low gear; that way, you won't suddenly see smoke coming from your brakes, and you won't destroy your brakes by riding them the whole way down.

6 More in Upcountry Maui

Come upcountry and discover a different side of Maui: On the slopes of Haleakala, cowboys, planters, and other country people make their homes in serene, neighborly communities like **Makawao** and **Kula,** a world away from the bustling beach resorts. Even if you can't spare a day or two in the cool upcountry air, there are some sights that are worth a look on your way to or from the crater. Shoppers and gallery hoppers might really want to make the effort; see chapter 7 for details.

On the slopes of Haleakala, Maui's breadbasket has been producing vegetables since the 1800s. In fact, during the gold rush in California, the Hawaiian farmers in Kula shipped so many potatoes that it was nickednamed Nu Kaleponi, a sort of pidgin Hawaiian pronunciation of "New California." In the late 1800s, Portuguese and Chinese immigrants, who had fulfilled their labor contracts with the sugarcane companies, moved to this area, drawn by the rural agricultural lifestyle. That lifestyle continues today, among the fancy gentlemen's farms that have sprung up in the past two decades. Kula continues to grow the well-known onions, lettuce, tomatoes, carrots, cauliflower, and cabbage. It is also a major source of cut flowers for the state: Most of Hawaii's proteas, as well as nearly all the carnations used in leis, come from Kula.

To experience a bit of the history of Kula, turn off the Kula Highway (Highway 37) onto Lower Kula Road. Well before the turnoff, you'll see a white octagonal building with a silver roof, the **Holy Ghost Catholic Church** (☎ **808/878-1091**). Hawaii's only eight-sided church, it was built between 1884 and 1897 by Portuguese immigrants. The church resembles something out of Portugal; it's worth a stop to see the hand-carved altar and works of art for the stations of the cross, with inscriptions in Portuguese.

✪ **Kula Botanical Garden.** Hwy. 377, south of Haleakala Crater Rd. (Hwy. 378), $7/10$ mile from Hwy. 37. ☎ **808/878-1715.** Admission $4 adults, $1 children 6–12. Daily 9am–4pm.

This 5-acre garden offers a good overview of Hawaii's exotic flora in one small, cool place. You can take a self-guided, informative, leisurely stroll through more than 700 native and exotic plants, including three unique collections of orchids, proteas, and bromeliads.

Tedeschi Vineyards and Winery. Off Hwy. 37 (Kula Hwy.); P.O. Box 953, Ulupalakua. ☎ **808/878-6058.** Free tastings. Winery tours daily 9am–5pm.

On the southern shoulder of Haleakala, you'll enter cattle country and the **Ulupalakua Ranch,** more than 20,000 acres once owned by legendary sea captain James Makee, celebrated in the Hawaiian song and dance *Hula O Makee.* Wounded in a Honolulu waterfront brawl in 1843, Captain Makee moved to Maui and bought Ulupalakua. He renamed it Rose Ranch and planted sugar as a cash crop. He grew rich and toasted life until his death, in 1879. Still in operation, the ranch is now home to Maui's only winery, established in 1974 by Napa vintner Emil Tedeschi, who began growing California and European grapes here and producing serious still and sparkling wines, plus a silly wine made of pineapple juice. The rustic grounds are the perfect place for a picnic. Pack a basket before you go, but don't BYOB: There's plenty of great wine to enjoy at Tedeschi. Spread your picnic lunch under the sprawling camphor tree, pop the cork on a Blanc du Blanc, and toast your good fortune in being here.

7 Driving the Road to Hana

Top down, sunscreen on, radio tuned to a little Hawaiian music on a Maui morning: It's time to head out to Hana along the Hana Highway (Highway 36), a wiggle of a road that runs along Maui's northeastern shore. The drive takes at least 3 hours—but take all day. Going to Hana is about the journey, not the destination.

There are wilder roads and steeper roads and even more dangerous roads, but in all of Hawaii no road is more celebrated than this one. It winds for 50 miles past taro patches, magnificent seascapes, waterfall pools, botanical gardens, and verdant rain forests, and it ends at one of Hawaii's most beautiful tropical places.

The outside world discovered the little village of Hana in 1926, when the narrow coastal road, carved by pickax-wielding convicts, opened with 56 bridges and 600 hairpin switchbacks. The mud-and-gravel road, often subject to landslides and washouts, was paved in 1962, when tourist traffic began to increase; it now sees more than 1,000 cars and dozens of vans a day, according to storekeeper Harry Hasegawa. That equals about 500,000 people a year on this road,

Hassle-free Discounts on Activities

You can save 10–25% on nearly 100 different activities statewide by buying an **Activity Owners Association of Hawaii Gold Card**, 355 Hukilike St., #202, Kahului, HI 96732 (☎ **800/398-9698** or 808/871-7947; www.maui.org), for just $30. The AOA Gold Card gives your entire family (up to four people) discounts on car rentals, helicopter tours, sailing tours, dinner cruises, horseback riding, kayaking, luaus, submarine tours, and more. Note that you must buy the card before you arrive in Hawaii.

which is way too many. Go at the wrong time, and you'll be stuck in a bumper-to-bumper rental-car parade—peak traffic hours are midmorning and midafternoon year-round, especially on weekends.

In the rush to "do" Hana in a day, most visitors spin around town in 10 minutes flat and wonder what all the fuss is about. It takes time to take in Hana, play in the waterfalls, sniff the tropical flowers, hike to bamboo forests, and take in the spectacular scenery; stay overnight if you can, and meander back in a day or two.

However, if you really must do the Hana Highway in a day, go just before sunrise and return after sunset: On a full-moon night, you'll believe in magic when you see the sea and the waterfalls glowing in soft white light, with mysterious shadows appearing in the jungle. And you'll have the road almost to yourself on the way back.

Akamai tips: Forget your mainland road manners. Practice aloha: Give way at the one-lane bridges, wave at oncoming motorists, let the big guys in four-by-fours with pig-hunting dogs in the back have the right of way—it's just common sense, brah. If the guy behind you blinks his lights, let him pass. Oh, yeah, and don't honk your horn—in Hawaii, it's considered rude.

THE JOURNEY BEGINS IN PAIA   Before you even start out, fill up your gas tank. Gas in Paia is mucho expensive ($2-plus a gallon), and it's the last place for gas until you get to Hana, some 42 miles, 54 bridges, and 600 hairpin turns down the road.

The former plantation village of Paia was once a thriving sugar-mill town. The mill is still here, but the population shifted to Kahului in the 1950s when subdivisions opened there, leaving Paia to shrivel up and die. But the town refused to give up, and it has proven its ability to adapt to the times. Now chic eateries and trendy shops stand next door to the ma-and-pa establishments that have been serving generations of Paia customers.

Plan to be here early, around 7am, when **Charley's,** 142 Hana Hwy. (☎ **808/579-9453**), opens. Enjoy a big, hearty breakfast for a reasonable price. After your meal, head up Baldwin Avenue; about a half block from the intersection of the Hana Highway and Baldwin Avenue, stop by **Pic-nics,** 30 Baldwin Ave. (☎ **808/579-8021**), to stock up for a picnic lunch for the road (see chapter 4).

As you leave Paia, on your right you'll see acres of sugarcane fields, the crop that kept Maui alive for more than a century. Just before the bend in the road, you'll pass the Kuau Mart on your left; a small general store, it's the only reminder of the once-thriving community of **Kuau.** The road then bends into an S-turn; in the middle of the S is the entrance to **Mama's Fish House,** depicted by a restored 1935 panel truck with Mama's logo on the side. Just past the truck on the ocean side is the entrance to Mama's parking lot and adjacent small sandy cove in front of the restaurant. Mainly surfers use this treacherous ocean access over very slippery rocks into strong surf, but the beach is a great place to sit and soak up some sun.

WINDSURFING MECCA A mile from Mama's, just before mile marker 9, is a place known around the world as one of the greatest windsurfing spots on the planet, **Hookipa Beach Park.** Hookipa ("hospitality") is where the top-ranked windsurfers come to test themselves against the forces of nature: thunderous surf and forceful wind. World-championship contests are held here (see "Maui Calendar of Events," in chapter 1), but on nearly every windy day after noon (the board surfers have the waves in the morning), you can watch dozens of windsurfers twirling and dancing in the wind like colored butterflies. To watch the windsurfers, do not stop on the highway, but go past the park and turn left at the entrance on the far side of the beach. You can either park on the high grassy bluff or drive down to the sandy beach and park alongside the pavilion. The park also has rest rooms, a shower, picnic tables, and a barbecue area.

Travel Tip

If you'd like to know exactly what you're seeing as you head down the road to Hana, we suggest renting a cassette tour, available from **Rental Warehouse,** in Lahaina at 578 Front St., near Prison Street (☎ **808/661-1970**), or in Kihei at Azeka Place II, on the mountain side of Kihei Road near Lipoa Street (☎ **808/875-4050**), for $10 a day.

The Road to Hana

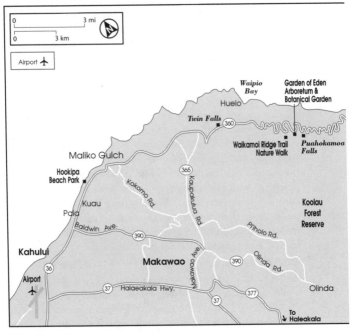

INTO THE COUNTRY Past Hookipa Beach, the road winds down into **Maliko** ("Budding") **Gulch** at mile marker 10. At the bottom of the gulch, look for the road on your right, which will take you out to **Maliko Bay.** Take the first right, which goes under the bridge and past a rodeo arena (scene of competitions by the Maliko Roping Club in summer) and on to the rocky beach. There are no facilities here except a boat-launch ramp. In the 1940s, Maliko had a thriving community at the mouth of the bay, but its residents rebuilt farther inland after a strong tidal wave wiped it out.

Back on the Hana Highway, as you leave Maliko Gulch, you'll see acres of pineapple fields on your right around mile marker 11. Don't be tempted to stop and pick pineapples, because they're the private property of Maui Land & Pineapple Co.; picking is considered stealing. For the next few miles, you'll pass through the rural area of **Haiku,** with banana patches, glimpses of farms, cane grass blowing in the wind, and forests of guava trees, avocados, kukui trees, palms, and Christmas berry. Just before mile marker 15 is the

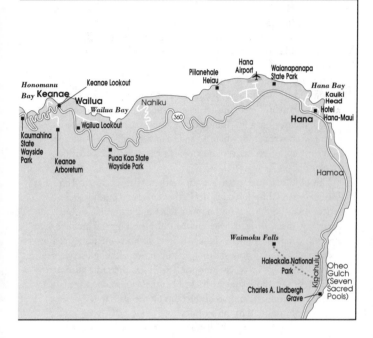

Maui Grown Market and Deli (☎ **808/572-1693**), a good stop for drinks or snacks for the ride.

At mile marker 16, the curves begin, one right after another. Slow down and enjoy the view of bucolic rolling hills, mango trees, and vibrant ferns. After mile marker 16, the road is still called the Hana Highway, but the number changes from Highway 36 to Highway 360, and the mile markers go back to 0.

A GREAT PLUNGE ALONG THE WAY A dip in a waterfall pool is everybody's tropical-island fantasy. The first great place to stop is **Twin Falls,** at mile marker 2. Just before the wide, concrete bridge, pull over on the mountain side and park (but not in front of the sign that says DO NOT BLOCK DRIVEWAY). Keep in mind that there have been thefts in this area, and remember that a good thief can get into your locked trunk faster than you can with your key. Hop over the ladder on the right side of the red gate and walk about 3 to 5 minutes to the waterfall and pool off to your left, or continue on another 10 to 15 minutes to the second, larger waterfall and pool (do not go in if it has been raining recently). What a way to start the trip to Hana.

HIDDEN HUELO   Just before mile marker 4 on a blind curve, look for a double row of mailboxes overseen by a fading HAWAII VISITORS BUREAU sign. Down the road lies a hidden Hawaii: a Hawaii of an earlier time, where ocean waves pummel soaring lava cliffs and where an indescribable sense of serenity prevails.

Protruding out of Maui's tumultuous northern coastline, hemmed in by Waipo and Hoalua Bays, is the remote, rural community of **Huelo.** Once, this fertile area supported a population of 75,000; today, only a few hundred live among the scattered homes on this windswept land, where a handful of bed-and-breakfasts and exquisite vacation rentals are known only to a select few travelers (see chapter 3).

The only reason Huelo is even marked is the historic 1853 **Kaulanapueo Church,** which sits in the center of a putting-green–perfect lawn, bordered with hog-wire fence and accessible through a squeaky, metal turnstile. Reminiscent of New England architecture, this coral-and-cement church, topped with a plantation-green steeple and a cloudy gray tin roof, is still in use, although services are held just once or twice a month. It still has the same austere, stark interior of 1853: straight-backed benches, a no-nonsense platform for the minister, and no distractions on the walls to tempt you from paying attention to the sermon.

Next to the church is a small graveyard, a personal history of this village in concrete and stone. The graves, facing the setting sun and bleached white over the decades, are the community's garden of memories, each well tended and oft-visited.

KOOLAU FOREST RESERVE   After Huelo, the vegetation seems lusher, as though Mother Nature had poured Miracle-Gro on everything. This is the edge of the **Koolau Forest Reserve.** Koolau means "windward," and this certainly is one of the greatest examples of a lush windward area: The coastline here gets about 60 to 80 inches of rain a year, and farther up the mountain, the rainfall is 200 to 300 inches a year.

Here you will see 20- to 30-foot-tall guava trees, their branches laden with green (not ripe) and yellow (ripe) fruit. The skin is peeled and the fruit inside the guava eaten raw, squeezed for juice, or cooked for jams or jellies. Also in this prolific area are mangos, java plums, and avocados the size of softballs. The spiny, long-leafed plants you see are hala trees, which the Hawaiians used for roofing material and for weaving baskets, mats, and even canoe sails. The very tall trees, up to 200 feet tall, are eucalyptus, brought to Hawaii from Australia to supply the sugarcane mills with power for the wood-burning engines. Unfortunately, in the nearly 100 years since the fast-growing tree was first introduced, it has quickly taken over Hawaiian forests, forcing out native plants and trees.

The 200 to 300 inches of rainfall up the mountain means a waterfall (and one-lane bridge) around nearly every turn in the road from here on out, so drive slowly and be prepared to stop and yield to oncoming cars.

DANGEROUS CURVES   About a half mile after mile marker 6, there's a sharp U-curve in the road, going uphill. The road is practically one lane here, with a brick wall on one side and virtually no maneuvering room. Sound your horn at the start of the U-curve to let approaching cars know you are coming. Take this curve, as well as the few more coming up in the next several miles, very slowly.

Just before mile marker 7 is a forest of waving **bamboo.** The sight is so spectacular that drivers are often tempted to take their eyes off the road. Be very cautious. Wait until just after mile marker 7, at the **Kaaiea** ("breathtaking") **Bridge** and stream below, to pull over and take a closer look at the hand-hewn stone walls. Then turn around to see the vista of bamboo, a photo opportunity that certainly qualifies as "breathtaking."

A GREAT FAMILY HIKE   At mile marker 9, there's a small state wayside area with rest rooms, a pavilion, picnic tables, and a barbecue area. The sign says Koolau Forest Reserve, but the real attraction here is the **Waikamoi Ridge Trail,** an easy ³/₄-mile loop that the entire family can do. The start of the trail is just behind the QUIET TREES AT WORK sign. The well-marked trail meanders through eucalyptus (including the unusual paper-bark eucalyptus), ferns, and hala trees.

THE GARDEN OF EDEN   Just past mile marker 10 is the **Garden of Eden Arboretum and Botanical Garden** (☎ **808/ 572-6453**), some 26 acres of nature trails, picnic areas, and more than 500 exotic plants and trees from around the Pacific (wild ginger, an assortment of ti plants, and an impressive palm collection). The Garden of Eden is the dream of arborist/landscape designer Alan Bradbury; he and his staff have been helping to restore a natural ecosystem and promote Hawaii's native and indigenous species since 1991. Don't be surprised if this place looks familiar—it's in the opening sequence of *Jurassic Park.* Hours are daily from 9am to 2pm; admission is $3 per person.

MORE GREAT PLUNGES   Another great waterfall is **Puohokamoa Falls,** a 30-foot falls that spills into an idyllic pool in a fern-filled amphitheater. Naturalist Ken Schmidt says that its name, loosely translated, means "valley of the chickens bursting into flight"—which is what hot, sweaty hikers look like as they take the plunge. Park at the bridge at mile marker 11 and take the short walk up the trail, which is lined with stone walls. The spectacular waterfall and deep swimming pool are surrounded by banana trees, colorful heliconias, and sweet-smelling ginger. Bring mosquito repellent. There's a picnic table at the pool.

Back at your car, be sure to check out the view toward the ocean from the bridge: Dozens of varieties of heliconias blanket the valley below.

CAN'T-MISS PHOTO OPS   Just past mile marker 12 is the **Kaumahina** ("moonrise") **State Wayside Park.** Not only is this a good pit stop (rest rooms are available here) and a wonderful place for a picnic under the tall eucalyptus trees (with tables and barbecue area), but it's also a great vista point. The view of the rugged coastline makes an excellent photo—you can see all the way down to the jutting Keanae Peninsula. Just past the park on the ocean side, there's another scenic turnoff (be careful crossing the oncoming traffic) and great photo opportunity.

Another mile and a couple of bends in the road, and you'll enter the Honomanu Valley ("valley of the bird"), with its beautiful bay. To get down to the **Honomanu Bay County Beach Park,** look for the turnoff on your left, just after mile marker 14, as you begin your ascent up the other side of the valley. The rutted dirt-and-cinder road takes you down to the rocky black-sand beach. There are no facilities here, except for a stone fire pit someone has made in the sand. This is a popular site among surfers and net fishermen. There are strong rip currents offshore, so swimming is best in the stream inland from the ocean. You'll consider the drive down worthwhile as you stand on the beach, well away from the ocean, and turn to look back on the steep cliffs covered with vegetation.

THE ROAD CLOSURE   Back on the Hana Highway, just beyond mile marker 14, the state highway crews will be at work. See "Road Closures on the Road to Hana," above.

MAUI'S BOTANICAL WORLD   Farther along the winding road, between mile markers 16 and 17, is a cluster of bunkhouses composing the YMCA Camp Keanae. A quarter-mile down is the **Keanae Arboretum,** where the region's botany is divided into three parts: native forest; introduced forest; and traditional Hawaiian plants, food, and medicine. You can swim in the pools of Piinaau Stream, or press on along a mile-long trail into Keanae Valley, where a lovely tropical rain forest waits at the end.

KEANAE PENINSULA   The old Hawaiian village of **Keanae** stands out against the Pacific like a place time forgot. Here, on an old lava flow graced by an 1860 stone church and swaying palms, is one of the last coastal enclaves of native Hawaiians. They still grow taro in patches and pound it into poi, the staple of the old Hawaiian diet; they still pluck *opihi* (shellfish) from tide pools along the jagged coast and cast throw-nets at schools of fish.

The turnoff to the Keanae Peninsula is on the left, just after the arboretum. The road passes by farms and banana bunches as it hugs the peninsula. Where the road bends, there's a small beach where fishers gather to catch dinner. A quarter-mile farther is the **Keanae Congregational Church** (☎ **808/248-8040**), built in 1860 of lava rocks and coral mortar, standing out in stark contrast to the green fields surrounding it. Beside the church is a small beach-front park, with false kamani trees against a backdrop of black lava and a roiling turquoise sea.

For an experience in an untouched Hawaii, follow the road until it ends. Park by the white fence and take the short, 5-minute walk along the shoreline over the black lava. Continue along the footpath through the tall California grass to the black rocky beach, separating the freshwater stream, **Pinaau,** which winds back into the Keanae Peninsula, nearly cutting it off from the rest of Maui. This is an excellent place for a picnic and a swim in the cool waters of the stream. There are no facilities here, so be sure you leave no evidence that you were here (carry everything out with you and use rest room facilities before you arrive). As you make your way back, notice the white PVC pipes sticking out of the rocks—they're fishing-pole holders for fishermen, usually hoping to catch ulua.

ANOTHER PHOTO OP: KEANAE LOOKOUT   Just past mile marker 17 is a wide spot on the ocean side of the road, where you can see the entire Keanae Peninsula's checkerboard pattern of green taro fields and its ocean boundary etched in black lava. Keanae was the result of a postscript eruption of Haleakala, which flowed through the Koolau Gap and down Keanae Valley and added this geological punctuation to the rugged coastline.

FRUIT & FLOWER STANDS   Around mile marker 18, the road widens; you'll start to see numerous small stands selling fruit or flowers. Many of these stands work on the honor system: You leave your money in the basket and select your purchase. We recommend stopping at **Uncle Harry's,** which you'll find just after the Keanae School around mile marker 18. Native Hawaiian Harry Kunihi Mitchell was a legend in his time. An expert in native plants and herbs, he devoted his life to the Hawaiian-rights and nuclear-free movements. Mitchell's family sells a variety of fruit and juices here, Monday through Saturday from 9am to 4pm.

WAILUA   Just after Uncle Harry's, look for the Wailua Road off on the left. This will take you through the hamlet of homes and churches of Wailua, which also contains a shrine depicting what the community calls a "miracle." Behind the pink **St. Gabriel's Church** is the smaller blue-and-white **Coral Miracle Church,** home of the **Our Lady of Fatima Shrine.** According to the story, in 1860, the men of this village were building a church by diving for coral to make the stone. But the coral offshore was in deep water and the men could only come up with a few pieces at a time, making the construction of the church an arduous project. A freak storm hit the area and deposited the coral from the deep on a nearby beach. The Hawaiians gathered what they needed and completed the church. This would make a nice enough miracle story, but there's more—after the church was completed, another freak storm hit the area and swept all the remaining coral on the beach back out to sea.

If you look back at Haleakala from here, on your left you can see the spectacular, near-vertical **Waikani Falls.** On the remainder of the dead-end road is an eclectic collection of old and modern homes. Turning around at the road's end is very difficult, so we suggest you just turn around at the church and head back for the Hana Highway.

Back on the Hana Highway, just before mile marker 19, is the **Wailua Valley State Wayside Park,** on the right side of the road. Climb up the stairs for a view of the Keanae Valley, waterfalls, and Wailua Peninsula. On a really clear day, you can see up the mountain to the Koolau Gap.

For a better view of the Wailua Peninsula, continue down the road about a quarter mile; on the ocean side, there will be a pull-off area with parking.

PUAA KAA STATE WAYSIDE PARK   You'll hear this park long before you see it, about halfway between mile markers 22 and 23. The sound of waterfalls provides the background music for this small park area with rest rooms, a phone, and a picnic area. There's a well-marked path to the falls and to a swimming hole. Ginger plants are everywhere: Pick some flowers and put them in your car so that you can travel with that sweet smell.

OLD NAHIKU Just after mile marker 25 is a narrow 3-mile road leading from the highway, at about 1,000 feet elevation, down to sea level—and to the remains of the old Hawaiian community of **Nahiku.** At one time, this was a thriving village of thousands; today, the population has dwindled to fewer than a hundred—including a few Hawaiian families, but mostly extremely wealthy mainland residents who jet in for a few weeks at a time to their luxurious vacation homes. At the turn of the century, this site saw brief commercial activity as home of the Nahiku Rubber Co., the only commercial rubber plantation in the United States. You can still see rubber trees along the Nahiku Road. However, the amount of rainfall, coupled with the damp conditions, could not support the commercial crop; the plantation closed in 1912, and Nahiku was forgotten until the 1980s, when multimillionaires "discovered" the remote and stunningly beautiful area.

At the end of the road, you can see the remains of the old wharf from the rubber-plantation days. Local residents come down here to shoreline fish; there's a small picnic area off to the side. Dolphins are frequently seen in the bay.

HANA AIRPORT After mile marker 31, a small sign points to the Hana Airport, down Alalele Road on the left. **Island Air** (☎ **800/323-3345** from the mainland or 800/652-6541 in Hawaii) has two flights a day to Kahului with connections to other islands. Newly formed commuter airline **Pacific Wings** (☎ **888/575-4546**) offers three flights daily to and from Hana, with connecting flights from Kahului as well. There is no public transportation in Hana. Car rentals are available through **Dollar Rent A Car** (☎ **800/800-4000** or 808/248-8237).

WAIANAPANAPA STATE PARK At mile marker 32, just on the outskirts of Hana, shiny black-sand Waianapanapa Beach appears like a vivid dream, with bright-green jungle foliage on three sides and cobalt blue water lapping at its feet. The 120-acre park on an ancient lava flow includes sea cliffs, lava tubes, arches, and the beach, plus 12 cabins, tent camping, picnic pavilions, rest rooms, showers, drinking water, and hiking trails. If you're interested in staying here, see chapter 3; also see "Beaches" in chapter 5.

8   The End of the Road: Heavenly Hana

Green, tropical Hana is a destination all its own, a small coastal village that's probably what you came to Maui in search of.

Here you'll find a rain forest dotted with cascading waterfalls and sparkling blue pools, skirted by red- and black-sand beaches. Beautiful Hana enjoys more than 90 inches of rain a year—more than enough to keep the scenery lush. Banyans, bamboo, breadfruit trees—everything seems larger than life in this small town, especially the flowers, such as wild ginger and plumeria. Several roadside stands offer exotic blooms for $1 a bunch. Just "put money in box." It's the Hana honor system.

Most visitors will zip through Hana, perhaps taking a quick look out their car windows at a few sights before buzzing on down the road. They might think they've "seen" Hana, but they definitely haven't "experienced" Hana. Allow at least 2 or 3 days to really let this land of legends show you its breathtaking beauty and quiet serenity.

As you enter Hana, the road splits about a half mile past mile marker 33, at the police station. Both roads will take you to Hana, but the lower road, Uakea Road, is more scenic. Just before you get to Hana Bay, you'll see the old wood-frame **Hana District Police Station and Courthouse.** Next door is the **Hana Museum Cultural Center,** on Uakea Road (☎ **808/248-8622;** fax 808/ 248-8620; www.planet-hawaii.com/hana), open daily from 10am to 4pm (most of the time). This small building has an excellent collection of Hawaiian quilts, artifacts, books, and photos. Also on the grounds are Kauhala O Hana, composed of four *hale* (houses) for living, meeting, cooking, and canoe building or canoe storage

Catercorner from the cultural center is the entrance to **Hana Bay.** You can drive right down to the pier and park. There are rest rooms, showers, picnic tables, barbecue areas, and even a snack bar here. The 386-foot, red-faced cinder cone beside the bay is **Kauiki Hill,** the scene of numerous fierce battles in ancient Hawaii and the birthplace of Queen Kaahumanu in 1768. A short, 5-minute walk will take you to the spot. Look for the trail along the hill on the wharf side, and follow the path through the ironwood trees; the lighthouse on the point will come into view, and you'll see pocket beaches of red cinder below. Grab onto the ironwood trees for support, because the trail has eroded in some areas. This is a perfect place for a secluded picnic, or you can continue on the path out to the

Hana

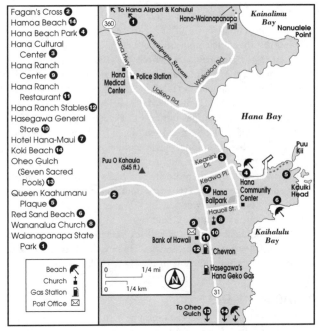

Fagan's Cross ❷
Hamoa Beach ⓮
Hana Beach Park ❹
Hana Cultural
  Center ❸
Hana Ranch
  Center ❾
Hana Ranch
  Restaurant ⓫
Hana Ranch Stables ⓬
Hasegawa General
  Store ❿
Hotel Hana-Maui ❼
Koki Beach ⓮
Oheo Gulch
  (Seven Sacred
  Pools) ⓭
Queen Kaahumanu
  Plaque ❺
Red Sand Beach ❻
Wananalua Church ❽
Waianapanapa State
  Park ❶

Beach ⚓
Church ✝
Gas Station ⛽
Post Office ✉

lighthouse. To get to the lighthouse, which sits on a small island, watch the water for about 10 minutes to get a sense of how often and from which direction the waves are coming. Between wave sets, either swim or wade in the shallow, sandy bottom channel or hop across the rocks to the island.

To get to the center of town, leave Hana Bay, cross Uakea Road, and drive up Keawa Place; turn left on Hana Highway, and on the corner will be the **Hotel Hana-Maui,** the luxurious hotel established by Paul Fagan in 1946 (for a review, see chapter 3). On the green hills above Hotel Hana-Maui stands a 30-foot-high white cross made of lava rock. Citizens erected the cross in memory of Paul Fagan, who founded the Hana Ranch as well as the hotel, and helped keep the town alive. The hike up to **Fagan's Cross** provides a gorgeous view of the Hana coast, especially at sunset, when Fagan himself liked to climb this hill.

Back on the Hana Highway, just past Hauoli Road, is the majestic **Wananalua Congregation Church.** It's on the National Historic Register not only because of its age (it was built from 1838 to 1842 from coral stones), but also because of its location, atop an old Hawaiian heiau.

Just past the church on the right side of the Hana Highway is the turnoff to the **Hana Ranch Center,** the commercial center for Hana, with a post office, bank, general store, the Hana Ranch Stables, and a restaurant and snack bar (see chapter 4). But the real shopping experience is across the Hana Highway at the **Hasegawa General Store,** a Maui institution (see chapter 7), which carries oodles of merchandise from soda and fine French wines to fishing line to name-brand clothing, plus everything you need for a picnic or a gourmet meal. This is also the place to find out what's going on in Hana: The bulletin board at the entrance has fliers and hand-written notes advertising everything from fund-raising activities to classes to community wide activities. You cannot make a trip to Hana without a stop at this unique store.

If you need gas before heading back, note that the two service stations, **Chevron** and **Hasegawa's Hana Geko Gas,** sit nearly side by side on the right side of the Hana Highway as you leave town.

OUTDOOR PURSUITS

Most day-trippers to Hana can't imagine what there is to do in this tiny community. The answer is: everything. One of the best areas on Maui for ocean activities, it also boasts a wealth of incredible nature hikes, remote places to explore on horseback, waterfalls to discover, and even lava tube caves to investigate.

For more information on the lava tubes, contact **Maui Cave Adventures** (☎ 808/248-7308). For details on horseback riding, check out **Oheo Stables** (☎ 808/667-2222). If you're a tennis player, you can take advantage of the free public courts located next to the Hotel Hana-Maui, available on a first-come, first-served basis.

BEACHES & OCEAN ACTIVITIES

Hana's beaches come in numerous varieties: white, black, gray, or red sand; perfectly shaped coves, crescents, or long stretches; and excellent for just about every kind of ocean activity you can think of.

HANA   The waters in the Hana Bay are calm most of the time and great for swimming. There's excellent snorkeling and diving by the lighthouse. Strong currents can run through here, so don't venture farther than the lighthouse. See Hana Bay, above, for more details on the facilities and hikes here.

RED SAND BEACH The Hawaiian name for this beach is Kaihalulu Beach, which means "roaring sea," and it's easy to understand why: The beach is as red as a Ferrari at a five-alarm fire. It's truly a sight to see. The beach is on the ocean side of Kauiki Hill, just south of Hana Bay, in a wild, natural setting on a pocket cove, where the volcanic cinder cone lost its seaward wall to erosion and spilled red cinders everywhere to create the red sands. Before you put on your bathing suit, there are two things to know about this beach: You have to trespass to get here (trespassing is against the law and you could face charges), and nudity (also illegal in Hawaii—arrests have been made) is common here.

To reach the beach, put on solid walking shoes (no flip-flops) and walk south on Uakea Road, past Haoli Street and the Hotel Hana-Maui, to the parking lot for the hotel's Sea Ranch Cottages. Turn left and cross the open field next to the Hana Community Center. Look for the dirt trail and follow it to the huge ironwood tree, where you turn right (do not go ahead to the old Japanese cemetery). If it's wet, do not attempt to go down the treacherous trail. Use the ironwood trees to maintain your balance as you follow the ever-eroding cinder footpath a short distance along the shoreline, down the narrow cliff trail. The trail suddenly turns the corner, and into view comes the burnt-red beach, set off by the turquoise waters, black lava, and vivid green ironwood trees.

The lava outcropping protects the bay and makes it safe for swimming. Snorkeling is excellent and there's a natural whirlpool area on the Hana Bay side of the cove. Stay away from the surge area where the ocean enters the cove.

KOKI BEACH One of the best surfing and boogie-boarding beaches on the Hana Coast lies just a couple of miles from the Hasegawa General Store in the Oheo Gulch direction. There is a very strong rip current here, so unless it is dead calm and you are a strong swimmer, do not attempt swimming here. In fact, a sign on the emergency call box—installed after a drowning in 1996—warns of the strong currents. It's a great place, though, to sit on the white sand and watch the surfers. The only facility is a big parking area. To get here, drive toward Oheo Gulch from Hana, where Highway 36 changes to Highway 31. About 1½ miles outside Hana, turn left at Haneoo Road.

HAMOA BEACH   For one of Hana's best beaches—great for swimming, boogie boarding, and lying out—continue another half mile down the Haneoo Road loop to Hamoa Beach. There is easy access from the road down to the sandy beach, and facilities include a small rest room and an outdoor shower. The large pavilion and beach accessories are for the guests of the Hotel Hana-Maui.

WAIOKA POND   Locally, this swimming hole in a series of waterfalls and pools is called Venus Pool, and the rumor is that in ancient Hawaii, only royalty was allowed to use this exquisite site. The freshwater swimming area is a great place to spend a secluded day. Only two warnings here: Don't go to the pond if it has been raining (flash floods), and don't go near the surf at the ocean end of the stream (strong undertow). To get here, park your car well off the Hana Highway at mile marker 48, before the bridge. Hop over the fence on the ocean side of the bridge, and follow the well-worn footpath that parallels the stream. At the stream, turn to your right to take the path down to the smooth rocks above the stream. There's a huge pond just off the white-rock waterfall with a little island you can swim to in the middle.

HIKING

Hana is woven with hiking trails along the shoreline, through the rain forest, and up in the mountains. Especially noteworthy is the hike to **Fagan's Cross,** a 3-mile walk to the cross erected in the memory of Hana Ranch and Hotel Hana-Maui founder Paul Fagan. It offers spectacular views of the Hana coast, particularly at sunset. The uphill trail starts across Hana Highway from the Hotel Hana-Maui. Enter the pastures at your own risk; they're often occupied by glaring bulls with sharp horns and cows with new calves, so beware. Watch your step as you ascend this steep hill on a Jeep trail across open °pastures; you'll be rewarded at the cross with the breathtaking view.

Another excellent hike leads you to **Blue Pool** and **Piilanihale Heiau.** This easy, 3-mile round-trip takes you to a freshwater, ocean-side waterfall and swimming pool at the halfway point. On the way back, you can tour a tropical botanical garden and see the largest heiau in the state. The hike is on a Jeep trail with some climbing over boulders, so wear good hiking boots or tennis shoes (no flip-flops) and bring a swimsuit and mosquito repellent. Go in the morning, when the sun lights up the ocean-side pool, and you'll have plenty of time for a picnic lunch before seeing the garden and heiau in the afternoon.

Turn toward the ocean on Ulaino Road, by mile marker 31. Drive down the paved road (which turns into a dirt road but is still drivable) to the first stream (about 1 1/2 miles). If the stream is flooded, turn around and go back. If you can forge the stream, cross it and park on the right side of the road by the huge breadfruit trees. The trees are part of the 122-acre **Kahanu Garden** (☎ 808/248-8912), owned and operated by the National Tropical Botanical Garden (www.ntbg.org), which also has two gardens on Kauai. Call before you go to reserve a spot on the guided tours of the garden and heiau. Tours (limited to 15) are given Monday through Friday from 1 to 3pm; they cost $10 for adults and are free for children 12 and under.

After you park your car, walk down the Jeep road that parallels the Kahanu Gardens. You'll have to ford two more streams before the road ends at the beach. Cross the rock-and-gravel beach. If it has been dry, you can just walk along the shoreline. If there has been rain, you will need to cross over the big boulders in the stream. Continue walking down the beach to the 100-foot waterfall on your left with its deep freshwater pool, known locally as **Blue Pool.** After a dip in the bracing spring water, you can sun yourself and eat a picnic lunch on the large boulders.

If you've made reservations for the tour of Kahanu Garden, be back at your car before the 1pm tour begins. The tour offers a history of Hawaii through a discussion of its native plants, plus the history of the Piilanihale Heiau and a chance to see the rugged coastline of this remote area. The 122 acres encompass plant collections from the Pacific Islands, concentrating on plants of value to the people of Polynesia, Micronesia, and Melanesia. Fringed by a vast native pandanus forest, Kahanu Garden contains the largest known collection of breadfruit cultivars. This collection serves as a germplasm repository for this important South Pacific food crop, housing cultivars from more than 17 Pacific Island groups and Indonesia, the Philippines, and the Seychelles.

The real draw here is the **Piilanihale Heiau** ("House of Piilani," one of Maui's greatest chiefs). Believed to be the largest in the state, it measures 340 feet by 415 feet, and it was built in a unique terrace design not seen anywhere else in Hawaii. The walls are some 50 feet tall and 8 to 10 feet thick. Historians believe that Piilani's two sons and his grandson built the mammoth temple, which was dedicated to war, sometime in the 1500s.

JUST BEYOND HANA
TROPICAL HALEAKALA: OHEO GULCH AT KIPAHULU

If you're thinking about heading out to the so-called Seven Sacred Pools, out past Hana at the Kipahulu end of Haleakala National Park, let's clear this up right now: There are more than seven pools—about 24, actually—and *all* water in Hawaii is considered sacred. It's all a PR scam that has spun out of control into contemporary myth. Folks here call the attraction by its rightful name, **Oheo Gulch,** and visitors sometimes refer to it as Kipahulu, which is actually the name of the area where Oheo Gulch is located. No matter what you call it, it's a beautiful sight. The dazzling series of waterfall pools and cataracts cascading into the sea is so popular that it now has its own roadside parking lot.

ACCESS POINTS   Even though Oheo is part of Haleakala National Park, you cannot drive from the summit. Even hiking from Halekala to Oheo is tricky: The access trail out of Haleakala is down Kaupo Gap, which ends at the ocean, a good 6 miles down the coast from Oheo. To drive to Oheo, head for Hana, some 60 miles from Kahului on the Hana Highway (Highway 36). Oheo is about 30 to 50 minutes beyond Hana, along Highway 31. The Highway 31 bridge passes over pools near the ocean; the other pools, plus magnificent 400-foot Waimoku falls, are reachable via an often-muddy but rewarding, hour-long uphill hike. Expect showers on the Kipahulu coast.

VISITOR CENTER   The **Kipahulu Ranger Station** (☎ 808/248-7375) is staffed from 9am to 5pm daily. Rest rooms are available, but no drinking water. Kipahulu rangers offer safety information, exhibits, books, and a variety of walks and hikes year-round; check at the station for current activities.

HIKING & CAMPING   There are a number of hikes in the park, and tent camping is allowed. Check with the Haleakala Park rangers before hiking up to or swimming in the pools, and always keep one eye on the water in the streams; the sky can be sunny near the coast, but flood waters travel 6 miles down from 8,000 acres of Kipahulu Valley and can rise 4 feet in less than 10 minutes.

7

Shops & Galleries

by Jocelyn Fujii

*S*o, what do you do on Maui when it's too late for a Haleakala sunrise, not quite happy hour, and not sunny enough for the beach? Go shopping, of course. And why not? You can leapfrog from one shopping center to the next simply by following the main road—and enjoy the views of Haleakala or the West Maui Mountains in between. Maui is also an arts center of the islands, with a large number of resident artists who show their works in dozens of galleries and countless gift shops.

As with any popular visitor destination, you'll have to wade through oceans of bad art and mountains of trinkets, particularly in Lahaina and Kihei, where touristy boutiques line the streets between rare pockets of treasures. If you shop in South or West Maui, expect to pay resort prices, clear down to a bottle of Evian or sunscreen. But Maui's gorgeous finds are particularly rewarding. Residents work, live, and shop for everyday needs in Central Maui, and it's home to first-rate boutiques for specialized tastes as well: Historic Wailuku has its own antiques alleys (N. Market and Main streets), and the Kaahumanu Center in neighboring Kahului is becoming more fashionable by the month. Upcountry, Makawao's boutiques are worth seeking out, despite some attitude and high prices.

1 Central Maui

KAHULUI

Kahului's best shopping is concentrated in two places. Almost all of the shops listed below are at one of the following centers:

Kaahumanu Center, 275 Kaahumanu Ave. (☎ **808/877-3369**), a commercial hub only 5 minutes from the Kahului Airport on Highway 32, has more than 100 shops, restaurants, and theaters. With a thoughtful selection of food and retail shops, Kaahumanu covers all the bases, from the arts and crafts to a **Foodland Supermarket,** with everything in between: a thriving food court; the island's best beauty supply, **Lisa's Beauty Supply & Salon** (☎ **808/877-6463**), and its sister store for cosmetics, **Madison Avenue Day Spa and Boutique** (☎ **808/873-0880**); mall standards

LINDBERGH'S GRAVE

A mile past Oheo Gulch on the ocean side of the road is **Lindbergh's Grave.** First to fly across the Atlantic Ocean, Charles A. Lindbergh (1902–74) found peace in the Pacific; he settled in Hana, where he died of cancer in 1974. The famous aviator is buried under river stones in a seaside graveyard behind the 1857 **Palapala Hoomau Congregational Church,** where his tombstone reads, "If I take the wings of the morning and dwell in the uttermost parts of the sea. . . ."

like **Sunglass Hut, Radio Shack,** and **Local Motion** (surf and beach wear); department stores **Liberty House** and **Shirokiya;** and attractive boutique/galleries such as **Ki'i** and **Maui Hands.** From 11:30am to 1:30pm on the last Friday of every month, there are food demonstrations and samplings, fashion shows, and live entertainment in the center's **Queen's Market Food Court.**

Rough around the edges and dramatically eclipsed by the Kaahumanu Center down the street, **Maui Mall,** 70 E. Kaahumanu Ave. (☎ **808/877-7559**), is still a place for everyday things, like Longs Drugs to 60-minute photo processing and a Star Market.

Caswell-Massey. Kaahumanu Center. ☎ **808/877-7761.**

Although part of a worldwide chain, this Caswell-Massey is unique for its selection of Maui-made soaps and bath products that use tropical fragrances and botanicals. Choose from hundreds of specialty products, from decadent bath salts with 23-karat gold flakes to Damask rose shampoo and bath gels. They prepare handsome, custom-designed baskets at no extra charge.

Cost Less Imports. Maui Mall. ☎ **808/877-0300.**

Natural fibers are everywhere in this tiny corner of the mall. You'll find lauhala, bamboo blinds, grassy floor and window coverings, shoji-style lamps, burlap yardage, baskets, tactile Balinese cushions—Asian, Indonesian, and Polynesian imports, as well as top-of-the-line, made-on-Maui soaps and handicrafts.

Hoaloha Heirlooms. Kaahumanu Center. ☎ **808/873-0461.**

Lavish koa ukuleles by Maui Ukulele and leis made of kukui nuts, wiliwili seeds, and Job's tears are part of the Hawaiian offerings at this wonderful gift shop. Paintings, koa tables, small Hawaiian quilts, children's clothes, muumuus and dresses, hair ornaments, handmade paper, fiber baskets, and hundreds of gift items from Hawaii, Indonesia, and the South Pacific are part of Hoaloha's offerings.

✪ **Ki'i Gallery.** Kaahumanu Center. ☎ **808/871-4557.**

The eclectic collection includes glass art and black pearls, as well as a wide assortment of made-on-Maui crafts. Chinese porcelains, clay teapots, jewelry, and hand-painted maple-wood bowls keep regulars returning. But it's the glass vases that dominate the room with their brilliance and luminosity. All handcrafted, of high quality, the glass reflects excellent craftsmanship and design, from Venetian and Czech glass to Pizzo from Maui and Vandemark Merritt from New Jersey.

Ki'i also has shops in the Grand Wailea Resort, Sheraton Maui, and the Hyatt Regency Maui.

Lightning Bolt Maui Inc. 55 Kaahumanu Ave. ☎ **808/877-3484.**

Here's an excellent selection of women's board shorts, aloha shirts, swimwear, sandals and shoes, and beach towels. Quality labels such as Patagonia and high-tech, state-of-the-art outdoor gear and moccasins attract adventurers heading for the chilly hinterlands as well as the sun-drenched shores.

Manikin. 55 Kaahumanu Ave. ☎ **808/877-1473.**

Women who like washable, flowing clothing in silks, rayons, and natural fibers will love Manikin. If you don't find what you want on the racks of simple bias-cut designs, you can have it made from the bolts of stupendous washable fabrics lining the shop.

Maui Hands. Kaahumanu Center. ☎ **808/877-0368.**

This is an ideal stop for made-on-Maui products and crafts of good quality; 90% of what's sold here was made on the island. Because it's a consignment shop, you'll find Hawaii-made handicrafts and prices that aren't inflated. The selection includes jewelry, glass marbles, native-wood bowls, tchotchkes for every budget, and paintings and prints aplenty, in all price ranges.

The original Maui Hands remains in Makawao at The Courtyard, 3620 Baldwin Ave. (☎ **808/572-5194**).

Maui Swap Meet. S. Puunene Ave. (next to the Kahului Post Office). ☎ **808/ 877-3100.**

Throughout the year, there are more than 100 vendors here. The colorful Maui specialties include vegetables from Kula and Keanae, fresh taro, plants, proteas, crafts, household items, homemade ethnic foods, and baked goods, including fabulous fruit breads. On Saturday from 5:30am to noon, vendors spread out their wares in booths, under tarps, in a festival-like atmosphere that is pure Maui with a touch of kitsch. Between the cheap Balinese imports and New Age crystals and incense, you may find some vintage John Kelly prints and 1930s collectibles. Admission is 50¢, and if you go early while the vendors are setting up, no one will turn you away.

✪ **Summerhouse.** In the Dairy Center, 385 Dairy Rd. ☎ **808/871-1320.**

Sleek, chic, tiny Summerhouse is big on style: linens by Russ Berens, FLAX, Kiko, and Tencel jeans by Signature—the best. We adore the hats, accessories, easy-care clothing, and up-to-the-minute evening dresses. The high-quality T-shirts, always a cut above, can take you from day to evening.

WAILUKU

Wailuku's attractive vintage architecture, numerous antiques shops, and mom-and-pop eateries imbue the town with a charm noticeably absent in the resort areas of west, south, and upcountry Maui. There is no plastic aloha in Wailuku. Of course there's junk, but a stroll along Main and Market streets usually turns up a treasure or two.

Hilo-based **Sig Zane Designs** plans a summer 1999 opening on Wailuku's Market Street, near Iao Theater. Zane and his partner, Punawai Rice, have redefined Hawaiian wear; their aloha shirts, women's clothing, and furnishings evoke a gracious Hawaii of an earlier time. Sig Zane Designs in Wailuku will likely become a cultural outpost.

✪ **Bailey House Gift Shop.** At the Bailey House Museum, 2375-A Main St. ☎ **808/244-3920.**

If you're shopping for made-in-Hawaii items and have time for only one stop in Wailuku, make it Bailey House. The small space contains a choice selection of remarkable gift items, from Hawaiian music albums to exquisite woods, traditional Hawaiian games to pareus and books. Hawaiian music often wafts in from a neighboring room, where a slack-key guitar class may be in session. This is a thoroughly enjoyable browse through authoritative Hawaiiana in a museum that's one of the finest examples of missionary architecture, dating from 1833.

✪ **Bird of Paradise Unique Antiques.** 56 N. Market St. ☎ **808/242-7699.**

Owner Joe Myhand loves furniture, old Matson liner menus, blue willow china, kimonos for children, and anything nostalgic that happens to be Hawaiian. The furniture ranges from 1940s rattan to wicker and old koa—those items tailor-made for informal island living and leisurely moments on the lanai. Myhand also collects bottles and mails his license plates all over the world. The collection ebbs and flows with his finds, keeping buyers waiting in the wings for his Depression glass, California pottery from the 1930s and 1940s, and vintage aloha shirts.

✪ **Brown-Kobayashi.** 160-A N. Market St. ☎ **808/242-0804.**

Graceful living is the theme here. Prices range from a few dollars to the thousands in this 750-square-foot treasure trove. Asian antiques mingle quietly with old and new French, European, and Hawaiian objects. Japanese kimono and obi, Bakelite and Peking glass beads, breathtaking Japanese lacquerware, cricket carriers, cloisonné, and a lotus-leaf basket carved of bamboo are among the many treasures here.

Memory Lane. 130 N. Market St. ☎ **808/244-4196.**

This 1,500-square-foot showroom is filled with art, Hawaiian collectibles, Asian antiques, kitsch, vintage textiles and aloha shirts, English crystal from the 1700s, Depression glass, antique silver, and furniture "from the very old to the 1950s and Federal," says the owner.

CENTRAL MAUI EDIBLES

The **Star Market,** in the Maui Mall; **Foodland,** in the Kaahumanu Center; and **Safeway,** at 170 E. Kamehameha Ave., will satisfy your ordinary grocery needs. On Saturday, you may want to check out the **Maui Swap Meet** (see above).

With a move from Wailuku to Kahului, both the service and the selection have improved at **Down to Earth Natural Foods,** 305 Dairy Rd. (☎ **808/877-2661**). Fresh organic Maui produce, a bountiful salad bar, sandwiches and smoothies, vitamins and supplements, freshly baked goods, chips and snacks, and whole grains have made Down to Earth a health-food staple for many years.

Established in 1941, the **Ooka Super Market,** 1870 Main St., Wailuku (☎ **808/244-3931**), Maui's ultimate home-grown supermarket, is a mom-and-pop business that has grown by leaps and bounds but still manages to keep its neighborhood flavor. Ooka sells inexpensive produce (fresh Maui mushrooms for a song), fresh island seafood, certified Angus beef, and Maui specialties such as manju and mochi. Proteas cut the same day, freesias in season, hydrangeas, fresh leis, torch gingers from Hana, upcountry calla lilies in season, and multicolored anthuriums compose one of Maui's finest and most affordable retail flower selections. Prepared foods are also a hit: bentos and plate lunches, roast chicken and lau lau, and specialties from all the islands.

Most of the space at **Shirokiya,** in the Kaahumanu Center (☎ **808/877-5551**), is devoted to food, with a well-stocked prepared-foods section, but check out the fresh produce (bananas, papayas), juices, and health-food supplements as well. The Dee Lite Bakery has a small corner, with its famous haupia cake and other white-and-bright pastries, but most of the other foods are local or Japanese plate-lunch fare offered in neatly packaged bento boxes or hot from the counter.

Ohana Farmers Market, Kahului Shopping Center, next to Ah Fook's Super Market (☎ **808/878-3189**), is where you'll find a fresh, inexpensive selection of Maui-grown fruit, vegetables, flowers, and plants in season.

Located in the northern section of Wailuku, **Takamiya Market,** 359 N. Market St. (☎ **808/244-3404**), is much loved by local folks and visitors, who often drive all the way from Kihei to stock up on picnic fare and mouth-watering ethnic foods for sunset gatherings and beach parties. This is for adventurous palates, local all the way. Unpretentious home-cooked foods from East and West are prepared daily and served on Styrofoam plates from an ethnic smorgasbord.

2 West Maui

LAHAINA

Lahaina's merchants and art galleries go all out from 6:30 to 9pm on Fridays, when **Art Night** brings an extra measure of hospitality and community spirit. The Art Night openings are usually marked with live entertainment and refreshments and a livelier-than-usual street scene.

If you're in Lahaina on the second or last Thursday of the month, stroll by the front lawn of the **Baldwin Home,** 696 Front St. (at Dickenson Street), for a splendid look at lei-making and an opportunity to meet the gregarious senior citizens of Lahaina. In a program sponsored by the American Association of Retired Persons, they gather from 10am to 4pm to demonstrate lei-making, to sell their floral creations, and equally important, to socialize.

What was formerly a big, belching pineapple cannery is now a maze of shops and restaurants at the northern end of Lahaina town known as the **Lahaina Cannery Mall,** 1221 Honoapiilani Hwy. (☎ **808/661-5304**). Find your way through the T-shirt and sportswear shops to **Lahaina Printsellers,** home of rare maps, antique originals, prints, paintings, and wonderful 18th- to 20th-century cartography representing the largest collection of engravings and antique maps in Hawaii. Follow the scent of coffee to **Sir Wilfred's Coffee House,** where you can unwind with espresso and croissants, or head for **Compadres Bar & Grill,** where the margaritas flow freely and the Mexican food is tasty. At **Enseres,** the Balinese home accessories include woven mats, coconut earrings and utensils, and carved coconut candle holders. The **Maui Chocolate Company** has a dangerously decadent selection of fudge and all things chocolate, which they will ship to the unsuspecting. In the central mall area, **Gertrude Mahi** sells gorgeous feather lei and lauhala hats of a fine weave. Other crafts, including some handsome hand-turned woods of koa, milo, and tamarind, are displayed in the **Simon-JonArt and Design Gallery** in the same center. Half of the gallery displays the landscapes, still lifes, and seascapes of **Julie Taylor Ellingboe.**

The **Lahaina Center,** 900 Front St. (☎ **808/667-9216**), is north of Lahaina's most congested strip, where Front Street begins. Across the street from the center, the seawall is a much-sought-after front-row seat to the sunset. There's plenty of free validated parking with easy access to more than 30 shops, a hair salon, restaurants, a nightclub, and a movie theater. Chef Sam Choy opened **Sam Choy's Lahaina** in January 1999, not long after **Ruth's Chris Steak House** opened its doors in the same center. **Maui Brews** serves lunch and dinner and offers live music nightly except weekends. Among the shopping stops: **Banana Republic,** the **Hilo Hattie Fashion Center** (a dizzying emporium of aloha wear), **McInerny** (wonderfully discounted designer clothes), and **ABC Discount Store**.

The conversion of 10,000 square feet of parking space into the re-creation of a traditional Hawaiian village is a welcome touch of Hawaiiana at Lahaina Center. With the commercialization of modern Lahaina, it's easy to forget that it was once the capital of the Hawaiian kingdom and a significant historic site. The village, called **Hale Kahiko,** features three main houses, called *hale:* a sleeping house; the men's dining house; and the crafts house, where women pounded lauhala for mats and baskets. Construction of the houses consumed 10,000 feet of ohia wood from the island, 20 tons of pili grass, and more than 4 miles of handwoven coconut sennit for the lashings. Artifacts, weapons, a canoe, and indigenous trees are among the authentic touches in this village, which can be toured privately or with a guide.

David Lee Galleries. 712 Front St. ☎ 808/667-7740.

This gallery is devoted to the works of David Lee, who uses natural powder colors to paint on silk. The pigments and technique create a luminous, ethereal quality.

Foreign Intrigue Imports. 505 Front St. ☎ 808/667-4004.

The intriguing selection of interior accents here puts a new spin on the often-tired world of Indian and Balinese imports: gorgeous hand-painted wooden trays, gilded Buddhas, cat benches, chests and armoires of all sizes, and sturdy hemp pouches and accessories. Hundreds of functional and decorative accessories line the shop and reflect Balinese artists' mastery of detail. Intrepid shoppers may find some deals among the vast and colorful selection, including one-of-a-kind, made-on-Maui necklaces of antique beads and jades.

Lahaina Body & Bath. 713 Front St. ☎ **808/661-1076.**

Lei Spa Maui. 505 Front St. ☎ **808/661-1178.**

The new Front Street location is an extension of Lei Spa, and both stores are worth a stop. It's a good sign that 95% of the beauty and bath products sold here are made on Maui, and that includes Hawaiian Botanical Pikake shower gel; kukui and macadamia-nut oils; Hawaiian potpourris; mud masks with Hawaiian seaweed; and a spate of rejuvenating, cleansing, skin-soothing potions for hair and skin. Scented candles in coconut shells, inexpensive and fragrant, make great gifts.

Martin Lawrence Galleries. In the Lahaina Market Place, 126 Lahainaluna Rd. ☎ **808/661-1788.**

The front is garish, with pop art, kinetic sculptures, and bright, carnivalesque glass objects. Toward the back of the gallery, however, there's a sizable inventory of two-dimensional art and some plausible choices for collectors of Keith Haring, Andy Warhol, and other pop artists. The focus is on national and international artists, with very little art from Maui.

Miki's. 762 Front St. ☎ **808/661-8991.**

See why aloha shirts are so fab: Tiny, busy, and bursting with color, Miki's has a tasteful assortment of aloha wear, from Tommy Bahama shirts and coordinates to Honu Bay T-shirts, Jams, surf shorts, and beach slippers.

Totally Hawaiian Gift Gallery. Lahaina Cannery Mall, 1221 Honoapiilani Hwy. ☎ **808/667-2558.**

A good browse for its selection of Niihau shell jewelry, excellent Hawaiian CDs, Norfolk pine bowls, and Hawaiian quilt kits. Hawaiian quilt patterns sewn in Asia (at least they're honest about it) are labor-intensive, less expensive, and attractive, although not totally Hawaiian.

○ **Village Galleries in Lahaina.** 120 and 180 Dickenson St. ☎ **808/661-4402** or 808/661-5559.

The 28-year-old Village Galleries is the oldest continuously running gallery on Maui, and it's highly esteemed as one of the few galleries with consistently high standards. The newer contemporary gallery offers colorful gift items and jewelry.

There's another location in the Ritz-Carlton Kapalua, 1 Ritz-Carlton Dr. (☎ **808/669-1800**).

Westside Natural Foods. 193 Lahainaluna Rd. ☎ **808/667-2855.**

A longtime Lahaina staple, Westside is serious about providing tasty food that's healthy and affordable. A healthy clientele is attracted to its excellent food bar.

KAANAPALI

Whalers Village, 2435 Kaanapali Pkwy. (☎ **808/661-4567**), has gone shockingly upscale, but there are some new additions that ease the pain somewhat. Our favorite shoe store, **Sandal Tree,** has moved here from the Hyatt Regency (see below). Another welcome addition is **Martin & MacArthur** and its Hawaii crafts: Larry DeLuz lidded koa bowls, Hawaiian-quilt cushion covers, jewelry, and a stunning selection of woodworks. You can also find award-winning **Kimo Bean** coffee at a kiosk, and an expanded **Reyn's** for aloha wear. **Cinnamon Girl,** a hit in Honolulu with its matching mother-daughter clothing and accessories, opened its third Hawaii store in Whalers Village. Once you've stood under the authentic whale skeleton or squeezed the plastic whale blubber at the **Whale Center of the Pacific,** you can blow a bundle at **Tiffany, Prada, Chanel, Ferragamo, Dolce & Gabbana,** or any of the 70 shops and restaurants that have sprouted up in this beachfront shopping center. The posh Euro trend doesn't bode well; even with the new-comers, there's too little here that's Hawaiian. Some of the village's mainstream possibilities: The **Body Shop** has the best and most globally conscious products for bath and home. **The Eye-catcher** has one of the most extensive selections of sunglasses on the island, located just across from the busiest **ABC** store in the state. The most comforting stop of all is the **Maui Yogurt Company,** where Maui-made Roselani ice cream is sold in mouth-watering flavors. The Whalers Village is open daily from 9:30am to 10pm.

Rhonda's Quilts. In the Hyatt Regency Maui, 210 Nohea Kai Dr. ☎ **808/667-7660.**

Rhonda's has increased its made-in-Hawaii selection. Some T-shirts, tote bags, mouse pads, and Hawaiian quilt designs are designed in house, but there are also dolls, children's and women's clothing, lo-cally made tiles in Hawaiian quilt patterns, books, stuffed animals, and other eclectic goods in this cheerful store.

✪ **Sandal Tree.** Whalers Village, 2435 Kaanapali Pkwy. ☎ **808/667-5330.**

It's unusual for a resort shop to draw local customers on a regu-lar basis, but the Sandal Tree attracts a flock of footwear fanatics for rubber thongs and topsiders, sandals and dressy pumps, athletic shoes and hats, Arche comfort footwear, and much more.

Accessories range from fashionable knapsacks to indulgences such as avant-garde geometric handbags. Prices are realistic, too.

Another Maui location is at the Grand Wailea Resort, 3850 Wailea Alanui Dr.

KAHANA

Those driving north of Kaanapali toward Kapalua will notice the spanking-new **Honokowai Marketplace** on Lower Honoapiilani Road, only minutes from the Kapalua Airport. The splashy new A Pacific Cafe is only one of its welcome features; there's also the flagship **Star Market, Hula Scoops** for ice cream, **Hawaiian Moons** for natural foods, a gas station, a copy shop, a dry cleaner, a few clothing stores, and the sprawling **Hawaiian Interiorz.**

Nearby **Kahana Gateway** is an unimpressive mall built to serve the condominium community that sprawls along the coastline between Honokowai and Kapalua. If you need women's swimsuits, however, **Rainbow Beach Swimwear** is a find. It carries a wide selection of suits for all shapes, at lower-than-resort prices, slashed even further during the frequent (and welcome) sales.

KAPALUA

Honolua Store. 502 Office Rd. (next to the Ritz-Carlton Kapalua). ☎ **808/ 669-6128.**

Walk on the old wood floors peppered with holes from golf shoes and find your everyday essentials: bottled water, stationery, mailing tape, jackets, chips, wine, soft drinks, paper products, fresh fruit and produce, and aisles of notions and necessities. One corner is dedicated to the Kapalua Nature Society, which leads hikes into the West Maui Mountains. There are always long lines of customers for the take-out counter offering deli items—and there are picnic tables on the veranda. Golfers and surfers love to come here for the morning paper and coffee.

Village Galleries. In the Ritz-Carlton Kapalua, 1 Ritz-Carlton Dr. ☎ **808/ 669-1800.**

Maui's finest exhibit their works here and in the other two Village Galleries in Lahaina. Take heart, art lovers: There's no clichéd marine art here. Translucent, delicately turned bowls of Norfolk pine gleam in the light, and watercolors, oils, sculptures, handblown glass, Niihau shell leis, jewelry, and all media are represented. The Ritz-Carlton's monthly Artist-in-Residence program features Village Gallery artists in demonstrations and special hands-on workshops— free, including materials.

3 South Maui

KIHEI

Kihei is one long strip of strip malls. Most of the shopping here is concentrated in the **Azeka Place Shopping Center** on South Kihei Road. Fast food abounds, as do tourist-oriented clothing shops like **Crazy Shirts** and the overly tropical **Tropical Tantrum.** Across the street, **Azeka Place II** houses several prominent attractions, including the popular restaurant called A Pacific Cafe, **General Nutrition Center,** the **Coffee Store,** and a cluster of specialty shops with everything from children's clothes to sunglasses, beauty services, and swimwear. Also on South Kihei Road is the **Kukui Mall,** with its movie theaters, **Waldenbooks,** and **Whaler's General Store.**

Aloha Books. In the Kamaole Beach Center, 2411 S. Kihei Rd. ☎ **808/ 874-8070.**

Thanks go to Tom Holland for adding an espresso bar with indoor-outdoor seating and live music, poetry, and theatrical performances. This is a community bookstore with character, and it has only gotten better with the years. Holland is a collector and dealer in Hawaiian antiques, collectibles, and art, and his bookstore reflects his passion: The shelves are stocked with books on Hawaii, and the walls are covered with vintage Hawaiian and Polynesian art. There are new, used, and rare books, and although this isn't a big bookstore, the titles cover a range of tastes, from popular fiction and historic novels to health, music, travel, and Dick Francis whodunits.

✪ Hawaiian Moons Natural Foods. 2411 S. Kihei Rd. ☎ **808/875-4356.**

Hawaiian Moons is a health-food store, and a great one, but it's also a mini-supermarket with one of the best selections of made-on-Maui products we've encountered on the island, plus a salad bar. The Mexican tortillas are made on Maui (and good!), and much of the produce here, such as organic vine-ripened tomatoes and organic onions, is grown in the fertile upcountry soil of Kula. There's locally grown organic coffee, Maui teas, gourmet salsas, Maui shiitake mushrooms, organic lemongrass and okra, Maui Crunch bread, and fresh Maui juices. Cosmetics are also top-of-the-line: sunblocks, fragrant floral oils, and the Island Essence made-on-Maui mango-coconut and vanilla-papaya skin lotions, the ultimate in body pampering.

Maui Sports & Cycle. In Dolphin Plaza, 2395 S. Kihei Rd. ☎ **808/875-2882.** Also at Long's Center, 1215 S. Kihei Rd. ☎ 808/875-8448.

These upbeat water-sports retail and rental shops are a hit among beachgoers and water-sports enthusiasts. Plans call for the addition of golf clubs, tennis racquets, and binoculars to the rental department, which is good news for golfers heading for the greens. A friendly, knowledgeable staff helps you choose from the mind-boggling selection of snorkel gear, boogie boards, kayaks, beach umbrellas, coolers, and view boards for "snorkeling lying down." You'll find swimwear and mountain bikes, too, and gear for riding on land or sea. Prescription snorkel masks are available, as are underwater cameras, sunscreens and lotions, jewelry, T-shirts, postcards, and hats and visors by the bushel.

☻ **Old Daze.** In Azeka I, 1280 S. Kihei Rd. ☎ **808/875-7566.**

Nineteenth-century Americana and Hawaiian collectibles are nicely wedded in this charming shop. Some recent finds: an 1850s German sideboard, a Don Blanding teapot, an old Noritake tea set, Royal Worcester china, 1960s ashtrays, Depression glass, a turn-of-the-century pie safe, antique kimonos, framed vintage music sheets, and Hawaiian silver collectible spoons. Choices range from hokey to rustic to pleasantly nostalgic, with many items for the kitchen.

Tuna Luna. Kihei Kalama Village, 1941 S. Kihei Rd. ☎ **808/874-9482.**

There are treasures to be found in this small cluster of tables and booths where Maui artists display their work. Ceramics, exotic wood photo albums, jewelry, candles and soaps, handmade paper, and fiber accessories are functional and not, and make great gifts to go.

WAILEA

Wailea consists largely of upscale resort shops that sell expensive souvenirs, gift items, clothing, and accessories for a life of perpetual vacations. **Sandal Tree** (see "Kaanapali," above), with its affordable-and-up designer wear, raises the footwear banner at the Grand Wailea Resort, while stores like **Mandalay,** in the Grand Wailea Shops and the Four Seasons Resort Maui, specialize in sumptuous Thai silks and Asian imports, from resort wearto the very dressy. **Lahaina Printsellers** has moved to the Grand Wailea from the Wailea Shopping Village, now under newownership and soon to become The Shops at Wailea. **Banana Republic, Louis Vuitton,** and **Tiffany** are among the new tenants at the yet-to-open Shops.

Grand Wailea Shops. At the Grand Wailea Resort, 3850 Wailea Alanui Dr. ☎ **808/875-1234.**

The sprawling Grand Wailea Resort is known for its long arcade of shops and galleries tailored to hefty pocketbooks. However, gift items in all price ranges can be found at **Lahaina Printsellers** (the premier store for old maps and prints), **Dolphin Galleries, H. F. Wichman, Sandal Tree,** and **Napua Gallery,** which houses the private collection of the resort owner. The sleek **Ki'i Gallery** is luminous with studio glass and the warm glow of exquisitely turned woods.

4 Upcountry Maui

MAKAWAO

Besides being a shopper's paradise, Makawao is the home of the island's most prominent arts organization, the ✪ **Hui No'eau Visual Arts Center,** 2841 Baldwin Ave. (☎ **808/572-6560**). Designed in 1917 by C. W. Dickey, one of Hawaii's most prominent architects, the two-story, Mediterranean-style stucco home that houses the center is located on a sprawling, manicured, 9-acre estate called Kaluanui. Its tree-lined driveway features two of Maui's largest hybrid Cook and Norfolk Island pines. A legacy of Maui's prominent kamaaina (native-born, longtime residents), Harry and Ethel Baldwin, the estate became an art center in 1976. Visiting artists offer lectures, classes, and demonstrations, all at reasonable prices, in basketry, jewelry-making, ceramics, painting, and diverse media. Half-day classes on Hawaiian art, culture, and history are also available. Call ahead for schedules and details. Hui No'eau's exhibits are drawn from a wide range of disciplines and multicultural sources, and include both contemporary and traditional art from established and emerging artists. Maui artists long to exhibit here, considering it the most prestigious of venues. There's also a unique gift shop worth a special stop, featuring many one-of-a-kind works by local artists and artisans. Hours are Monday through Saturday from 10am to 4pm.

✪ **Collections.** 3677 Baldwin Ave. ☎ **808/572-0781.**

This longtime Makawao attraction is showing renewed vigor after more than 2 decades on Baldwin Avenue. Its selection of sportswear, soaps, jewelry, candles, and marvelous miscellany reflects good sense and style. Dresses, separates, sweaters, home and bath accessories, and a shop full of good things make this a Makawao must.

Cuckoo for Coconuts. 1158 Makawao Ave. ☎ **808/573-6887.**

The owner's quirky sense of humor pervades every inch of this tiny shop, barely bigger than a large walk-in closet and brimming with vintage collectibles, gag gifts, silly coconuts, 1960s and '70s aloha wear, tutus, sequined dresses, vintage wedding gowns, and all sorts of oddities, arranged around an old claw-foot bathtub in the middle of the shop.

Gecko Trading Co. Boutique. 3621 Baldwin Ave. ☎ **808/572-0249.**

The selection here is eclectic and always changing: One day it's St. John's Wort body lotion and mesh T-shirts in a dragon motif; the next day it's soaps from Provence and antique lapis jewelry. We've seen everything from hair scrunchies to handmade crocheted bags from New York, clothing from Spain and France, collectible bottles, T-shirts, and Mexican hammered-tin candle holders. The prices are reasonable, the service is friendly, and it's not self-consciously stylish.

Holiday & Co. 3681 Baldwin Ave. ☎ **808/572-1470.**

Attractive women's clothing in natural fibers hangs from racks, while jewelry to go with it beckons from the counter. Recent finds include lotus-fiber bags from Bali and sumptuous Ambre bubble bath, expensive and French and worth it.

Hot Island Glassblowing Studio & Gallery. 3620 Baldwin Ave. ☎ **808/ 572-4527.**

You can watch the artist transform molten glass into works of art and utility in this cordial studio in Makawao's Courtyard, where an award-winning family of glassblowers built its own furnaces. It's fascinating to watch the shapes emerge from glass melted at 2,000°. The colorful works displayed in the studio range from small paperweights to large vessels, and they're shipped around the world. Four to five artists participate in the demonstrations, which begin when the furnace is heated, about half an hour before the studio opens at 10am.

Hurricane. 3639 Baldwin Ave. ☎ **808/572-5076.**

This chic boutique carries clothing, gifts, accessories, and books that are two steps ahead of the competition. Tommy Bahama silk piqué aloha shirts and aloha print dresses, Sigrid Olsen's line of clothing, hats, art by local artists, and hard-to-find, eccentric books and home accessories are part of the Hurricane appeal.

The Mercantile. 3673 Baldwin Ave. ☎ **808/572-1407.**

The jewelry, home accessories, dinnerware, Italian linens, plantation-style furniture, and clothing are tastefully selected, a salute to the

good life. Soothing eye pillows filled with flaxseeds, handmade
designer dolls, hand-carved armoires, down-filled furniture and
slipcovers, and a large selection of Kiehl's products will make it easy
to part with your time and money. The clothing—comfortable
cottons and upscale European linens—is for men and women, as are
the soaps, including Maui Herbal Soap products and some unusual
finds from Provence.

✪ **Ola's Makawao.** In the Paniolo Building, 1156 Makawao Ave. ☎ **808/
573-1334.**

You'll always find a Doug Britt painting or two, which is reason
enough to stop by Ola's. Britt's scintillating paintings and furniture
assemblages (vanities and lockers of found wood!) are among the
great art finds of Hawaii. Owners and sisters Cindy Heacock and
Shari O'Brien add a personal touch to the delightful environment
they've created in this bright, thoughtfully designed space. Handmade American art by more than 160 artists includes Hawaii's best
in glassware, ceramics, wood, jewelry, paper, and other media. Enjoy the studio glass, porcelain vases, koa chopsticks, outrageous martini glasses, toys, letter openers, dolls, silks, and sumptuous bath
products, but don't forget Bella's at Ola's, a line of handmade
chocolates.

Silk Angel. Corner of Baldwin and Makawao aves. ☎ **808/573-1124.**

This tiny corner boutique is filled with all things silk and angelic,
gathered from the owner's Asian and Indonesian travels: hand-
painted sarongs, batiks, scarves from India, capes, and a gorgeous
selection of sarongs made from Indian sari material.

Tropo. 3643 Baldwin Ave. ☎ **808/573-0356.**

Tropo, the sister store of Hurricane (see above), gives men equal
shopping time and an equally delectable selection. Find the latest in
shirts and the literary tomes to go with them, as well as Tommy
Bahama silk piqué trousers and shorts; tasteful T-shirts; Western
shirts (with snap buttons, made by Rockmount, whose clothes Robert Redford wore in *The Horse Whisperer*); stylish winter wovens by
Toes on the Nose; great aloha shirts by Que and Kahala; and an
intoxicating selection of fragrance and bath products for men and
women.

✪ **Viewpoints Gallery.** 3620 Baldwin Ave. ☎ **808/572-5979.**

The island's only fine-arts cooperative showcases the work of
dozens of Maui artists in an airy, attractive gallery located in a

restored theater with a courtyard, glassblowing studio, and restaurants. The cooperative maintains a high degree of professionalism, as the artists involved (all full-time professionals) have passed a rigorous screening.

UPCOUNTRY EDIBLES

Working folks in Makawao who long to eat in arrive at the **Rodeo General Store,** 3661 Baldwin Ave. (☎ **808/572-7841**), to pick up their spaghetti and lasagna, sandwiches, salads, and specials from the deli. You can get all the necessary accompaniments here—fresh produce, wine, soft drinks, paper products, baked goods, and sweets.

Down to Earth Natural Foods, 1169 Makawao Ave. (☎ **808/ 572-1488**), always has fresh salads and sandwiches, a full section of organic produce, bulk grains, vitamins and supplements, beauty aids, herbs, juices, snacks, condiments, tofu, seaweed, soy products, and aisles of vegetarian and health foods—canned, packaged, prepared, and fresh.

In the more than 6 decades that the **T. Komoda Store and Bakery,** 3674 Baldwin Ave. (☎ **808/572-7261**), has spent in this spot, untold numbers have creaked over the wooden floors to pick up the famous cream puffs. Old-timers know to come early, or they'll be sold out. Then the cinnamon rolls, doughnuts, pies, and chocolate cake take over, keeping the aromas of fresh baking wafting through the old store.

FRESH FLOWERS IN KULA

Like anthuriums on the Big Island, proteas are a Maui trademark and an abundant crop on Haleakala's rich volcanic slopes. They also travel well, dry beautifully, and can be shipped worldwide with ease. Among Maui's most prominent sources is **Sunrise Protea** (☎ **808/ 876-0200**), in Kula at the base of Haleakala National Park. Sunrise offers a walk-through garden and gift shops, friendly service, and a larger-than-usual selection. If you want the freshly cut flowers, they arrive from the fields on Tuesday and Friday afternoons. You can order individual blooms, baskets, arrangements, or wreaths for shipping all over the world. **Proteas of Hawaii** (☎ **808/878-2533**), another reliable source, offers regular walking tours of the University of Hawaii Extension Service gardens across the street in Kula.

For flower shopping in other parts of Maui, **Ooka Super Market** (see "Central Maui Edibles," above) and the Saturday-morning **Maui Swap Meet** (see "Kahuhlui," above) are among the best and least expensive places for tropical flowers of every stripe.

5 East Maui: On the Road to Hana

PAIA

Biasa Rose Boutique. 104 Hana Hwy. ☎ **808/579-8602.**

Unusual gift items and clothing with a tropical flair are the Biasa Rose specialties: capri pants in bark cloth, floating plumeria candles, retro fabrics, dinnerware, children's clothes, stylish FLAX wrap skirts in a vintage wallpaper pattern. If the aloha shirts don't get you, the candles in the shape of nude males and females will surely catch your eye.

Big Bugga Sportswear. 18 Baldwin Ave. ☎ **808/579-6216.**

Someone decided to take care of the Little Buggas (6 months to size 4) and the Big Buggas (up to size 10X), and this wonderful store in Paia was born. You have to be microsized or ultrahuge to shop here. Togs for tots are a small part of the inventory of T-shirts and surf wear; the rest begins at XL and goes up to 10X, with aloha shirts as large as 7X. Sorry, mediums and larges, there's nothing for you here. The great selection of sportswear goes from shorts for 40-inch to 60-inch waistlines to T-shirts for the ultra-ample girth. They'll even take special orders for sweatpants and sweatshirts up to size 10X.

Katie's Place Gifts & Collectibles. At Baldwin Ave. and Hana Hwy. ☎ **808/ 579-8660.**

Hula dolls galore! Find the wiggling collectibles here in all price ranges, a good match for the Don Blanding dinnerware (popular and hard to find), Depression glass, salt and pepper shakers, Matson liner menus, music sheets, vintage 1940s bark-cloth curtains, and countless other snippets of the past, in prices that won't break the bank.

Maui Crafts Guild. 43 Hana Hwy. ☎ **808/579-9697.**

The old wooden storefront at the gateway to Paia houses local crafts of high quality and in all price ranges, from pit-fired raku to bowls of Norfolk pine and other Maui woods fashioned by Maui hands. Basketry, fabrics, glass, musical instruments, Hawaiian quilts, hand-made paper, ceramics, jewelry, bamboo flutes, hand-turned bowls, koa accessories, prints, pressed flowers, and hundreds of items are displayed in the rustic two-story gift gallery. They ship anywhere, and all artists are selectively screened. **Aloha Bead Company** (☎ 808/579-9709) in the back of the gallery is a treasure trove of beads.

Moonbow Tropics. 36 Baldwin Ave. ☎ **808/579-8592.**

If you're looking for a tasteful aloha shirt, Moonbow has one of the best selections in town—not exhaustive, but a few carefully culled racks of the top labels in aloha wear. There are shorts, a few purses, and a small jewelry selection, but mostly it's shirts, in good-quality fabrics.

EDIBLES ON THE ROAD TO HANA

Nahiku Coffee Shop, Smoked Fish Stand, and Ti Gallery. Hana Hwy., mile marker 28, Nahiku. No phone.

What a delight to stumble across this comfort on the long drive to Hana! The small coffee shop, open daily from 6:30am to 4:30pm, serves locally made baked goods, while the Ti Gallery, open daily from 9:30am to 4:30pm, sells locally made crafts. The cast-iron smoker (our favorite part of the operation) puts out smoked and grilled chicken, beef, and fresh local fish, sending seductive smoky aromas wafting through the moist Nahiku air, daily from 10am to 5pm. The teriyaki-based marinade, made by the owner, adds a special touch. There are a few roadside picnic tables, or you can take your lunch on to Hana for a beachside picnic.

6 At the End of the Road in East Maui: Hana

✪ **Hana Coast Gallery.** Hotel Hana-Maui. ☎ **808/248-8636.**

This gallery is known for its high level of curatorship and commitment to the cultural art of Hawaii. There are no jumping whales or dolphins here—and except for a section of European and Asian masters (Renoir, Japanese woodblock prints), the 3,000-square-foot space is devoted to Hawaii artists. Dozens of well-established local artists display their sculptures, paintings, prints, feather work, stone work, carvings, and three-dimensional works in displays that are so natural they could well exist in someone's home.

Hasegawa General Store. Hana Hwy. ☎ **808/248-8231.**

Established in 1910, immortalized in song since 1961, burned to the ground in 1990, and back in business in 1991, this legendary store is indefatigable and more colorful than ever in its third generation in business. The aisles are choked with merchandise: Hana-blend coffee specially roasted and blended for the store, Ono Farms organic dried fruit, fishing equipment, every tape and CD that mentions Hana, the best books on Hana to be found, T-shirts, beach and garden essentials, mugs, baseball caps, film, and other necessities for the Hana life.

8

Maui After Dark

by Jocelyn Fujii

The island's most prestigious entertainment venue is the $28-million
Maui Arts and Cultural Center in Kahului (☎ **808/242-7469**),
a first-class center for the visual and performing arts. It has proved
to be a great success, a Maui star: Since its 1994 opening, the state-
of-the-art facilities have attracted first-rate performers and sold-out
shows. Bonnie Raitt has performed here, as have Hiroshima, Pearl
Jam, Ziggy Marley, and Tony Bennett, not to mention the finest in
local and Hawaii talent. It has booked world-class cultural exhibits,
rock and reggae, the Lakota Sioux Indian Dance Theatre, Carlos
Santana, the Maui Symphony Orchestra, the stars of the Moscow
Ballet, John Mayall, Kenny Loggins, magic shows, top Hawaiian
performers, the Hawaii International Film Festival, and many other
notable acts. The center is as precious to Maui as the Met is to New
York, with a visual-arts gallery, an outdoor amphitheater, offices,
rehearsal space, a 300-seat theater for experimental performances,
and a 1,200-seat main theater. Whether it's hula, the Iona Pear
Dance Company, Willie Nelson, or Hawaiian-music icon Keali'i
Reichel, only the best will appear at the Maui Arts and Cultural
Center. The center's activities are well publicized locally, so check
the *Maui News* or ask your hotel concierge what's going on during
your visit.

HAWAIIAN MUSIC

Except for Casanova in Makawao, Hapa's in Kihei, Tsunami in
Wailea, and Maui Brews in Lahaina, nightlife options on this island
are limited. The major hotels generally have lobby lounges offering
regular Hawaiian music, soft jazz, or hula shows beginning at sunset. If the duo called **Hapa, Willie K and Amy Gilliom,** or the so-
loist **Keali'i Reichel** are playing anywhere on their native island,
don't miss them; they're a Hawaiian music bonanza, among the finest Hawaiian musicians around today.

JAZZ & BLUES

To find out what's happening in jazz or blues, look in at **Hapa's
Brew Haus** (☎ **808/879-9001**) in Kihei (see "South Maui,"

below). It seems to be the nightlife nexus for this genre, with quality music and overflow crowds that linger into the wee hours. The thriving blues scene throughout Hawaii can be credited to the efforts of Louie Wolfenson, his partner Kurt Kangas, and the **Maui Blues Association** (☎ **808/879-6123**), which books sold-out events at clubs throughout the state. Check the papers to see what's on while you're on Maui. Their annual Islands Blues Mele, a festival around Memorial Day, grows by the year and has assumed a life of its own.

1 West Maui: Lahaina

Maui Brews, 900 Front St. (☎ **808/667-7794**), opens daily from 11:30am, with happy hour from 3 to 6pm; it turns into a nightclub from 9pm to 1:30am. Swing, salsa, reggae, and late-night jams draw a crowd to this corner of the Lahaina Center. There's live music every night except weekends, and Ladies' Night is on Thursday.

At **Longhi's,** 888 Front St. (☎ **808/667-2288**), live music spills out into the streets from 9:30pm to midnight on some weekends. Usually it's salsa or jazz, but call ahead to confirm. Other special gigs can be expected if rock 'n' rollers or jazz musicians who are friends of the owner happen to be passing through. It wouldn't hurt to ask what's happening here.

You won't have to ask what's going on at **Cheeseburger in Paradise,** 811 Front St. (☎ **808/661-4855**), the two-story green-and-white building at the corner of Front and Lahainaluna streets. Just go outside and you'll hear it: loud, live, and lively tropical rock blasting into the streets and out to sea daily from 4:30 to 11pm. There's no cover.

AN INTIMATE AFFAIR: LUAU, MAUI STYLE

Most of the larger hotels in Maui's major resorts offer luaus and Polynesian entertainment on a regular basis. You'll pay about $65 to attend one. To protect yourself from disappointment, don't expect it to be a home-grown affair prepared in the traditional Hawaiian way; the labor-intensive nature of this feast makes achieving that an impossible endeavor for large-scale commercial operations offered on a regular basis. There are, however, commercial luaus that capture the romance and spirit of the affair with quality food and entertainment in outdoor settings.

Maui's best luau is indisputably the nightly **Old Lahaina Luau,** (☎ **808/667-1998**), an even bigger hit at its new 1-acre site just ocean-side of the Lahaina Cannery. We thought it couldn't get better, but it did. Local craftspeople display their wares only a few feet

It Begins with Sunset

Nightlife in Maui begins at sunset, when all eyes turn westward to see how the day will end. Like spotting the same whale or school of spinner dolphins, sunset viewers seem to bond in the mutual enjoyment of a natural spectacle. And what better way to take it all in than over cocktails? Maui is a haven for lovers of both.

Sunset viewers along south and west Maui shorelines need only head for the ocean and find a seat. Our favorite sunset watering holes begin with **The Bay Club at Kapalua** (☎ 808/669-5656), where a pianist plays nightly and the northwesterly view of Molokai and Lanai is enhanced by the elegant surroundings. It's quiet here, removed from the hubbub that prevails in the more populated Kaanapali Beach Resort to the south.

In Kaanapali, park in Whalers Village and head for **Leilani's** (☎ 808/661-4495) or **Hula Grill** (☎ 808/667-6636), next to each other on the beach. Both have busy, upbeat bars and tables bordering the sand. These are happy places for great people watching, gazing at the lump of Lanai that looks to be a stone's throw away, and enjoying end-of-day rituals like mai tais and margaritas. Hula Grill's Barefoot Bar appetizer menu is a cut above, offering such treats as macadamia-nut/crab wontons, fresh fish-and-chips, and pizza. Leilani's has live music daily from 2:30 to 6pm, while Hula Grill offers hula from 3 to 5pm and at 6:30pm.

Now, Lahaina: It's a sunset-lover's nirvana, lined with restaurants that hang over the ocean and offer fresh fish in a multitude of preparations—and mai tais elevated to an art form. If you love loud rock, head for **Cheeseburger in Paradise** (☎ 808/661-4855). A few doors away, **Lahaina Fish Company** (☎ 808/661-3472) and **Kimo's** (☎ 808/661-4811) are magnets all day long and especially at sunset, when their open decks fill up with

from the ocean. Seating is provided on lauhala mats for those wishing to dine as the traditional Hawaiians did, but there are tables for everyone else. Although there is no fire dancing in the program, you won't even miss it. Thatched buildings, amphitheater seating, excellent food and entertainment, and the backdrop of a Lahaina sunset are among its unforgettable features. This is the consummate luau, with a healthy balance of entertainment, showmanship, authentic high-quality food, educational value, and sheer romantic beauty. (No watered-down mai tais, either; these are the real thing.)

revelers. These three restaurants occupy the section of Front Street between Lahainaluna Road and Papalaua Street.

At the southern end of Lahaina, in the 505 Front Street complex, **Pacific'o** (☎ **808/667-4341**) is a solid hit, with a raised bar, seating on the ocean, and a backdrop of Lanai across the channel. Besides the view and the friendly service, the food is notable, having won many awards for seafood.

Moving south toward Wailea, the harbor stop called Maalaea is famous for its whale sightings during the winter months. Year-round, **Buzz's Wharf** (☎ **808/244-5426**) is a formula restaurant with a superb ocean view and continuous service between lunch and dinner. Those are the basic makings of a sunset-viewing way station. Add an ice-cold beer or mai tai and a steaming order of fish-and-chips, and the sunset package is complete.

In Wailea, our favorite stop is the **Hula Moons** outdoor terrace at Outrigger Wailea Resort (☎ **808/879-1922**)—for the ambience, if not the food. It's more open than its fancier neighbors and, in a corny but romantic touch, live Hawaiian music with a hula dancer is offered daily from 5:30 to 9:30pm. In Makena resort further south, you can't beat the Maui Prince's **Molokini Lounge** (☎ **808/874-1111**), with its casual elegance and un-equalled view of Molokini islet on the ocean side and, on the mauka side, a graceful, serene courtyard with ponds, rock gardens, and lush foliage. Adding to the setting is the appetizer menu, which comes from the esteemed Prince Court kitchen. From 5:30pm nightly, the pupu menu features a Molokini sampler platter (Thai-style spring rolls, shrimp summer rolls, ahi sashimi), a seared ahi seaweed salad on a tortilla shell, and panfried tiger shrimp. There's live Hawaiian entertainment nightly from 6 to 6:45pm.

The luau begins at sunset and features Tahitian and Hawaiian entertainment, including ancient hula, hula from the missionary era, modern hula, and an intelligent narrative on the dance's rocky course of survival into modern times. The entertainment is riveting, even for jaded locals, and the food is as much Pacific Rim as authentically Hawaiian, served from an open-air thatched structure: imu-roasted kalua pig, baked mahimahi in Maui onion–cream sauce, guava chicken, teriyaki sirloin steak, lomi salmon, poi, dried fish, poke, Hawaiian sweet potato, sautéed vegetables, seafood salad, and

the ultimate taste treat, taro leaves with coconut milk. The cost is
$65 for adults, $30 for children, plus tax.

The **Maui Marriott Luau** (☎ 808/667-1200) is beachside in
Kaanapali and costs $65 for adults and $26 for children, free for
those under 5. An open bar, outdoor stage, Hawaiian games, and
after-dinner show appeal to those with Las Vegas tastes, with fire
dancers and hula. The luau is offered from 5 to 8pm nightly.

2 South Maui

KIHEI

Hapa's Brew Haus, Lipoa Shopping Center, 41 E. Lipoa St.
(☎ 808/879-9001), is the liveliest game in town, with local icon
Willie K. packing them in every Wednesday night. He is a powerful musical presence who is worth the drive to Kihei. The intimate
environment, tiered seating, and state-of-the-art sound and lighting
show off his virtuoso guitar playing and unmistakable vocals to great
advantage. Call the hot line (☎ 808/875-1990) to find out whether
jazz, blues, rock, reggae, funk, Jawaiian (a fusion of Jamaican and
Hawaiian), the Maui Symphony Orchestra band (MSO), or the duo
named Hapa will be filling the house.

WAILEA

The Grand Wailea Resort's **Tsunami,** 3850 Wailea Alanui Dr.
(☎ 808/875-1234), Maui's most high-tech club, happens to be
south Maui's only nightspot for dancing. But what a club: 10,000
square feet, with marble, laser lights, huge video screens, futuristic
decor, and well-dressed revelers. It's all disco, no live music, and is
open Thursday, Friday, and Saturday from 9pm to 2am with a
$5 cover. The DJ plays everything from 1980s hits to Top 40 on
weekends. Thursday is ladies' night: no cover charge for women,
drink specials, and a flower or other memento for the wily females
who turn out to "dress and impress." On Friday, "Flashback Fever"
(music from the 1970s and 1980s) takes over.

3 Upcountry Maui

Upcountry in Makawao, the partying never ends at **Casanova,** 1188
Makawao Ave. (☎ 808/572-0220), the popular Italian ristorante
(see chapter 4 for a review) where the good times roll with the pasta.
This is a restaurant, nightclub, bar, and dance spot all in one. If a
big-name mainland band is resting up on Maui following a sold-out
concert on Oahu, you may find its members setting up for an

impromptu night here. On Maui, word spreads quickly. DJs take over on Wednesday (ladies' night) and Thursday nights. Every other Thursday is a fundraiser for the Maui AIDS Society, and on Friday and Saturday, live entertainment draws fun-lovers from even the most remote reaches of the island. Entertainment starts at 9:45pm and continues to 1:30am. Expect good blues, rock 'n' roll, reggae, jazz, Hawaiian, and the top names in local and visiting entertainment. Elvin Bishop, the local duo Hapa, Los Lobos, and many others have filled Casanova's stage. The cover charge is usually $5.

Index

See also separate Accommodations and Restaurants indexes, below.
Page numbers in *italics* refer to maps.